PSYCHOLOGY GETS IN THE GAME

Psychology Gets in the Game

SPORT, MIND,
AND BEHAVIOR,
1880–1960

*Edited by Christopher D. Green
and Ludy T. Benjamin Jr.*

UNIVERSITY OF NEBRASKA PRESS

LINCOLN AND LONDON

Library of Congress Cataloging-
in-Publication Data
Psychology gets in the game:
sport, mind, and behavior, 1880–
1960 / edited by Christopher D.
Green and Ludy T. Benjamin Jr.
p. cm. Includes bibliographical
references and index.
ISBN 978-0-8032-2226-7
(paperback : alkaline paper)
1. Sports – Psychological aspects.
I. Green, Christopher D.
II. Benjamin, Ludy T., 1945–
GV706.4.P684 2009
796.01 – dc22   2009025856

Set in Minion by Bob Reitz.
Designed by Nathan Putens.

Contents

Illustrations

PSYCHOLOGY GETS IN THE GAME

INTRODUCTION

THE ORIGINS OF SPORT PSYCHOLOGY

Ludy T. Benjamin Jr. and Christopher D. Green

Ninety percent of this game is half mental.
YOGI BERRA

Sport is a trillion-dollar enterprise, a dominant source of year-round entertainment. It is a microcosm of society in which the critical social issues of the day are often dealt with on the field of play (Davies 2007). People play sports, they watch sports, they watch movies about sports, they read about sports, they gamble on sports, they argue about sports, they join fantasy leagues, they pay thousands of dollars to attend fantasy camps, they live out their athletic dreams through their children, they idolize their sport heroes, they view rival athletes with utter detestation, and in the off-season of their favorite sport they suffer miserably from Seasonal Affective Disorder (SAD), which sports fans know has nothing to do with the hours of sunlight.

The overwhelming majority of people who participate in sports do so at the amateur level, playing without any form of compensation. This level of competition stands in stark contrast to the world of professional sports that involves millionaire athletes and billionaire owners. Average salaries for professional athletes have reached astronomical levels in the twenty-first century. Basketball players earn an average of $3.7 million, followed by baseball players at $2.5 million; hockey players at $1.8 million; and football players at $1.3 million. Professional golfers aren't on food stamps, but on average they don't do nearly as well with PGA players earning average salaries of $875,000. Evidence of the disparity in women's sports is shown by an average salary of $196,000 for LPGA players (LeUnes 2009). And these salaries do not reflect incomes from other sources such as advertising and other endorsements.

As the promise of extraordinarily lucrative paydays has escalated, so too have means by which to improve athletic performance. Witness the scandals surrounding performance enhancing drugs in a number of sports including baseball, football, track and field, weightlifting, and cycling. Given the high stakes of fame and exorbitant incomes, many athletes have sought whatever advantages they can acquire — some legal, some not. Indeed, athletes, coaches, scientists, and backroom "pharmacists" are working diligently to push the envelope on athletic performance. Hoberman (2001) has called it a national obsession.

Athletes and those who study athletic competition have long realized that although much of an athlete's success comes from physical talents, mental factors play a hugely important role. At the elite levels physical talents often seem closely matched among athletes, meaning that mental factors often decide between coming in first and finishing second. The desire for gaining every possible edge has led many athletes to seek the services of psychologists as part of their training and coaching team. Today, psychologists work as sport psychologists for Olympic teams and professional teams and as personal coaches with many elite athletes such as Greg

Norman, Nick Faldo, David Duval, Evander Holyfield, Gabriela Sabatini, Jim Courier, Mary Jo Fernandez, Eric Lindros, John Smoltz, Nancy Kerrigan, Picabo Street, and countless others.

The modern profession of sport psychology has its roots in the 1960s when, at a meeting in Italy in 1965, the first international sport psychology organization was formed in Europe, followed by national organizations in the United States in 1966 and Canada in 1969. These organizations provided a forum in which early sport psychologists could discuss their work and plan for the future of their profession. By the mid-1980s the field had come of age with additional organizations that were better aimed at promoting professional interests. These organizations include the Association for Applied Sport Psychology (AASP), which was formed in 1986 and which is the largest organization of sport psychologists in the world. Also in 1986 sport psychologists created a division of the American Psychological Association, the Division of Exercise and Sport Psychology (Division 47).

The initial journal devoted exclusively to sport psychology was the *International Journal of Sport Psychology*, founded in 1970. The leading American journal, the *Journal of Sport Psychology*, appeared about a decade later in 1979. Today, there are sport psychology journals published in many countries including more than thirty-five English-language journals that could be considered to be devoted to sport psychology or to closely related fields such as sports medicine, kinesiology and exercise science, sport sociology, and sport management.

Today, the Association for Applied Sport Psychology has a membership in excess of 1,300, several of whom have built lucrative practices working with teams and individual athletes. For example, psychologist David Cook left his position at the University of Kansas to form his own sport psychology consulting service based in San Antonio, Texas. He has worked individually with numerous golfers in the PGA and LPGA as well as with professional athletes in baseball, basketball, and football. He has also worked with Olympic teams as well as professional teams such as the San Antonio Spurs and the Washington Wizards (LeUnes 2009).

Fran Pirozzolo began working with professional golfers more than twenty-five years ago and emphasizes stress inoculation and other cognitive techniques to help athletes deal with the pressure inherent in competition. In 1996 he became the mental skills coach for the New York Yankees. His six-year position with the Yankees saw them win four World Championships. He has since worked with the Houston Astros, Detroit Tigers, and Texas Rangers. Since 2002 he has served as player development coach for the Houston Texans of the National Football League.

Kenneth Ravizza is in the Department of Kinesiology at California State University–Fullerton where he has built a reputation for his expertise in helping athletes achieve peak performance. He has worked with the Los Angeles Angels baseball team, the football teams at the University of Nebraska and Arizona State University, and the very successful baseball team at his own university. He has also consulted in such diverse sports as field hockey, gymnastics, water polo, and softball.

Some sport psychologists have tended to specialize more in a single sport such as Richard Coop of the University of North Carolina–Chapel Hill who has worked with professional and amateur golfers for more than twenty years. His impressive client list includes Corey Pavin, Ben Crenshaw, Larry Mize, Mark O'Meara, Donna Andrews, and the late Payne Stewart.

Although fewer in number, women too have been involved at the elite levels of sport psychology. Colleen Hacker of Pacific Lutheran University has focused her expertise on soccer and since 1995 has worked with the women's U.S. National Soccer Team that finished first at the 1996 Olympic Games, the 1998 Goodwill Games, the 1999 World Cup, and the 2004 Olympic Games. She has also consulted with professional athletes in baseball, football, and basketball as well as amateurs in such sports as track and field, swimming, speed skating, and crew. Her emphases have been on strategies to reach peak performance and in team sports working to build leadership and team cohesion.

Cook, Pirozzolo, Ravizza, Coop, and Hacker represent the breadth of impact of the field of sport psychology and the sports world's recognition that psychology has a role to play in the enhancement of athletic performance. Given the financial stakes of sports competition, the opportunities for sport psychologists look evermore promising (Gardner 2001; Meyers, Coleman, Whelan, and Mehlenbeck 2001).

Two Origin Paths

These five successful sport psychologists also evidence the dual origins of the field and the controversy surrounding the practice of modern sport psychology. Cook, Coop, and Pirozzolo came to sport psychology with backgrounds in psychology. Ravizza and Hacker received their training in kinesiology and exercise science.

It can be argued that the origins of the modern profession of sport psychology lie predominantly in the field of physical education and that many of the earliest practitioners in the 1960s had their graduate education and training in the pertinent academic departments. It would not be until the 1980s that psychologists would enter the field in any significant numbers. The entrance of psychologists in the field continues today both because of the growing success of sport psychology and because of the need for psychologists to find other venues for practice due to the loss of psychotherapy income brought about by the cost-containment outcomes of managed care.

Not surprisingly there has been a turf war in sport psychology with vociferous arguments about who is qualified to offer services under such a professional label. The result is a field served by two very differently trained classes of practitioners. Those who come from a sport science or physical education background complain that the psychologists typically have never played or coached sports nor had any training in sport science. The psychologists counter that the individuals trained in sport science and physical education have weak backgrounds in psychology. In truth, because of licensing laws for psychology, only a licensed psychologist can use the label "sport psychologist" in offering his or her services to the public. The field has avoided this problem by offering certification from AASP to individuals who have a doctoral degree from an accredited university and substantial education in both psychology and sport science (LeUnes 2009).

This bifurcated road is important for historical purposes because it defines the historical paths used by contemporary sport psychologists in identifying their origins or at least their prehistory (see Wiggins 1984). Psychologists look to the earlier studies by psychologists, whereas those trained in sport and exercise science look to the field of physical education and motor learning for their ancestry. Although there are studies from physical education faculty that would qualify as sport psychology research (see McCloy 1930), much of the motor-learning research, especially before 1940, would not. These latter studies were about practice, about fatigue, and about the rate of acquisition of motor skills, but they were not about sport. It is not the purpose of this book to cover both paths. Instead, our focus in the chapters that follow is on the work by early psychologists such as Edward Scripture, John Watson, Karl Lashley, Coleman Griffith, and others who were interested in the questions relating psychology and sport.

An Overview of the Prehistory

Although sport psychology as a profession, with its organizations, journals, and specialty certification, has its origins in the 1960s, there are many earlier studies that would qualify as sport psychology research and practice. This prehistory is the subject of this book, and it begins on a bicycle.

Treatises on the psychology of sport appear as early as the 1880s: for instance, there was Emil du Bois-Reymond's 1881 argument for the improvement of sensory-motor integration through exercise (as cited in Hoberman 2001). The earliest research studies on sport psychology, however, were not published until the 1890s. The first such were by French physician Philippe Tissié and American psychologist Edward Scripture, both of whose studies were published in 1894, and by American psychologist Norman Triplett in 1898. Both the Tissié and Triplett studies dealt with the psychology of cycling, the first with endurance, the second with speed, whereas the Scripture study investigated reaction time in fencers.

Tissié, best known in the history of medicine for his description of the first case of a "mad traveler," or fuguer (see Hacking 1998), was interested in both the physiology and psychology of extreme exertion. In 1893 he conducted a field study of a cyclist riding for twenty-four consecutive hours on a velodrome track. Tissié recorded a number of physiological and biochemical measures postrace and wrote about the physiological changes produced by the long duration event but also about the psychological factors involved in that kind of endurance (Hoberman 2001; Tissié 1894a, 1894b).

Triplett's 1898 cycling study was conducted while he was a graduate student in psychology at Indiana University as part of research for his master's thesis. He sought to measure racing times for cyclists when they raced alone compared to racing in competition with other cyclists. He found that competition resulted in faster times, a phenomenon that social psychologists have since labeled social facilitation, indicating the enhanced performance that occurs when well-practiced individuals perform in the presence of others.

Scripture's 1894 experiment comparing expert fencers with

novices examined reaction times, for which he found no differences between the two classes of fencers, and speed of movement, which he found superior in the expert fencers. Both the Triplett and Scripture studies are discussed in later chapters of this book.

It is interesting to note that although the Tissié and Scripture studies predate the work by Triplett, it is Triplett who has typically been identified as conducting the first sport psychology study based on his 1898 research. In a survey of thirty-three English-language sport psychology textbooks published between 1980 and 2002, nineteen of them identify Triplett as the father or founder of sport psychology or as the individual who published the first research in sport psychology. None of those sources identify Scripture or Tissié in a similar way. Why is that? Most likely the labeling has to do with the accessibility of the publications. Tissié's work appeared in French journals, whereas Scripture's work was published in his in-house journal *Studies from the Yale Psychological Laboratory*, a journal that can be found in very few libraries and one that ceased publication in 1902 after only ten years. Triplett's article, however, was published in the most visible journal of its time, the *American Journal of Psychology*. Once his study was identified as the beginning study in the field of sport psychology, other books and articles followed suit in recognizing his priority.

Other than these initial endeavors Tissié, Triplett, and Scripture published no further research related to sport psychology. This one-shot involvement in the field was typical of the early researchers in both motor-learning research and psychological studies. For example, University of Iowa psychologist George T. W. Patrick (1903) published a single article on the psychology of football that dealt not with the athletes but with the spectators, specifically proposing a cathartic purpose in watching the violent game of football. Likewise, Karl Lashley (1915) authored a single study investigating the effects of the distribution of practice on learning archery skills (see Dewsbury, this volume). Psychologists Harold Burtt of Ohio State University (Burtt and Nichols 1924), Vern Ruble (1928) of Indiana University, and Donald Paterson of the University of Minnesota (Paterson and Peterson 1928) each conducted a single study on the psychology of football players and other athletes.

The exceptions to this rule of single studies were Robert Werner Schulte (1897–1933), a psychologist at the German and Prussian College for Physical Education in Berlin (Bäumler 1997), and Coleman R. Griffith (1893–1966), a psychologist at the University of Illinois. Both developed sustained research programs in sport psychology and produced multiple publications on the subject. Schulte established what may be the first sport psychology laboratory in the world in 1924, and Griffith followed suit in 1925. Schulte worked in the field for a decade until his untimely death; Griffith was active as a sport psychologist for more than twenty years including professional consultation with the Chicago Cubs (Green 2003). Both of these individuals are discussed in greater detail in chapters in this book: Bäumler on Schulte and Green on Griffith.

Because they were the first psychologists to sustain activity in sport psychology, it is no surprise that Schulte and Griffith have been designated by contemporary sport psychologists as the founders of the field. But as Green (2006) has noted, such claims are origin myths because it is clear that there is nothing that links the work of these earlier researchers to the modern-day discipline of sport psychology. This early work can be described as anticipatory but not foundational (Sarup 1978). Schulte and Griffith had no students who would carry on their work. Moreover, there are no intellectual ties in the 1960s to their sport psychology of the 1920s. This work is more accurately described as prehistory and, as noted earlier, is the subject of this book.

In the chapters that follow we hope to give the reader a sense of the impetus for this early work as the new experimental psychologists sought to validate their new science in a world of pragmatism and psychotechnics, that is, to demonstrate the applicability of their scientific psychology. These stories tell of ingenuity, of optimism, of frustration, and of success and failure. They tell of the early pioneers who sought to bring science to bear in understanding the relationship of behavior and mental processes to athletic success.

Overview of the Chapters

Günther Bäumler begins our coverage with a description of the origins of sport psychology in Europe by covering the years 1890 to 1930. His coverage is extensive, noting in particular the pioneers from France, Germany, Italy, and Russia. He provides a detailed picture of the work of Philippe Tissié, including the latter's work on extended exertion, but also Tissié's writing on the psychopathology of sport, or more positively, sport hygiene. Bäumler argues that Schulte's laboratory provided for the institutionalization of sport psychology in Germany. Schulte set out to develop tests of athletic ability for various sports and in doing so devised many of the measures and apparatuses used in making those assessments. Because of such work, he can be viewed as part of the psychotechnics movement in Germany that led to industrial, human factors, and engineering psychology.

Our coverage of the American precursors to sport psychology begins with a chapter by James Goodwin on Edward Scripture. Scripture earned his doctorate in experimental psychology from Wilhelm Wundt and in 1892 was hired to develop the psychology laboratory at Yale University. As Goodwin notes, Scripture was a thoroughgoing positivist who argued that the only valid accounts of mental events were those that involve precise measurement. He was also much influenced by American pragmatism, publishing his first two books in part to emphasize the applicability of the new science of psychology for human betterment (Scripture 1895, 1897). Scripture began his studies on athletics in 1894 by studying gymnasts, runners, boxers, and fencers. His dependent measures were typically measures of reaction time, a common method of studying athletes because of the emphasis on speed and quickness of reaction in many sports. Further, reaction time as a measure of the speed of mental processing was a quite common method of investigation in the early psychology laboratories, including Wundt's laboratory where Scripture had studied. Like Schulte, Scripture built several pieces of unique apparatus in order to test the performance of the athletes he was studying. Goodwin provides a rich description of these studies. He concludes that Scripture's work in this field was not designed to promote the psychological study of athletes but instead to demonstrate the value of experimental psychology for solving human problems outside the laboratory. This characterization of Scripture's studies is also accurate for many of the other figures described in this book.

The next chapter by Stephen Davis, Matthew Huss, and Angela Becker describes the work of Norman Triplett. As noted earlier, Triplett's studies on the effects of competitors on cycling performance were conducted while he was a graduate student, and according to the authors, this work was important because unlike the reaction-time studies of others, it recognized the crucial dimension of athletics, namely competition. The impetus for this master's thesis study is not known, but it would be Triplett's first and last contribution to the experimental literature on sport psychology. Unlike Scripture who seemed to have little interest in athletics beyond his few studies, Triplett remained a devoted fan to athletics throughout his life and his career at Kansas Normal School (KNS). He had been a star sprinter in his youth and played on the faculty baseball team at KNS. He was one of the planners of the school's grandstand in 1903, and when it burned in 1923, he helped design the new full-scale stadium. He was often seen at athletic practices in many sports and was especially involved with the KNS track team, serving as their faculty advisor for thirty years. Kansas Normal School, as the name implies, was a university where teaching was of utmost importance. Triplett spent his life there and consequently his research record is fairly meager. Yet his single study of cycling competition and social facilitation has earned him a place in the histories of sport psychology and social psychology.

In the next chapter Donald Dewsbury tells the interesting story of archery studies conducted by two of the most famous psychologists of the twentieth century — John B. Watson and Karl Lashley. The research began in 1913 on the Dry Tortugas islands off the coast of the Florida Keys and concluded two years later in Baltimore. The researchers did not set out to contribute to the literature on sport psychology. Instead, their research was a study of learning, and the authors sought to find a task that would be little influenced by language and sufficiently interesting to motivate subjects to perform well over a large number of trials. Specifically, the studies were concerned with the nature of the learning curve and changes in its continuity (that is, what induces plateaus?), with fatigue, and with the optimal distribution of practice. The last of these questions especially concerned Watson. Dewsbury argues that Watson wanted to discover the effectiveness of varying distributions of trials on learning. What training regimen would produce the most efficient learning? Like Scripture, Watson was interested in demonstrating the practicality of psychology. He believed that the nature of learning in the archery task provided the kind of model needed to answer the question about how best to teach a skill, both for human and animal learning. After the publication of these studies, Watson and Lashley never returned in any subsequent research to the field of sport psychology nor to the study of archery. Although the archery studies were clearly a diversion in research, the well-designed research proved the power of scientific psychology in defining an efficient training program for the acquisition or improvement of that skill.

No athlete may be better known in North America than the Bambino, the Home Run King, the Sultan of Swat, the Colossus of Clout, the Maharajah of Mash, the Wali of Wallop, the Wazir of Wham, and other aliases. George Herman "Babe" Ruth was a truly exceptional athlete who was one of the best pitchers of his day, but whose excellence as a hitter, both for average and power, forced him into an everyday role as an outfielder. Had steroids been in existence in 1920, it is likely that Ruth would have been accused of using them. In that year he hit fifty-four home runs, a number that was greater than the total accumulated by all the players on fourteen of the sixteen teams playing major league baseball. Ruth wasn't just a great player; his accomplishments put him in a league of his own.

In 1921 the Babe would meet up with psychology in the laboratory at Columbia University. Alfred Fuchs tells this fascinating story of how Babe Ruth was put through a series of psychological tests aimed at identifying the secrets of his remarkable ability. The idea for the testing came from Hugh Fullerton, a baseball writer who arranged for the assessment at Columbia. The studies were actually conducted by two psychology graduate students. According to Fuchs, Fullerton had two goals for testing Ruth: first, to determine the factors that were responsible for Ruth's ability to hit home runs that traveled such formidable distances and, second, to provide baseball scouts with measurement standards they could use in searching for other ballplayers with Ruthian skills. Fuchs covers the testing in considerable detail, describing the mental, sensory, and motor testing that were common to the psychology laboratories of the time, especially at Columbia, a department founded by James McKeen Cattell, who coined the term *mental test* and pioneered the development of psychological tests in America. Fuchs closes his chapter with an epilogue describing an almost identical testing in 2006 of St. Louis Cardinals' superstar Albert Pujols in the psychology laboratories at Washington University.

In the chapter by Frank Baugh and Ludy Benjamin the topic switches to college football in the 1920s, specifically to the teams of Pop Warner at Stanford University. In 1926 B. C. Graves, a young football coach at Sul Ross College in Alpine, Texas, arrived on the Stanford campus to pursue his master's degree. He was eager for the chance to work with the fabled Warner and to do his thesis research on the subject of football, specifically on the subject of the offensive line charge at the snap of the ball. Knowledge of the snap count was judged to be one of the chief advantages enjoyed by the offensive team. Such knowledge offered the offensive line the ability to move a fraction of a second before the defensive players, thus enhancing chances for success of the play. In the 1920s there was considerable controversy over the nature of the snap signals. Should the count be based on words or numbers? If numbers, should they be single digit or double digit? Should the cadence be uniform or should it vary? What was the optimum time interval in which the snap count should appear?

Graves would team with psychologist Walter Miles for his thesis work. Miles had played college football but had shown no interest in sport psychology. Likely he was drawn to Graves's project because of the need for an apparatus that would simultaneously measure the initiation of movement by seven linemen. Miles relished the challenges of designing complicated apparatus for complex psychology problems. The result was what he called the multiple chronograph. This ingenious device not only measured the individual reaction times of each of the seven subjects being tested, but it also showed the time of initiation of movement of each, thus allowing the uniformity of the offensive line charge to be measured. The studies reached important conclusions about the nature of signal calling that are consistent with the way signals are called in football today. Miles never pursued other sport psychology work throughout his long and distinguished career, but the football charging studies represented a meaningful collaboration between a coach and psychologist that resulted in well-designed research that answered several important questions about how football should be played.

Christopher Green's chapter describes the career of Coleman Griffith, whom Green acknowledges has been "adopted" as the father of sport psychology in North America by contemporary sport psychologists looking to establish the legitimacy of their profession in a more distant past. Although Griffith spent more than twenty years investigating the relationship of psychology and sport, he produced no students who would carry on that work, nor is his work linked intellectually to the rise of sport psychology in the 1960s. But he was the first psychologist in North America to make a career as a sport psychologist, both as a researcher and practitioner. He wrote popular books on the subject such as *The Psychology of Coaching* (1926) and *Psychology and Athletics* (1928), and he published articles on sport psychology intended for coaches and athletes. Interestingly, he published few accounts of the research conducted in the sport psychology laboratory that he founded at the University of Illinois in 1925. In 1938 at the invitation of chewing gum-magnate Phillip K. Wrigley, Griffith began an almost three-year association with the Chicago Cubs. This grand experiment is the focus of Green's chapter as he contrasts the scientific efforts of the college professor with the overt and covert resistance of major league ballplayers and managers. Green takes the reader to spring training and into the clubhouse for this fascinating account of a clash of cultures, in which science, suspicion, and superstition face off.

From major league baseball the next chapter moves to the National Football League and to the description by Stephen

Graef, Alan Kornspan, and David Baker of the use of physical and mental testing for the evaluation of professional football players. The chapter's emphasis is on Paul Brown, famed coach of the Cleveland Browns and the Cincinnati Bengals, and on his use of both intelligence and personality tests. Brown's interests in testing began during the 1930s when he coached in high school in Massillon, Ohio. That such data could be said to be useful in player selection and assignment is evidenced by Brown's Massillon coaching record, which included eighty wins in nine years against eight defeats and six state championship trophies. Brown had athletes complete tests in five domains: intelligence, aggression, character, personality, and physical reaction. The most important of those tests was the test of intelligence. Brown believed that players needed to be smart, that success in football was about the ability to learn and to adapt in changing situations on the field. That the test results were taken seriously is indicated by the fact that players who scored poorly did not make the team even when other physical skills might recommend them. Brown brought his testing program with him into college football and then into the National Football League. Eventually other NFL teams adopted the use of intelligence testing leading to the current method of rookie screening that occurs annually in the NFL Scouting Combine, an event that showcases the physical skills of the crop of potential NFL draftees but also assesses each athlete in terms of intelligence testing.

Alan Kornspan is also the author of the next chapter that covers the use in sports of relaxation methods, especially hypnosis. Research and practice are discussed beginning in the 1930s; however, the chapter largely covers work done in the 1950s and 1960s. A focus of the chapter is the work of psychologist and hypnotist David Tracy who among other accomplishments worked in the 1950s with the St. Louis Browns baseball team and the New York Rangers hockey team. Tracy's work received a great deal of publicity in newspapers, magazines, and on television, and Kornspan argues that it served notice to a number of coaches and owners of the potential value of psychologists, especially in helping athletes reduce tension in those situations in which it was particularly detrimental to performance. Other individuals who would enter the field as early sport psychology practitioners included Bruce Ogilvie, George Crane, and Arthur Ellen. The importance of their work is discussed in the context of the beginnings of the modern profession of sport psychologist.

The conclusion by Christopher Green and Ludy Benjamin provides a historical context for the creation of a discipline and profession of sport psychology in the 1960s that has risen to levels of research and practice far beyond what Schulte and Griffith might have envisioned for the field. The authors discuss the changes in the field of physical education within universities and the factors that led to its dramatic makeover as a scholarly discipline. That transformation is integral to the development of a scholarly emphasis in the study of sport and eventually of the field of sport psychology. It is a story that involves government intervention; the Cold War; the public's growing fascination with professional sports; the economic changes spurred by that ever-growing audience; the needs of athletes, coaches, and team owners; and the ambitions of individuals from psychology and kinesiology and exercise science to demonstrate their relevance to the world of sport.

The stories detailed in the chapters that follow illustrate the varied motives that contributed to research and practice linking psychology and sport. There were those psychologists who conducted this research because they wished to demonstrate the applicability of the new science of psychology. There were those who were involved because of the methodological challenges of the research. There were those who found in sport a useful dependent variable to investigate core human behavior, namely learning. And there were those who merged their love of sport with their expertise in psychology. Collectively these chapters tell the story of sport psychology before there was an identifiable field as such. We hope that readers will find much enjoyment in these chapters and a better appreciation for the early ventures of psychologists into the world of sport.

References

Bäumler, G. 1997. Sports psychology. In *A pictorial history of psychology*, ed. W. G. Bringmann, H. E. Lück, R. Miller, and C. E. Early, 485–89. Chicago: Quintessence Publishing.

Burtt, H. E., and J. H. Nichols. 1924. Intelligence of varsity athletes. *American Physical Education Review* 29:125–28.

Davies, R. O. 2007. *Sports in American life: A history.* Malden MA: Blackwell.

Gardner, F. L. 2001. Applied sport psychology in professional sports: The team psychologist. *Professional Psychology: Research and Practice* 32:34–39.

Green, C. D. 2003. Psychology strikes out: Coleman R. Griffith and the Chicago Cubs. *History of Psychology* 6:267–83.

———. 2006. Coleman Roberts Griffith: "Adopted" father of sport psychology. In *Portraits of pioneers in psychology*, ed. D. A. Dewsbury, L. T. Benjamin, Jr., and M. Wertherimer, 151–66. Vol. 6. Washington DC: American Psychological Association and Lawrence Erlbaum.

Griffith, C. R. 1926. *The psychology of coaching: A study of coaching methods from the point of view of psychology.* New York: Scribner.

———. 1928. *Psychology and athletics: A general survey for athletes and coaches.* New York: Scribner.

Hacking, I. 1998. *Mad travelers: Reflections on the reality of transient mental illnesses.* Charlottesville: University of Virginia Press.

Hoberman, J. 2001. *Mortal engines: The science of performance and the dehumanization of sport.* Caldwell NJ: Blackburn.

Lashley, K. S. 1915. The acquisition of skill in archery. *Papers from the*

Department of Marine Biology of the Carnegie Institution of Washington 7 (211): 105–28.

LeUnes, A. 2009. *Sport psychology.* 4th ed. New York: Francis and Taylor.

McCloy, C. 1930. Character building through physical education. *Research Quarterly* 1:41–61.

Meyers, A. W., J. K. Coleman, J. P. Whelan, and R. S. Mehlenbeck. 2001. Examining careers in sport psychology: Who is working and who is making money? *Professional Psychology: Research and Practice* 32:5–11.

Paterson, D. G., and I. E. Peterson. 1928. Athletics and scholarship. *University of Minnesota Department of Physical Education Research Bulletin* 1:1–16.

Patrick, G. T. W. 1903. The psychology of football. *American Journal of Psychology* 14:104–17.

Ruble, V. W. 1928. A psychological study of athletes. *American Physical Education Review* 33:219–34.

Sarup, G. 1978. Historical antecedents of psychology: The recurrent issue of old wine in new bottles. *American Psychologist* 33:478–85.

Scripture, E. W. 1894. Tests of mental ability as exhibited in fencing. *Studies from the Yale Psychological Laboratory* 2:122–24.

———. 1895. *Thinking, feeling, doing.* Meadville PA: Flood and Vincent.

———. 1897. *The new psychology.* New York: Scribner.

Tissié, P. 1894a. Observations physiologiques concernant un record velocipédique. *Archives de Physiologie* 5:823–37.

———. 1894b. Psychologie de l'entraînement intensif. *Revue Scientifique*, 31e année, 4e série, tome II: 481–93.

Triplett, N. 1898. The dynamogenic factors in pacemaking and competition. *American Journal of Psychology* 9:507–33.

Wiggins, D. K. 1984. The history of sport psychology in North America. In *Psychological foundations of sport*, ed. J. M. Silva, III, and R. S. Weinberg, 9–22. Champaign IL: Human Kinetics.

1

The Dawn of Sport Psychology in Europe, 1880–1930

EARLY PIONEERS OF A NEW BRANCH OF APPLIED SCIENCE

Günther Bäumler

This sketch of the psychological investigation of sport in Europe between 1880 and 1930 covers a variety of different aspects of the science. The chronological order of the contributions between and within the sections is observed as far as possible. The researchers selected for inclusion are representative of European sport psychology to an acceptable degree, although many have of necessity been left out. Certain articles were also not available to the author, especially those from Russian investigators between 1925 and 1930.

Science and Society in the Nineteenth Century

At the end of the nineteenth century, the so-called fin de siècle, conditions were favorable for the growth of the psychological investigation of sport as a new applied science. Physiology had already attained a high scientific standard and had developed concepts that would later prove important for sport psychology as well. These included the concepts of automatism, ideo-motor action (Carpenter 1853, [1876] 1993), imagination (Tuke 1872), and dynamogeny (Brown-Séquard 1882, 1884; Féré 1885, 1887, 1892, 1904). Another movement of importance for society at this time was hygiene, from which also gymnastics, bathing, and swimming became popular.

At the same time sport itself was experiencing a kind of popular renaissance through the English sports, alpinism, and the nordic and alpine winter sports. In addition, the new safety bicycle, invented in the 1880s, made riding a popular pastime, and this activity subsequently became integrated into the modern life style.

Since the time of the Romantics (the first half of the nineteenth century), a scientific interest in the inner life of the human being had come into fashion in Europe and, in combination with experimental methodology, gave rise to a new experimental approach to psychology. Early publications on this type of psychology were Fechner's *Elemente der Psychophysik* (1860), Sergi's *Principi di Psicologia sulla Base delle Scienze Sperimentali* (1873–74), and Wundt's *Grundzüge der Physiologischen Psychologie* (1874) (see Saffiotti 1920). Shortly afterward, the first laboratory of experimental psychology was founded at Leipzig by Wilhelm Wundt in 1876.[1] Thus the so-called New Psychology had been established within only a few years (see Dewey 1886; Scripture 1897). Finally, as a consequence of the developments mentioned above (physiology-hygiene-sport-psychology), interest in a psychology of sport also arose toward the end of the nineteenth century.

Sport Psychology

As far as we know, the word *psychology* was not used in connection with the word *sport*, at least as a title, before the late 1890s. But a first indication of such a concept was in "Psychologie de l'Entraînement Intensif" (Psychology of Intensive Training), an article by the French hygienist Philippe Tissié published in 1894. Only a few years later in 1899 and 1900, the designation "psychology of sport" appeared as the title of two articles. The first one was by Balduin Groller.[2] It was published in two parts in October and December of 1899 in the journal *Die Wage* (Vienna) under the title "Zur Psychologie des Sportes" (About the Psychology of Sport).[3] Groller pointed to "certain psychological phenomena which are released by sportive activities but which are not scientifically researched as yet." And he considered it "questionable whether the most competent scientists even know of their existence" (337).[4] Only a few months later, in May 1900, a programmatic essay by the founder of the modern Olympic movement, Pierre de Coubertin, appeared under the nearly identical title "La Psychologie du Sport."[5] Since the contents of this essay were very different from that of Groller's, it is unlikely that Coubertin knew of Groller's article when he wrote his own. Therefore it seems that phrases cognate to *sport psychology* were coined by both authors independently of each other at the very end of the nineteenth century, with Groller possessing a slight priority.

Precursors of Sport Psychology

The first signs of a growing interest in the psychology of sport came from psychological outsiders. Around 1875 the Russian anatomist Pyotr Francevich Lesgaft began to develop a system of physical education.[6] His aim was to promote harmony between body and soul (or mind). The method Lesgaft recommended was to learn conscious control of the body. He supposed that the nervous system could be trained by this method and could then serve as the basis for the development of character and mind.

A few years later, the German physiologist Emil du Bois-Reymond (1881) concluded that motor exercise means "exercise of the central nervous system" and, therefore, such exercise is not only "gymnastics of the muscles" but even more so "gymnastics of the nerves," that is, gymnastics of the "psychical functions."[7] Similar thoughts were presented by the Hungarian Karoly Budinszky in his article "A Tornázás és az Akarat Fejlesztése" (About Gymnastic Activity and the Development of Will) (1884–85).[8] Budinszky's opinion was that strengthening the nervous system through physical exercise strengthens self-control and willpower.

Even more detailed suggestions of psychological phenomena related to sport were given by the French physiologist Fernand Lagrange (1888).[9] Examples of the phenomena Lagrange stressed include to be *en train* (nowadays called flow, or peak experience), warming up mentally, fixation in a highly motivated competitive state, mental work in gymnastics, and many others. It must be supposed that these suggestions of Lagrange had an instigating effect on researchers who came after him.

Angelo Mosso and Philippe Tissié

Two scientists and sport enthusiasts stand at the beginning of European sport psychology: Angelo Mosso and Philippe Tissié. The Italian physiologist Angelo Mosso had a great interest in the scientific study of the problems of physical education, physical exercise and sport.[10] He was therefore called the *apostolo dello sport* (Ferretti 1951). Mosso found in his experimental studies that intensive mental work causes a transitory weakening of muscle strength and that physical work weakens mental performance. From these findings he concluded that gymnastics in school cannot counteract the "brain exhaustion" produced by intensive mental learning, and the hours of gymnastics should accordingly not be interspersed among the normal hours of school learning (Mosso 1891, 1892, 1904).

In 1894 Mosso, together with his brother Ugolino Mosso and ten Italian mountain soldiers (*alpini*), ascended Monte Rosa in the Alps.[11] Here the party stayed in a hut at a height of 4,560 meters for about ten days, with the soldiers having to perform physical exercises (dumb-bell lifting).[12] Many physiological and biochemical measurements were recorded from the subjects.

Discussing the results published in 1897, Mosso pointed out two effects that are of interest for sport psychology. The first one we can call a pioneer effect: in mountain climbing, the person who is leading the group will be fatigued more quickly than his followers (Mosso 1897, ch. 6). Mosso suggested that the reason for this increased fatigue is that the person in front of the group has the additional load of attention and emotion (anxiety and care). The other effect noted by Mosso can be called the rivaling effect: he observed that the soldiers, especially in periods of boredom, spontaneously developed a tendency to compete with each other in their weight lifting tests. As a result the number of repetitions (up to exhaustion) increased with an unexpected rapidity.

Like Mosso, Philippe Tissié was interested in studying psychological phenomena of sport, especially cycling, and he pursued two lines of research.[13] First was the study of the psychological phenomena of training and of competition, and second was the search into the possibility of the therapeutic use of sport and physical exercise against psychopathological disorders. With this research Tissié did pioneering work in the field of sport psychology, beginning around 1891.

Psychology of Training and Competition

Tissié was the first to study the training and competition of sportsmen from the perspective of psychology. The relevant papers are "Psychologie de l'Entraînement Intensif" (Psychology of Intensive Training) (1894) and "Observations Physiologiques Concernant un Record Vélocipédique" (Physiological Observations Concerned with a Cycling Record) (1894). The phenomena that Tissié studied with cyclists were automatism, suggestion, and fatigue.[14] For example, he showed that during long-distance races exceptional mental states can come forward: such states include a regression to primitive emotional states, personality-doubling, hallucination, hypermnesia, and fixed ideas.[15] Some of the factors that can improve performance during competition are self-reliance, hope of success, and enthusiasm of the spectators. For training Tissié claimed that suggestion and autosuggestion are the most important.

Balduin Groller (1899) also reported psychological effects of competition. Referring to cycling, he pointed to the different roles of guiding and following: for example, the strict fixation of attention of the follower on the back wheel of the guiding man so as to keep in line. Groller further referred to the pacemaking effect.[16] As Groller pointed out, this effect can also be seen in horse racing; he expressed the conviction that race horses have a "will to win," an eager desire to fight for victory. This and many other observations made by Groller concerning tactics, moral depression, and so on show that he possessed a good insight into certain psychological phenomena of sport.

An interesting contribution from the view of statistics to the management of competitions concerns the question — first raised by Sir Francis Galton of England in 1902 — of how a certain sum, which is available for two prizes, should be divided between the first- and the second-place finishers. Employing the normal distribution and taking the number of competitors as large, the answer given by Galton was that about seventy-five percent of the available prize sum should go to the first place and about twenty-five percent to the second place. Karl Pearson (1902) corroborated the Galton's solution in a mathematical analysis of the problem.[17]

Like Groller, Hanns Georg Hartgenbusch (1926; English translation 1927) described psychological phenomena that he had observed as a sportsman.[18] However, he viewed all of these phenomena from the perspective of an established psychological perspective, Gestalt theory. For example, he pointed to the importance of a phenomenal representation of the performance in sports like high jump or broad jump.[19] He also stressed the "urgency of the spatial distance" (*Eindringlichkeit der-zu überbietenden-Raumstrecke*) for the discus and javelin thrower. Other topics he examined were the different sorts of behaviors seen among audience members at different athletic events, phenomenal centering, observable in football, skiing, and other sports, and the psychological dynamics in bicycle street races.[20] The contributions of Hartgenbusch are of special value on account of his use of established academic psychological terminology.

Another article that dealt with the psychological problems of training and competition was that of Philip Ewart Vernon (1928) in which the psychological phenomena of an eight-man rowing team and a college boat club were described and discussed.[21] Vernon considered autosuggestion to be very important since it can influence the performance of an oarsman in either a positive or negative way.[22] He further considered self-confidence rather than self-pity as most important for the individual oarsman. For example, ideas of desperation have an autosuggestive character and prevent the oarsman from doing his best, and therefore a coach should pay special attention to the mental aspects of the oarsman in order to establish self-confidence. Rowing as a crew requires harmony and a close interconnection among the members of the crew. A condition of success, Vernon argued, is the sentiment of "group self-respect," which depends on the crew's expectations about the success or failure of the boat. The first aim of the coach must be to manage this group's self-respect.

Yet another article of interest is that by Otto Klemm (1930) in which he stressed the concept of mental set (*Einstellung*) in sport.[23] For example, "set toward the goal" is essential for further endurance when the athlete is already exhausted. In this case the psychological attitude is crucial. Here imagination (mental representation, or *Einbildungskraft*) is not enough to attain the goal since only the goal-oriented will, or willpower, can combine the elements of an action to its totality. Set or will was therefore for Klemm an important condition and a matter of the right inner attitude, the confidence of victory, the belief into success.

A more fundamental but nevertheless important research was the paper by the psychiatrist Rudolf Allers and the physiologist Ferdinand Scheminsky, both of Vienna, on "Über Aktionsströme der Muskeln bei Motorischen Vorstellungen und Verwandten Vorgängen" (Concerning the Action Potentials of the Muscles during Motor Imaginations and Similar Processes) (1926). The two researchers showed by experiment that imagining the movement of certain parts of the body (for example, clenching the fist) can induce electrical action potentials of the muscles of the respective part but not of other parts. This finding can, of course, be considered a verification of the principle of William B. Carpenter's ideo-motor action, which is the basis, for instance, of mental training.[24] But application of this principle to sport was not present in Europe before 1930. This late introduction is also the case for other psychological training techniques, such as suggestion with and without hypnosis, autosuggestion (Couéism), yoga, systematic relaxation (Hirschlaff 1911), and autogenic training, that were even better known at that time.[25]

Valuable contributions to psychological knowledge about sport also came from athletes who described their own sport experiences. Very elaborate examples of this are reports by the Austrian alpinist Eugen Lammer.[26] His reflections show a striking similarity to some of the psychoanalytic ideas later expressed by Sigmund Freud (such as the concept of a mind divided among various dispositions and the efficacy of the unconscious). It is therefore interesting that Lammer as a student and young teacher lived in Vienna at the same time as that during which Freud developed his psychoanalytic theory there (see Lammer 1893; Bäumler 2002).

Another early sport report was that of the French cyclist Jiel, better known as Jiel-Laval, who in 1891 participated in the famous 1,200-kilometer (for him seventy-four-hour) road race from Paris to Brest and back again without any prescribed rest pauses.[27] In the same year Jiel-Laval published his mental experiences from this race, among which were some exceptional states of consciousness such as somnolence, hypervigilance, dissociation of the ego, and hallucination. Many other famous reports were published between 1900 and 1930, especially by French sportsmen.[28] An example of these are the reports by the solitary (one-handed) sailor Alain Gerbault.[29]

In Quest of Mental and Physical Overburdening in School

Between about 1875 and 1925 the hygienical problem of overwork, or overburdening, with mental stress in school was extensively discussed and studied in Europe.[30] One pressing question was whether sport in school could compensate for the mental fatigue produced by normal (academic) school subjects. Only a few of the numerous studies dealing with this question are noted here. The first one was a study by the Swiss Robert Keller (1894b) at a secondary school in Winterthur.[31] He found that twenty minutes of gymnastics produced a deterioration of performance in a subsequent reading test and that one hour of gymnastics produced more mental fatigue than one hour of normal (mental) school work. Like Mosso had before him, Keller concluded that school gymnastics is not a means for recovering from mental fatigue. Some years later, Ludwig Wagner (1898) performed another fatigue study.[32] He used skin-aesthesiometry in order to compare the fatiguing effect of an hour of school gymnastics (*Turnen*) with that of twelve other special school subjects.[33] The result was that mathematics and Latin, followed by gymnastics (*Turnen*), produced the highest degrees of fatigue (measured by desensitation of the skin) as compared with all other subjects. Wagner, however, showed that the fatiguing effect of gymnastics could be mitigated by a milder, more playful form of gymnastics that, among other things, included ball sports as well. Max Oker-Blom (1910) from Helsingfors, Finland, used serial addition as a measure of fatigue, and he observed a negative influence of gymnastics on mental performance in the subsequent school hour.[34] From this finding he concluded that the best hour for physical education in school is the last hour of the school day.

The view of the role of school gymnastics changed when Hanns Sippel (1923) introduced a more agreeable form of physical education.[35] With this innovation he showed that physical exercise can indeed reactivate the psychological energies of pupils. He therefore recommended that a mild form of physical exercise should be practiced daily in school for about thirty-five minutes.

Finally, Jacobus Meiring (1925) investigated the psychological effect of gymnastics upon the mental state during the following day.[36] He performed a formal experiment (though only carried out with a few subjects) with the experimental factor gymnastics versus no sports and the dependent variables of serial addition and cancellation. With this experiment he observed that physical exercise had a positive effect on mental ability during the next day that he called the law of delayed performance enhancement. The results of these studies, especially those of Sippel and Meiring, supported the claim of the Academy of Medicine of Paris, as presented by M. G. Langneau in 1888, that the intellectual overburdening and sedentary life style in school must be overcome by daily physical exercises suitable to the age of the children.

Psychopathology, Psychotherapy, and Psychohygiene

In several papers published between 1894 and 1909, Philippe Tissié called attention to the existence of such psychopathological phenomena as overmotivation and hallucinations in sport and also to the suitability of sports as a therapy for psychopathological disorders. He recommended a combination of sport, gymnastics, and psychological methods for the treatment of diseases like phobia, neurasthenia, and hysteria. But he also pointed to the negative psychological effects of sport abuse, as for example automatisms and disintegration of the personality. About the same time the French doctor Charles du Pasquier, in his article "Le Plaisir D'aller à Bicyclette" (The Pleasure of Riding a Bicycle) (1896), proposed bicycle sport as a therapy for neurasthenia whereby the symptoms of apathy and melancholy can be mitigated or even removed, and well-being, contentment, and optimism can be restored. For him the decisive therapeutic factor was the pleasure of speedy bicycle rides. Later, Toby Cohn (1913) recommended sport as an apt method for the treatment of psychopathological conditions such as tics, psychoneuroses and intestinal neuroses.[37] In his opinion the different sports can effectuate a broad range of psychological functions and traits such as self-confidence, emotional stability, and goal orientation.

Supposedly the first psychoanalysis of motivation for sport was performed by Helene Deutsch (1926) when she reported the case of a patient suffering from impotence, anxiety, and depression who could temporarily overcome his feelings of inferiority only by engaging in sport.[38] The first symptoms appeared when the patient as a young boy had come to see sports balls as threatening objects and had developed a phobia of them. In compensation he developed a keenness for ball sports, especially soccer and tennis. With this individual the danger threatening from within was displaced to the outside world and the phobia waned. Deutsch's general conclusion was that sport functions as a safety valve through which the harassed human being tries to ward off his or her fears.

Already in 1888 Fernand Lagrange had expressed his conviction that physical exercise influences the nervous system and may therefore be of use for psychohygienic purposes. After him Tissié and du Pasquier also advocated sports as a means of psychohygiene, with du Pasquier stressing the general psychohygienic effect of speedy bicycle rides. Du Pasquier also pointed to an interactive effect of the sort that nervously irritated persons are sedated by the rides while depressive persons experience a mood arousal.

Another proponent of sport as a means of psychohygiene was Eduard Bertz (1900), who stated that moderate bicycle sport may be a useful means for the healthy to maintain a "wellness of body and soul" (mind).[39] The factors that produce the healthy state are not only training of the body in the ride but also the exposure to fresh air, the experience of self-efficacy, and the pleasure that in this case is produced by the speed of the bicycle.

An empirical study of the psychohygienic effects of environmental factors in combination with free forms of sports and physical exercises is that by Bernhard Berliner (1913–14), who performed a psychological test study on children who spent weeks of recuperation in a holiday camp on the seacoast.[40] The primary result was an increase in their ability to concentrate.

Personality

The topic of character formation through sport was very popular in the nineteenth century, especially in connection with gymnastics. Among others, Lesgaft between 1875 and 1900 was an advocate of the thesis of character formation through sport. He stated that the sportive games encourage group spirit, unselfishness, social awareness, among other things, and create a better control of feelings, a stronger willpower, and a higher intelligence (see Wonneberger 1952; Rudik 1963, 342, 351; Riordan 1977, 236; Kulinkovic 1983, 657). Similarly J. Küppers (1891) expressed the opinion that gymnastics is not only exercise for the body but also, and primarily, for the mind.[41] The character traits this sport develops are willpower, courage, resolution, daring, and self-reliance. After Küppers Julius Baumann (1897) also praised the value of gymnastics and sports for the development of character.[42] Likewise, Konrad Koch

(1900) held the same position.[43] A very sensibly written booklet was that of B. Barth (1912) in which he stated that every sport is accompanied by mental activity and that this mental activity is the reason why character (that is, self-control and public spirit, among other traits) can be developed by means of sport.

Despite these claims, no empirical studies of character formation through sport were performed during this period. The reason may be that character measurement was not well developed and thus not practical for studies in sport, even though Schulte (1925a) and Knappe (1925) conceived character profiles of boxers and soccer players. With respect to empirical research, Heinrich Steinitzer (1907–8, 1910–11) was an exception of sorts. By means of graphology, he searched for characterological signs of alpinists. According to Steinitzer, the typical alpinist strives more intensively, approaches his or her goals more directly, and is personally more involved in his or her actions than are nonalpinists. Although the methodology of Steinitzer is questionable, his collection of specimens from the writings of famous mountaineers is of historical value.

Another empirical approach was that of Vernon (1929), who in his former study (1928) had characterized the personality of successful rowers as possessing qualities such as high suggestibility, determination, and extraversion. In his 1929 study Vernon developed a Will-Temperament test that was a modification of the Downey Will-Temperament Test of 1923. Vernon used his test to study the differences between rowers and nonrowers. The results seemed to correspond with Vernon's impressions of the personality of the rowers.

Causes and Correlates of Sport Ability

It was Francis Galton who in *Hereditary Genius* ([1869] 1892) pointed to athletic ability as an important differential aspect of character.[44] His collection of family relations contained, among others, able oarsmen and wrestlers, and his conclusion was that the exceptional ability to row must in part be hereditary in origin.

Alfred Binet in his 1893 study of the ability to play chess claimed that the memory ability which is necessary in order to play blindfold chess has to do more with abstract thinking than with concrete imagination.[45] Also the psychotechnical test-study of Djakow, Petrowski, and Rudik (1927) in which members of the Laboratory of Experimental Psychology and Psychotechnics of Moscow used participants of the International Chess Tournament of Moscow 1925 is pertinent here. The authors found that these very successful chess players revealed only an average performance in general tests of memory, attention, and thinking. But they were superior (a) in memorizing constellations of chessmen on the chessboard, (b) in a simultaneous regard of different parameters of the perceptual field (multidimensional attention, or range of attention), (c) in dynamic multidimensional attention (simultaneously registering the structures of the movements of different objects), and (d) in apprehension of regularities (logical induction, or synthetical thinking). The conclusion of the authors was that chess players are only superior in tests of more abstract thinking or in tests that are somehow more related to the task of playing chess.

In another study performed by Wilhelm Nolte (1925), it was found that general quickness of action (sprint running) is a fundamental individual characteristic in certain sports, as for example in boxing.[46] Somewhat amazing — though plausible as a result of a correlation with physical stature — is the study by Cambridge psychologists Banister and Blackburn (1930–31), who showed that the interpupillary distance correlated positively with the ability at ball games.

Several studies were also performed with school children or older students in order to find out whether an ability in sport relates to intelligence. A very early study was that performed by

Karl Pearson (1906–7), who found that "the athletic character in children ('athletic capability') is markedly associated with intelligence" (133).[47] Mabel Jane Reaney (1914), Heinrich Schüssler (1915), and Werner Schulte (1925c, 277) also reported positive correlations between measures of athletic and mental ability.[48]

Coubertin and the International Congress of the Psychology and Physiology of Sport

In his 1900 essay "La Psychologie du Sport" (The Psychology of Sport) Pierre de Coubertin judged sport psychology to be very important to the Olympic movement. His opinion was that in view of the rapid spread of sport it was necessary to understand this cultural phenomenon from the perspective of psychology. He therefore tried to analyze sport with respect to such psychological aspects as instinct, personality, harmony, ecstasy, collectivity, and morality. Coubertin demonstrated his conviction that psychology plays a leading role in the scientific study of sport. Afterward, he wrote several other essays about the psychology of sport that were published between 1906 and 1912 in the *Revue Olympique* and as a collection in *Essais de Psychologie Sportive* (1913a).

Coubertin was also the initiator of the first sport psychological congress, which was held in Lausanne in May 1913 as the International Congress of Psychology and Physiology of Sport. To this congress former president of the United States Theodore Roosevelt contributed a lecture about the psychological benefits of sport. According to Coubertin, the intent of the congress was "to make known a new science, or more exactly a branch of science which is unknown up to now by the public: the psychology of sport" (Coubertin 1913c; Coubertin 1913b, 20; Comité International Olympique 1913). For him this science was an important aid in developing the New Olympism as a "physical pedagogy" that is "intellectual, moral and aesthetical" in its character.[49]

Philosophical Psychology of Sport as Culture

The psychology of sport as a phenomenon of culture was studied in a more philosophical manner by Heinrich Steinitzer (1910).[50] Steinitzer's intent was to compare the cultural phenomena of alpinism and sport. In the final analysis his opinion was that sport and alpinism in its idealistic form are not compatible. He further concluded that alpinism is not compatible with culture because the alpinist goes to the mountains in order to flee from the cultural world. To obtain this result, Steinitzer first defined sport psychologically as "jede Tätigkeit . . . , soweit sie ausschließlich zu dem Zwecke ausgeführt wird, Kräfte mit anderen unter bestimmten Ausführungsbedingungen zu messen" ("every act that is performed exclusively to the end of measuring one's powers against another person under certain defined conditions") (7).

A few years later, the psychologist Wilhelm Benary (1913) also tried to define sport from the standpoint of psychology.[51] His opinion was that the essence of sport is the idea of perfect mastery of a skill. This formulation means that the condition of sport is a very exclusive one and that the difficulty is that in every instance the person engaged in sport can only approximately attain his or her goal. In other words, the sportsman competes against an ideal opponent who is infinitely superior to him. But, according to Benary, this concept of sport does not mean that sport is the opposite of culture as Steinitzer has thought. In spite of this opposition between Steinitzer and Benary, both are important to sport psychology insofar as they showed, like Coubertin, that a psychological definition of sport appeared to be possible if not mandatory.

Following the work of these researchers, Fritz Giese, in his book *Geist im Sport* (Mind in Sport) (1925), stated that sport must be conceived as the opposite of "physical culture" (*Körperkultur*) since it is action, or "deed," and is not primarily oriented to things like health. Sport is a special form of living (a *Lebensform*) and, as such, an objective (and autonomous) cultural phenomenon of human life. The three essential aspects of this *Lebensform* are the aesthetic, the heroic (according to Giese one such hero of sports was Babe Ruth), and the collective (that is, the affiliative or gregarious tendencies). Giese's central claim was that sport has mental values, and therefore it is much more than mere physical exercise, having its own specific effects upon the mind. The highest goal of sport, he said, is to influence human culture in a positive way.

Soon after, Alfred Peters (1927) also undertook a psychological analysis of the phenomenon of sport in relation to play and combat.[52] His main thesis was that play and combat can bring meaning to the life of humans while sport, with its infantile striving for records, cannot. Sport rather creates an idle type of human that serves only sensual pleasure and the social recognition of the individual. It uses the instincts of combat and of pleasure-play in a domesticated manner so that their primordial contents — the courage and the ecstasy — are eliminated. The results are theatricality, official control, and pseudoheroism. Psychologically sport is a trial to overcompensate psychical emptiness in a narcotizing manner. On the whole the contribution of Alfred Peters was a harsh critique especially of record sport from the standpoint of psychology and cultural anthropology.

The preface to the monograph of Alfred Peters was written by the philosopher Max Scheler who used the opportunity to present a short sketch of his own opinion of sport that differed markedly from that of Peters.[53] Scheler emphasized the close connection between physical culture and sport and saw the two in opposition to the spiritual asceticism that has dominated human culture throughout the Christian era. For Scheler modern sport serves as a resublimation of drive-energy to the body by means of artificial regulations in order to restitute the hitherto neglected values of bodily existence.

A further contribution to the philosophical or cultural psychology of sport was Hanns Sippel's paper "Vom Sinn und Wesen der Leibesübungen" (On the Meaning and Essence of Physical Exercises) (1928). For Sippel sport was first and foremost a matter of soul, that is, of the inner drives, wishes and needs, and not primarily a matter of the body. Only when these psychological energies are present is physical exercise also sport and can be used as a means for the development of the mental and psychical powers as well.

Rhythm and the Physical Culture Movement

Physical Culture (*Körperkultur*) was an ideological movement of the 1920s whose aim was to educate body, soul, and mind as a unity and which was influenced mainly by Ludwig Klages and other representatives of the then popular *Lebensphilosophie* (life philosophy).[54] One of the origins of the physical culture movement was the newly developed rhythmic gymnastics.

Extensive literature about the psychology and philosophy of rhythm and about rhythmic gymnastics exists, even from such well-known psychologists as Ernst Meumann, Kurt Koffka, and David Katz and also from Ludwig Klages. But only a very few of the publications about this topic can be mentioned here. An early work on rhythm was Karl Bücher's *Arbeit und Rhythmus* (Work and Rhythm) (1896).[55] It was an overview of anthropological research into the customs of folks around the world who ease the burden of heavy work through the use of rhythms. Among these types of work was rowing, in which many different rhythmical songs and forms of command have existed since antiquity.

A strong interest in the phenomenon of rhythm arises at the beginning of the twentieth century when the Swiss music teacher Emile Jaques-Dalcroze from Geneva, Switzerland, created rhythmic gymnastics, or eurhythmics.[56] The idea was that rhythm, not sound, is the primary form of movement. On the whole, the theoretical considerations of Jaques-Dalcroze about this subject (see 1907, 1919) contained much psychological and philosophical thinking concerning the efficacy of rhythm in human life.

Later, during the 1920s, his former pupil Rudolf Bode developed his own system of expression-gymnastics, or expressive calisthenics (*Ausdrucksgymnastik*), and he too based his system on psychology and philosophy.[57] Bode's opinion was that the expression of the psychological impulses through movement is a source of health, and rhythm is a means to increase the expressive power of the organism so that the latent psychic energies can be freed. With regard to teaching his form of gymnastics, relaxation and concentration seemed most important to Bode (Bode 1922, 1925, 1931).

The ideas of the dancer Rudolf von Laban, the founder of choreutics (*Bewegungschöre*) and dance gymnastics, were very fruitful for research into movement rhythm.[58] Laban's contributions to the psychology of human movement were authentic, and with his choreutic conception of kinesthetic motor space and his choreutic laws, he built a closed theory of movement in dance and dance calisthenics. His movement notation system, the Labanotation, or Kinetography Laban, was an ingenious invention too (see Hutchinson 1977; Longstaff 2000). Of special value for sport psychology was Laban's 1920 book *Die Welt des Tänzers* (The World of the Dancer) in which he presented many insightful psychological statements about dance as an art of space harmony and about rhythmic movement.

An experimental study of rhythm was performed by the German Ewald Sachsenberg (1927).[59] His subjects had to perform a rhythmical gymnastic movement sequence repeatedly in a stereotypic manner under the influence of different sorts of rhythmic acoustic stimulation. With this method Sachsenberg ascertained an interactive influence of supporting versus counteracting acoustic rhythm on the quality of the movement rhythm.

A theoretical treatment of the physical culture movement in which rhythm played a prominent role was the book *Körperseele* (Body-Mind) (1924) by the psychologist Fritz Giese. By body-mind Giese meant that a physical-psychical unity exists with regard to expression. According to Giese, the aim of the physical culture movement was to educate the total person in order to allow for interaction between body and mind, and a harmony between body and mind therefore had to be established.

The Attractiveness of Sport: Motives and Interests

Besides the early statement by Charles du Pasquier (1896) that the primary motive of bicycle sport is a pleasure of speed, the question of motives for sport was dealt with mainly in respect to mountaineering. Eduard Richter (1903), for example, tried to indicate the motives that urge humans to ascend mountains "without necessity."[60] Among other things his list of motives contained the thrill of novelty, oddness, and adventure, the pleasure of wild life (regression to nature and the conquest of pains and dangers), the aesthetic delight in viewing the mountains, and the wish to experience one's own power and agility.

Another very lively contribution was that from the English alpinist Geoffrey E. Howard (1920–21).[61] Howard tried to find out why he went to the mountains "again and again" since, as he stated, "I die several deaths on a mountain" (68). Yet his experiences in the mountains fascinated him, for example a vision he had in the Selkirks of the Canadian Rockies, "a vision of [the god] Pan himself" (66). Howard continued, "The Canadian Rockies bring me a thousand thoughts and a thousand compensations" (66), for "among the hills, great or small, you get back . . . to the beginnings of things, to . . . a wholesome sense of the exceeding littleness of the trifles which absorb and stultify our foolish hearts" (68–69). Howard's thoughts about his motives are, of course, not science, but they are the profound reflections of an intelligent "mountain-maniac" and thus are at least valuable insights into motivation for this sport.

A further contribution to motivation for mountaineering is that from Else Voigtländer (1923).[62] Her main assertion was that mountaineering is of interest to people because it opens a new, unknown world, a world that lies "there above" in a prominent position between heaven and earth and represents grandeur, solitude, stateliness, and freedom. An essential condition for experiencing these feelings is the shift of the visual perspective that occurs with the ascent to the high mountains. Compared with this perspective, the pleasure of overcoming the dangers and pains of ascent is only of secondary importance as a motive. Of course, a great pleasure and reinforcement is the summit ecstasy that can even take on a religious dimension.

A very sophisticated approach to sport motivation was presented in Mabel Jane Reaney's dissertation "The Psychology of the Organized Group Game" (1916).[63] One of Reaney's intents was to present a theory of the attraction of organized group games (football, hockey, and so on). Basic to these games are certain primitive instincts (instincts to chase and to fight, among others) as well as some higher instincts (instincts to compete with rivals and of group consciousness or gregariousness). In Reaney's opinion the organized group game can serve as a security valve to provide a catharsis for these drives or instincts. This catharsis is mediated by sublimation, a sort of intellectualization of the satisfaction of the involved instincts by a complex of sport-related ideas, the so-called game-group of ideas. Though only theoretical in nature, the conclusions that Reaney reached about the development of the attraction of certain sports were thought out carefully (see Bäumler 2007).

In the search for sport motivation, several empirical studies about the interest of pupils in school gymnastics were carried out. Marx Lobsien (1903, 1909) from Kiel, Germany, asked school children which school subject they liked best. The result was that younger boys as well as girls (up to fourteen) liked gymnastics (and also arithmetic) very much. With increasing age however, gymnastics was more and more displaced by history. This finding was corroborated by several other studies, such as that by the Swede Georg Brandell (1915) that showed unequivocally that interest in school gymnastics decreased as the children aged while other subjects, such as mathematics, gained in interest.

Social Psychology

The social-psychological aspect of sport was vaguely touched upon by Mosso and Tissié and in the self-reports of sportsmen, and afterward the first experimental investigation in this area was performed by the American Norman Triplett (1898).[64] He was followed by Walther Moede, who in 1914, 1920, and 1920–21 published the results of experimental studies of performance in isolated versus other-oriented (that is, competitive) work tasks.[65] Moede used sportlike tasks in which a maximum of action speed or a maximum of force had to be attained (that is, a tug-of-war). Different situations were compared: single work, duel, and parties competition, competition of one group against another.[66] Moede found that parties competition produced the most effort, followed by the duel. He concluded that aside from a competitive effect, there also exists a solidarity effect in groups.

Group behavior was also the main interest of Vernon (1928), who studied behavior in a rowing club.[67] Vernon's supposition was that rowing as a crew requires harmony and close interconnections among the members of the crew. He also regarded as an important condition of success the self-confidence of the whole group, the sentiment of group self-respect. This group self-respect depends, he argued, on the crew's expectations about the success or failure of the boat. Therefore the first aim of the coach of rowers must be to manage the group self-respect. As to the relation between the individual and the crew, it is important to see that every technical fault in one member must instantly be compensated for by the crew as a whole. Accordingly, it is understandable that the whole group life of the boat club is based on the rapport between its members and that its optimal character is that of a "peculiar gregarious self-satisfaction."

Werner Schulte and the Institutionalization of Sport Psychology

The early contributions (up to 1930) to sport psychology in Europe were only by-products of ongoing academic research. But over time a tendency emerged that institutionalized and professionalized sport psychology. The first signs of such developments were at the Olympic Congresses of 1897 in Le Havre, France, at which, among others, a lecture about the "Psychology of Physical Exercises" was presented and at the Congrès International de Psychologie et Physiologie Sportives of 1913 in Lausanne, Switzerland (see above).

The most prominent step toward the institutionalization of sport psychology was gained in connection with the foundation in May 1920 of the Deutsche Hochschule für Leibesübungen in Charlottenburg, near Berlin (Janssen 1997).[68] That same year, a psychological laboratory was installed there under the direction of Robert Werner Schulte.[69] The task of the laboratory was to develop methods of aptitude testing in sport (see Diem 1922, 43).[70] With verve and originality, Schulte began to invent psychotechnical apparatuses in order to objectively measure sport-related abilities. Beginning in 1920, he also gave lectures about sport psychology to physical education students. As early as 1921 he published his first book about sport psychology: *Leib und Seele im Sport* (Body and Mind in Sport). During the next few years he wrote several other books and many articles about sport psychology. It was a great loss for both German and the wider European sport psychology when he died as a young man of thirty-five in January 1933 (Janssen 2006, 137).

Schulte's best-known contribution to sport psychology is the 1925 monograph *Eignungs- und Leistungsprüfung im Sport* (Aptitude- and Performance-Testing in Sport). It contained eighteen chapters, the main concern of which was the methodological problems of aptitude measurement in sport. One of Schulte's more prominent ideas was the formulation of a law of the optimal amount of physical exercise (*Gesetz der Optimaldosis*) (Schulte 1925b, 48–50). This principle was an application of the Arndt-Schulz law (Arndt 1885).[71] The monograph also contained four chapters authored by others that dealt with strength, boxing, football and precompetition fright.

Werner Schulte had a good reputation as a creative psychotechnician, as can be seen from the memorial address that was dedicated to him in 1933 by the French psychotechnician Jean-Maurice Lahy.[72] Also in reviewing Schulte's monograph *Psychologie der Leibesübungen* (The Psychology of Physical Education) (1928), Christian Ruckmick (1930) of the University of Iowa praised the work for its "lucid discussions" and for a "mental attitude that is in keeping with modern psychology."

In 1925 Schulte changed to the Preußische Hochschule für Leibesübungen and the Psychotechnische Hauptprüfstelle für Sport und Berufskunde (Vocational Guidance in Sport) in Berlin. Here he again established a well-equipped laboratory of sport psychology and extended his research activities. Schulte's last contribution to sport psychology, "Psychologische Erfahrungen als Sportflieger und Fallschirmspringer" (Psychological Experiences as a Sport Aviator and Parachutist), was published in 1931, about fourteen months before his death.

The publications of Werner Schulte concerning sport psychology were many-sided and sometimes also of a philosophical nature. Most characteristic of Schulte, however, is his invention of psychotechnical apparatus for research and aptitude testing in sport, a discussion of which is presented in his monographs of 1925 and 1927.

We might conclude therefore that 1920 was the year of the first formal attempt to institutionalize sport psychology as an academic discipline. It was Robert Werner Schulte who first engaged in this task, and consequently he might be called the first professional sport psychologist in Europe, if not in the world. However, the professionalization of sport psychology was not to survive long. Schulte's early death and the turmoil of the 1930s and 1940s interrupted the development of the discipline of sport psychology until the 1960s.[73]

The Russian Sport Psychologists

Beginning with Lesgaft, Russian scientists also participated in the research on the psychological effects of physical exercise and sport. As far as we can gather from some remarks by the well-known Russian sport psychologist Petr Antonovic Rudik in 1963, research departments of sport psychology were established around 1930 at the institutes of physical culture in Moscow and Leningrad. But even before the appearance of these departments, beginning about 1925, sport psychological experiments were performed at these institutes by psychologists such as Kudisch, Nikitin, Netchayev, Puni, Rudik, and Tchutchmaryev (see Puni 1961, 7; Rudik 1963, 342).[74] Rudik, for example, worked at the Central State Institute of Physical Culture in Moscow but was also associated with the Laboratory of Experimental Psychology and Psychotechnics in Moscow, as can be surmised from the monograph *Psychologie des Schachspiels* (Psychology of Chess) published by Djakow, Petrovski, and Rudik in 1927.[75]

As to methodology and contents the research of these psychologists was of course in line with the psychological mainstream of the 1920s, that is, experimental and psychotechnical.[76] But the details of this research are not known to us, with the exception of the monograph by Djakow, Petrovski, and Rudik. We only know that Rudik did research around 1925 on the development of skills, on the influence of muscular work on the reaction process, and on reactions during sport performance and that in 1930 he developed a psychotechnical methodology for studying the processes of perception, attention, memory and reaction. Further, Alexander Netchayev (Netschajew), the former director of the pedological research institute at St. Petersburg (then Leningrad), performed research on the influence of physical exercise on the power of perception, memory, imagination and attention (1926).[77] Also, we know that Tchutchmaryev worked on the influence of physical education on the development of the intellectual processes (1928) and Puni (in Leningrad) on the influence of competitions on the psyche of skiers (1929) (see Rudik 1963, 342).[78]

But some twenty years earlier, around 1905, studies of behavior during gymnastics and play and of psychomotor ability as an aspect of personality (that is, agility, speed, and richness of movement) had been performed at the Laboratory of Experimental and Pedagogical Psychology of St. Petersburg by the differential and experimental psychologist Lasurski and his coworkers A. J. Nekljudowa, N. E. Rumiantsev (Rumjanzew), L. J. Palmin, N. N. Tytschino, and others (see Rumiantsev 1914, 419; Lasurski 1913).[79] Tytschino (1908), for example, developed a typology of motorial behavior and wrote about the *Correlations of the Speed of Different Psychomotor Processes*. About 1905 Rumiantsev may have studied the motor behavior of some youths, or in 1909, together with Lasurski, he may have studied the characterological aspects of the speed of reaction tasks (Tytschino 1908; Lasurski 1913, 88, 110–12; Rumiantsev 1914, 420). Nevertheless, the most active Russian researcher of sport psychology until the 1930s was of course P. A. Rudik, whom P. Kunath (1963) called the "past master of the Soviet sport psychology."

Psychotechnics, Aptitude Testing, and Motor Skills

Psychotechnics was the forerunner of industrial psychology and ergonomics.[80] Its peculiar method was aptitude measurement by use of apparatuses that simulated the work situations (Gundlach 1996, 132). Related to sport, the leading psychotechnician was Werner Schulte. A special part of psychotechnics was the study of motor skills that was considered important for industry as well as for sport. A popular introduction to this subject was provided by T. H. Pear in a booklet (1924), the original title of which was *Skill in Work and Play*.[81] When this booklet was translated into German in 1925 the title was changed to *Geschicklichkeit in Sport und Industrie*, which seems to be more representative of its contents.[82]

Pear presented a concise introduction to the principles of learning motor skills used in sport and industry. Pear employed many examples to demonstrate the applicability of these principles in skill development, and it is interesting to read that it was an oarsman who has detected the parallels in learning the skills of a mine-cutter, a chocolate-packer, and a rower, all of whom must learn to perform regular arm movements. Pear's booklet was a model of how scientific results may be made known to teachers or trainers. And it also showed that sport psychology has applications to motor learning as well.

In Germany Otto Klemm (1929) analyzed skilled behavior and skill acquisition at slot machines, the handling of which was also a matter of perceptual-motor skill and therefore considered at the time a sport. As to the development of skill through practice, Wilhelm Cohnen (1927) experimented with the throwing underarm of a small leather ball. The primary result was that only after a long period of practice (eighty-eight days) did the individual differences become stable. From this study Cohnen concluded that a diagnosis of aptitude based on only one or at most a few test trials cannot be considered valid as related to later performance, for example in a profession or sport.

In respect to psychotechnical aptitude testing, the tests for clinical assessment also deserve mention. According to the assessment of motor ability, the Russian neurologists Oseretzky and Gourevitch were the pioneers. Encouraged by Gourevitch, N. Oseretzky began in 1921–22 to develop a metrical scale for assessment of motor ability in children.[83] The first conception of the scale was published by Oseretzky in 1923 in Russian and then in 1925 in German. Soon the test was further elaborated upon.[84] Later still, it was also adapted for international use (the Vineland adaptation and the Lincoln-Oseretsky Scale) (see Cassel 1950–51). In its elaborated form and as a prototype of further motor tests, the Oseretzky scale is a valuable means of measurement in sport psychology too.

A peculiar field of psychotechnics was the investigation of the psychological problems of aviation; most of the studies were performed as military research in connection with World War I. Many psychologists from different European nations, such as Italy, France, England, and Germany, participated in this research into the qualifications of an aviator.[85] Later, during the 1920s, Schulte also published papers on the psychology of sky sports, that is, flying sport airplanes and gliders as well as parachute descents (1926, 1927b, 1931).

Finally, it should be mentioned that a large amount of literature also exists concerning the influence of low or high environmental (air or water) pressure upon the psychological functions of humans at great heights (as with mountaineering, balloon sport, and aviation) or depths (as with scuba diving). But the early history of this research deserves a special article to deal with it.

All the research in Europe between 1880 and 1930 that is described here was due to the effort of true pioneers of sport psychology. In many cases they were rather inexperienced researchers whose main support was their own enthusiasm. Accordingly, nearly all of these studies were based on weak theories and even weaker methodologies. Nevertheless, many new ideas, questions, phenomena, and concepts were developed so that a body of knowledge grew that when we include the results from America, was large enough to establish (or more correctly to bring on the "dawn" of) this new branch of the applied sciences that was to be called sport psychology.

Notes

This contribution to the history of sport psychology is dedicated to Professor Dr. Heinz Schmidtke, emeritus of ergonomics at the Technische Universität München, as an expression of gratitude for his decisions made as president of this university in favor of sport psychology in Munich at about the time of the Olympic Games in 1972.

I am highly indebted and grateful to the editor Professor Christopher Green for many valuable suggestions, corrections, critiques, and contributions concerning the manuscript and also to Dr. E. Beese (Munich) for his help in correcting the English.

1 Often the foundation of Wundt's laboratory is dated 1879. Zusne (1984) gives the date as 1875 and so does Chu (1982, 25). But James McKeen Cattell, who had been an assistant of Wundt, had reasonable arguments for dating the establishment of the laboratory to 1876 (Cattell 1928).

2 The original name of Balduin Groller (1848–1916) was Albert Goldscheider. He was born in Arad (a town then in Hungary but since 1920 in Romania) and became a writer and journalist in Vienna.

3 Professor Dr. Jürgen Court (University of Erfurt) has kindly informed me about the existence of Groller's article.

4 Obviously Groller had overlooked the beginnings of the sport psychological research activities in the 1890s in Europe and America.

5 Pierre Frédy, Baron de Coubertin (1863–1937), the founder of the

Olympic Games in modern times, was a historian, philosopher, humanist, and essayist. He considered psychology as being important to sports science because sport is a phenomenon of human culture and personal interest.

6 Pyotr Francevich Lesgaft (1837–1909) was a professor of anatomy in St. Petersburg, Russia. As early as 1874 he began to write about the usefulness of physical education to train the mental abilities of normal and handicapped children. His collected papers *Guide to Physical Education of School Children* appeared as two volumes in 1888 and 1901 and again between 1951 and 1952. His memoirs were published in 1912. See Wonneberger 1952; Rudik 1963, 342, 351; Schuwalow 1963; Riordan 1977, 1987, 392; Kulinkovic 1983.

7 Emil Du Bois-Reymond (1818–96) was professor of physiology at the University of Berlin. He is best known for his studies of animal electricity (Zusne 1984).

8 Karoly Budinszky, said to be a teacher in Budapest, published his article in the Hungarian language in the journal *Tornaügy* (Gymnastics) (Rókusfalvy 1974; Bäumler 1989).

9 Fernand Lagrange (1848–1909) was supposedly a physiologist or a medical doctor in Limoge, France, where nowadays a Collège Fernand Lagrange exists. In 1888 he also published an article, "La Fatigue et l'Entrainement," *Revue Scientifique* 16, 2e semestre: 632–38.

10 Angelo Mosso (1846–1910), a professor of physiology at the University of Turin, Italy, invented the Mosso ergograph and was a pioneer in psychophysiology of nervous fatigue and fear. See Mosso 1884, 1891.

11 Ugolino Mosso was professor of pharmacology at the University of Genoa, Italy.

12 The ascent took about twenty-four days to study acclimatisation, while the total expedition lasted about six weeks.

13 The hygienist Philippe Tissié was born in 1852 in La Bastide-sur-l'Hers (in the Ariège) and died in 1935 in Pau (the French Pyrénées). He was conservator at the Anthropological Society of Bordeaux, received his medical degree in 1887, and published his first monograph, *L'hygiène du Vélocipédiste* (The Hygiene of

the Bicyclist), in 1888. Tissié was an active member of the French Society of Psychiatry and Neurology, Inspector of Physical Education in Bordeaux, and founder of the Physical Education League of the Gironde in southern France. See Thibault 1985; Klecker and Bäumler 1995.

14 The concept of automatism (unconscious automatic action) was discussed particularly by Pierre Janet (1859–1947) in 1889. It is partly based on the theory of the two from the neurologist Jean-Baptiste Charcot (1825–93).

15 An example of an emotional state is a fit of rage.

16 Groller did not mention the 1898 article by Norman Triplett (see Davis, Huss, and Becker, this volume), and it is not clear whether he knew of it (see Bäumler 1998; Lück 1998) because it appeared only one year before Groller's own work. With respect to the pacemaking effect, Groller wrote that "science has not dealt with that problem up to now" (1899, 339). Groller theorized that the pacemaking effect has to do with a sort of hypnosis and with autosuggestions. Earlier in 1887, in his *Sensation et Mouvement*, the Parisian psychiatrist Charles Féré (1852–1907) had shown by experiment that the strength of muscular contraction is increased by "even apparently irrelevant external stimulation" (Zusne 1984). He explained this effect with the principle of dynamogeny (dynamogènie) that was detected about 1880 by the French neurologist Charles Edouard Brown-Séquard (1817–94).

17 Pearson valued Galton's solution as "a sound rule for practical purposes," which is applicable "in the educational world" as well as in "rifle, athletics, sporting and agricultural competitions" (1902, 397). He also considered the solution of Galton's Difference Problem as "a real advance in statistical theory" since "we fix our attention no longer to the whole population, but on definite individuals in its ordered array" (390).

18 Hartgenbusch was a pupil of the Gestalt psychologist Kurt Koffka at the University of Giessen, Germany. Koffka was later at Smith College.

19 For example, phenomenal representation is given in high jump by the visible bar, indicating the performance (height) that the jumper has to master at the moment.

20 Phenomenal centering means unintended and unwished fixity of
the attention (and consequently of action) on certain objects of
the perceptual field: for instance, in ball games the fixation of the
forward upon the prominent Gestalt of the goal keeper.

21 Born in 1905 at Oxford, England, Philip Ewart Vernon was an
educational psychologist and psychometrician. He died in 1987 in
Calgary, Canada. Earning a BA in 1927 and an MA in 1930 at St. John's
College, Cambridge, Vernon was later professor of psychology at the
University of Glasgow, psychological research adviser of the British
Army and Navy (1942–49), and professor of educational psychology
at the University of London. From 1968 to 1975 he was professor at
the University of Calgary. Among his many writings are *Studies in
Expressive Movement (1933), The Measurement of Abilities* (1940),
Personality Assessment (1963), and *Intelligence* (1979).

22 The concept of autosuggestion has been discussed since the
middle of the nineteenth century. Vernon used it in the sense of
an often unconscious, affective disposition, a self-confidence or
self-pitying, a certain conviction or belief, which can be a positive
or negative influence on performance. For example, any "fears [of
an oarsman] as to his being able to last out while rowing a course
always seem to realize themselves by autosuggestion" (Vernon
1928, 317). Intentional autosuggestion by use of a repeatedly
spoken, stereotyped formula so as to convince oneself was the main
principle of Couéism, the method of self-mastery of the French
Emile Coué (1857–1926). See Baudouin 1920; Coué 1913, 1922.
Tissié (1894b) observed autosuggestions of cyclists in the form
of soliloquies, and J. H. Schultz (1927) identified his method of
autogenic training as a form of conscious "autosuggestive training."

23 Gustav Otto Klemm (1884–1939) was a member of the Leipzig
school of Ganzheitspsychologie and professor of applied psychology
and experimental pedagogy at the University of Leipzig. For
comprehensive information about Klemm, see Loosch 2008.

24 William B. Carpenter (1813–85) was registrar at the University of
London and later at the University of Edinburgh (Zusne 1984). He
was author of the important book *Principles of Mental Physiology*
(1876) in which he described the ideo-motor principle.

25 Autogenic training is relaxation technique that involves conscious control of normally not controllable (vegetative) physiological functions by autosuggestion. It is commonly attributed to the German neurologist Johannes H. Schultz. In an article from 1929 he envisioned autogenic training as a form of inner gymnastics.

26 Eugen Lammer (1863–1945) was teacher at a grammar school in Stockerau, Austria. As an alpinist he wrote many articles about mountaineering, and he promoted climbing without a guide. See Messner and Höfler 1999.

27 Jiel-Laval's original name was Pierre-Joseph Laval, or Joseph Laval. The name Jiel was at first a nickname made out of his personal initials J and L. It was later combined with the right surname Laval and the designation "Jiel-Laval" became usual also in publications. Jiel-Laval was born in 1855 in Saint Junien, near Limoges, in France. In 1877 he came to Bordeaux, where together with friends he founded the Veloce-Club Bordelais, became one of the founders of the Ligue Francaise de l'Education physique, and became one of the most prominent cyclists of France. Philippe Tissié from Bordeaux was his psychological and physiological coach and studied the mental experiences made during Jiel-Laval's cycle races. In the race Paris–Brest–Paris Jiel-Laval finished second among 206 competitors. He died in 1917 at the age of sixty-one. "Èloge funebre de Joseph Laval dit Jiel Laval" (Funeral Oration for Joseph Laval, Called Jiel-Laval), the funeral oration for him, was held by Maurice Martin, then the most influential sport journalist and, according to Tissié (1917), the grand maitre du cyclisme in France. This oration, which ran sixteen pages, should have been published in 1917, but it could not be found by the present author. Philippe Tissié also wrote a necrology, and this one is preserved (Tissé 1917). Photographs of Jiel-Laval, who seems to have been the first athlete to be studied in a sport psychological research (around 1890), can be found in *Le Progrès Illustre*, no. 25, June 7, 1891, as well as in *Revue des Jeux Scolaires*, 1917: 58. For further information on the Paris–Brest–Paris race of 1891, see also Deon 1997.

28 For an overview of such French reports in the 1920s, see Jossmann 1931.

29 Alain Gerbault (1893–1941) came from Laval, a town between Le Mans and Rennes, on the road from Paris to Brest. He wrote several books about his sailing adventures, mostly as diaries from on board.

30 In later times the study of this question belonged to the experimental education movement of which professor Ernst Meumann (1862–1915) was the most prominent representative. See Meumann 1907–14.

31 Dr. Robert Keller was the headmaster of a secondary school in Winterthur, Switzerland.

32 Ludwig Wagner was a medical doctor and a teacher at a secondary school in Darmstadt, Germany.

33 The method was developed by H. Griesbach (1895), who was professor in Mülhausen (Mulhouse), Alsace (France).

34 Maximilian Oker-Blom (1863–1917) was professor of hygiene at the University of Helsingfors (now Helsinki), Finland. See Burgerstein 1920.

35 Hanns Sippel (1892–1973) was a physical educator and a medical doctor. He prepared his dissertation, "The Influence of Gymnastics upon the Performances of School Children," in 1922 at the Sportpsychologisches Laboratorium of the Deutsche Hochschule für Leibesübungen in Berlin under Robert Werner Schulte and received his doctorate from the University of Erlangen, Germany, under Otto Stählin. His dissertation was then published under the title *Physical Education and the Mental Work of the School Child* (Berlin, 1923). See Lück 2006b.

36 Jacobus Meiring, born 1898 in Johannesburg, then Republic Transvaal, South Africa, received a BS in Natural Science and a bachelor's in education at the University of Stellenbosch, where he also was a teacher at the secondary school. He studied psychology at the University of Leipzig and in 1925 received his PhD there under Felix Krueger and Otto Klemm.

37 Dr. Cohn was a neurologist in Berlin.

38 Born in Przemysl, Galizia (now Poland), Helene Deutsch (1884–1982) was a pupil of Sigmund Freud and from 1925 to 1935 was director of the Vienna Institute of Psychoanalysis. Starting in 1935, she was a professor at Boston University. See Slovenko and

Knight 1967, 8; Roazen 1985. Her article appeared first in 1925 in German and then in 1926 in English. A part of the English version was reproduced under the title "Some Dynamic Factors in Sport" (Slovenko and Knight 1967).

39 The writer and journalist Eduard Bertz (1853–1931) lived from 1881 to 1883 in the community of Thomas Hughes in Rugby, Tennessee, where he installed the library. One of his novels was *Das Sabinergut* about Rugby; the novel later appeared under the title *Amerika, du Hast es Besser* (America, You Have It Better). See Debruyn 1976; Schenkel 2006.

40 Bernhard Berliner was from the Zentralstelle für Balneologie in Berlin.

41 Dr. J. Küppers was director of a teacher's training college in Siegburg, Germany.

42 Julius Baumann was professor of philosophy at the University of Göttingen, Germany.

43 Konrad Koch (1846–1911) was professor of history and ancient languages at the secondary school of Braunschweig and a member of the German Zentralausschuß für Volks-und Jugendspiele, which was founded in 1891. See Court 2006.

44 The anthropologist and general scientist Sir Francis Galton (1822–1911) was called the father of the study of individual differences, especially in psychology. He tried to prove his conviction that mental traits are inherited in the same way as physical traits (Zusne 1984).

45 Alfred Binet (1857–1911) was the most prominent French psychologist of his time and director of the psychological laboratory at the Sorbonne in Paris (Zusne 1984). He was an early expert of hypnotism, suggestion, and thought processes and is best known for his development along with Théodore Simon of the first intelligence test in 1905. Binet's paper of 1893 was published in 1966 in English under the title "Mnemonic Virtuosity: A Study of Chess Players."

46 Wilhelm Nolte was assistant at the Psychotechnische Hauptprüfstelle für Sport und Berufskunde in Berlin. In the study cited, he used the Boxing-Quickness Test from Schulte.

47 See also Pearson 1904–5. Karl Pearson (1857–1936) was professor of mathematics at the University College of London. He invented the product-moment correlation coefficient *r*.

48 Mabel Jane Reaney performed her study at the Psychological Laboratory of King's College, University of London.

49 The preparations and some results of the congress were described in Coubertin 1913b. The proceedings were edited by Coubertin as a monograph in 1913. A constructive critique by Coubertin appeared in the *Revue Olympique*, 1914, in four parts (nos. 97–100). See Coubertin 1914.

50 Heinrich Steinitzer (1869–1947) of Munich was a writer and graphologist as well as an alpinist. His father, an Austrian officer, was born, like Groller, in the Hungarian (now Romanian) town of Arad. See Märtin 2006, 50–51.

51 Wilhelm Benary (1888–1955) was born in Erfurt, Germany, and died in California. He studied philosophy and prepared his dissertation "Die psychologische Theorie des Sports" (The Psychological Theory of Sport) in Breslau, Germany (now Wroclaw in Poland), where he received his PhD in 1913 studying under William Stern. During World War I he was an aviation psychologist. In psychology he is known by his study of a 1922 case of psychic blindness and by the so-called Benary cross, an optical illusion that demonstrates the brightness contrast (1924). See Court and Janssen 2003.

52 The sociologist and journalist Alfred Peters (1888–1974) received his PhD at the University of Cologne in 1925 under the philosopher Max Scheler. His dissertation "Der Begriff des Sports" (The Concept of Sport) was published in 1927 under the title *Psychologie des Sports* (The Psychology of Sport). See Court and Nitsch 2006.

53 Max Scheler (1874–1928) was professor of philosophy at the University of Cologne. His special interests were ethics, religion, and philosophical anthropology.

54 The German-Swiss philosopher Ludwig Klages (1872–1956), who from 1919 lived in Kilchberg, near Zurich, is known by his metaphysique of life. In his opinion all living things have a soul that is the essence (the meaning) of life. Additionally, humans are able to represent sensations in images and therefore acquire a *geist*

(spirit) that is always in combat with the soul within the person (that is, nature). See Klages's 1929 book *Der Geist als Widersacher der Seele* (Spirit as the Opponent of the Soul). Klages considered that the psychic aspects of life can be apprehended only in expressive movements, and he therefore developed his own mode of graphology as well as the so-called characterology. Heinrich Steinitzer (see above) was his pupil in graphology and characterology as well as a lifelong friend. Klages stressed the significance of the unconscious, instincts, intuition, feelings, and ecstatic states. His main predecessors were Friedrich Nietzsche (1844–1900) and the French philosopher Henri Bergson (1859–1941). Klages's neoromantic ideas are even nowadays of significance for sport psychology (athletics, calisthenics, and dance), as can be seen, for example, by the concepts of Csikszentmihalyi 1975. See Zusne 1984, among others.

55 Karl Bücher was from Leipzig, Germany.

56 Jaques-Dalcroze (1865–1950) was born in Vienna, Austria.

57 The music teacher Rudolf Bode was born in 1881 in Kiel, Germany, and he died in 1971 in Munich. In 1911 he founded his Institute of Music and Rhythm (Bode-School) in Munich.

58 The dancer Rudolf von Laban (1879–1958) was called the Grandseigneur of dance. He was born in Pressburg, Hungary (now Bratislava, Slovakia); studied dance and the arts in Paris, Vienna, and Munich); and founded the Laban School of dance gymnastics (Zurich and elsewhere) and the Choreographic Institute (Würzburg and Berlin) in which he created his great choreutics, for example "Terpsichore." He later had a Dance-Notation Bureau in New York and an Art of Movement Studio in Manchester. In 1953 he founded the Rudolf von Laban Trust and the Laban Art of Movement Guild in Addlestone, Woburn Hills, near London. See Schuftan 1929; Seybold-Brunnhuber 1952; Günther 1959; Preston-Dunlop 1998.

59 Ewald Sachsenberg was professor of management science at the Technische Hochschule of Dresden.

60 Eduard Richter (1847–1905) was professor of geography at the University of Graz, Austria, and an enthusiastic alpinist. Richter had great merit in promoting scientific research among the alpine clubs of Austria and Germany.

61 Howard's paper was read before the Alpine Club of London in 1920.

62 Else Voigtländer, born 1882, was the daughter of the publisher R. Voigtländer, Leipzig. She studied psychology and philosophy in Munich under Lipps and Pfänder and received her PhD in 1909. Later, she was the author of several interesting studies in psychology.

63 Mabel Jane Reaney received her doctor of science at the University of London. The paper from which statements are reported here appeared in 1916 and was the theoretical part of Reaney's doctoral thesis. Reaney also wrote the "Psychology of the Boy Scout Movement" (1914).

64 For Triplett, see Lück 1998. The first quasi experimental study in sport psychology of all was actually performed by the American psychologist E. W. Scripture in 1894 (Scripture 1894; see also Bäumler 1996, 1998, 2002).

65 Walther Moede (1888–1958) was born in Sorau, Prussia (now Zary, Poland). He was professor of psychotechnics and director of the Institute of Industrial Psychotechnics at the Technische Hochschule of Charlottenburg, near Berlin, and like Norman Triplett, he was a pioneer social psychologist through his experiments (Zusne 1984; Haak 1996).

66 Five persons built a group, or party, and each person performed his task in presence of his group so as to obtain a maximum performance for the whole group.

67 Vernon's paper was a publication from the psychological laboratory of Cambridge, England. He made his observations employing a college boat club from Cambridge, probably St. John's.

68 For the founding of the Deutsche Hochschule für Leibesübungen, see Diem 1923, 151–54.

69 Dr. Robert Werner Schulte (1897–1933) was a pupil of Wilhelm Wundt and Wilhelm Wirth in Leipzig. From 1919 he was an assistant to Walther Moede at the Institute of Industrial Psychotechnics and Work-Technique at the Technische Hochschule in Charlottenburg, near Berlin, as well as lecturer at the Humboldt Hochschule of Berlin. In 1920 he became lecturer of sport psychology at the Deutsche Hochschule für Leibesübungen and in

1921 director of the department of educational science. See Janssen 2006, 135–42; Diem 1923, 154. The psychological laboratory was located in the Stadion of Berlin (Hoske 1922).

70 At the same time Schulte was also director of the sport psychological laboratories at the Preußische Hochschule für Leibesübungen, the Psychotechnical Examination Board for Sport and Vocational Guidance (Psychotechnische Hauptprüfstelle für Sport und Berufskunde), and the Research Institute of School Psychology, all of them in Spandau, near Berlin. See Schulte 1924, 354.

71 The Arndt-Schulz Law, which was called the fundamental law of biology, proposed an inverted-u relation between the strength of a stimulus and the physiological or biochemical reactive force: weak stimuli slightly fan the vital activity, middle strong stimuli accelerate it, strong stimuli inhibit it, and very strong ones halt it (Arndt 1885, 1892; Schulz 1887, 1918; Orlob 1992). Rudolf Arndt (1835–1900) was professor of psychiatry, while Hugo Schulz (1853–1932) was professor of pharmacology. Both taught and conducted research at the University of Greifswald, Germany.

72 Lahy's memorial address may be found in the journal Le Travail Humain 1 (1933): 219. Jean-Maurice Lahy (1872–1943) was director of the psychological institute at the University of Paris. See Lück 1994; Janssen 2006.

73 See also Janssen 1986. Working in the United States at nearly the same time as Schulte, Coleman R. Griffith started his deserving researches in sport psychology. He also quit them in 1932 without leaving a successor. See Bäumler 1993.

74 According to Rudik, the head of the sport psychological department at the Central Institute of Physical Education at Moscow was Professor W. W. Gorinewski.

75 The psychologist Petr Antonovic Rudik (1893–1983) was associated with the Central State Institute of Body Culture in Moscow from 1919 on. At least from 1924 he was also assistant at the Psychological Institute of the University of Moscow. Beginning in 1932, he was director of the chair of Pedagogy and Psychology and from 1949 on, professor at the Institute of Sport Education and School Hygiene (supposedly in Moscow).

76 See also Riordan 1987.

77 The then well-known psychologist Alexandr Petrovitch Netchayev (1870–1948) studied psychology in Germany under Wilhelm Wundt in Leipzig and Georg Elias Müller in Göttingen. In 1901 he founded the first Laboratory of Experimental Pedagogical Psychology at the Pedagogical Museum in St. Petersburg and until 1917 was professor at the military academy in St. Petersburg. From 1922 to 1926 he was director of the psychoneurological institute in Moscow. In 1930–31 he was again in Leningrad, but in 1935, for political reasons, he was compelled to go to Kasachstan, where he eventually became a teacher (Rumiantsev 1914).

78 Avksenty Zesarevitch (Cesarevich) Puni was born in 1898 in Vyatka (northwestern Russia). In 1917 he began to study medicine at the University of Perm but soon he joined the Red Army at the time of the October Revolution and Civil War. Afterward he became sport organizer in his native town, where, among other things, in 1927 he began to examine the psychophysiological effects of training table tennis. In 1929 he entered the Lesgaft Institute of Physical Culture in Leningrad (St. Petersburg) and completed his graduate studies. In 1938 he received his PhD in pedagogy from the institute, and in 1946 he launched the department of sport psychology there. Eventually he received this department's first chair and directed the department for thirty years. He died in 1986. See Ryba, Stambulova, and Wrisberg 2005.

79 Several of these researches, published in Russian, have appeared in the years after 1905 in *Wjestnik Psychologii.*

80 The term *psychotechnics* was coined by the German-American psychologist Hugo Münsterberg, who wrote *Grundzüge der Psychotechnik* (Outlines of Psychotechnics) in 1914. Münsterberg (1863–1916) was born in Danzig, Germany (now Gdansk, Poland), and died in Cambridge, Massachusetts. He received his MD in 1887 from Heidelberg under Wilhelm Wundt and from 1897 to 1916 was professor at Harvard University, where he developed the applied psychology of America. See Zusne 1984.

81 T. H. Pear was professor of psychology at the University of Manchester, England, and director of the psychological laboratory that was associated with the Industrial Fatigue Research Board.

82 The translator was Margot Isbert, the wife of Wilhelm Benary. See Court and Janssen 2003, 19.

83 N. Oseretzky was scientific assistant at the Moscow psychoneurological children's clinic, which was directed by Professor Gourevitch. Later, Oseretzky was professor and director of the institute of child research in Leningrad. See Oseretzky 1931.

84 For further developments, see also Oseretzky 1929, 1931.

85 For overviews, see, for example, Benary et al. 1919; Dockeray and Isaacs 1921; Herlitzka 1928.

References

Allers, R., and F. Scheminsky. 1926. Über aktionsströme der muskeln bei motorischen vorstellungen und verwandten vorgängen [Concerning the action potentials of the muscles during motor imaginations and similar processes]. *Pflügers Archiv für die gesamte Physiologie* 212:169–82.

Arndt, R. 1885. *Die neurasthenie* [Neurasthenia]. Wien.

———. 1892. *Biologische studien I: Das biologische grundgesetz* [Biological studies I: The fundamental law of biology]. Greifswald.

Banister, H., and J. M. Blackburn. 1930–31. An eye factor affecting proficiency at ball games. *British Journal of Psychology* 21:382–84.

Barth, B. 1912. *Willens-und charakterbildung durch leibesübungen* [The formation of will and character through physical exercises]. Leipzig.

Baudouin, C. 1922. *Suggestion and autosuggestion.* Trans. E. Paul and C. Paul. London: Allen and Unwin.

Baumann, J. 1897. *Über willens-und charakterbildung auf physiologisch-psychologischer grundlage* [About the formation of will and character based on psychophysiology]. Berlin.

Bäumler, G. 1989. The beginning of modern sport psychology. In *Proceedings of the "Pierre de Coubertin and the Psychological Basis of Olympism Memorial Meeting 1988,"* ed. P. Rókusfalvy, 12–21. Budapest: Hungarian University of Physical Education.

———. 1993. Anfänge der sportpsychologie (1894–1928) [The beginnings of sport psychology, 1894–1928]. In *Illustrierte geschichte der psychologie*, ed. H. E. Lück and R. Miller, 263–68. München.

———. 1996. The contributions to sport psychology by E. W. Scripture and his Yale group: Part II; Scripture's 1894 experiment on the reaction-time of fencers. *Sportonomics* 2:21–24.

———. 1998. The life and personality of Norman D. Triplett: I; From birth to PhD (1861–1900). *Sportonomics* 4:95–96.

———. 2002. Sportpsychologie zwischen 1884 und 1900: Die generation der pioniere [Sport psychology between 1884 and 1900: The generation of the pioneers]. In *Sportmedizin und sportwissenschaft: Historisch-systematische facetten*, ed. G. Bäumler, J. Court, and W. Hollmann, 287–318. Sankt Augustin.

———. 2007. Von Patrick bis Welte: Sechs historische essays zur psychologie des fußballspiels [From Patrick to Welte: Six historical essays on the psychology of football]. In *Jahrbuch 2006 der Deutschen gesellschaft für geschichte der sportwissenschaft e. V.: Fussballsport und Wissenschaftsgeschichte*, ed. J. Court, A. Müller, and C. Wacker, 119–62. Berlin.

Benary, W. 1913. *Der sport als individual-und sozialerscheinung* [Sport as an individual and social phenomenon]. Berlin.

Benary, W., A. Kronfeld, E. Stern, and O. Selz. 1919. *Untersuchungen über die psychische eignung zum flugdienst* [Investigations into the psychological aptitude for air service]. Leipzig.

Berliner, B. 1913–14. Experimentalpsychologische untersuchungen über die wirkung des seeklimas [Experimental psychological studies on the effect of the sea climate]. *Zeitschrift für Balneologie, Klimatologie und Umwelthygiene* 6:246–53, 275–80, 313–17, 349–56, 379–87, 409–13.

Bertz, E. 1900. *Philosophie des fahrrads* [Philosophy of the bicycle]. Dresden.

Binet, A. 1893. Les grandes mémoires: Résumé d'une enquête sur les joueurs d'échecs [The great memories: Summary of a study on chess players]. *Revue des Deux Mondes* 117, année 63: 826–59. Later published in 1966 as Mnemonic virtuosity: A study of chess players. Trans. M. L. Simmel and S. B. Barren. *Genetic Psychology Monographs* 74:127–62.

————. 1894. *Psychologie des grandes calculateurs et jouers d'échecs* [Psychology of great arithmeticians and chess players]. Paris.

Bode, R. 1922. *Ausdrucksgymnastik* [Expression-gymnastics]. München.

————. 1925. *Der rhythmus und seine bedeutung für die körperliche erziehung* [Rhythm, its significance for physical education]. Jena.

————. 1931. *Expression-gymnastics.* Trans. S. Forthal. New York.

Brandell, G. 1915. *Das interesse der schulkinder an den unterrichtsfächern* [The interest of school children in school subjects]. Leipzig. Original Swedish title We skolbarns intressen: En psykologisk-pedagogisk undersökning, 1913.

Brown-Séquard, C. E. 1882. Recherches expérimentales et cliniques sur l'inhibition et la dynamogénie [Experimental and clinical research on inhibition and dynamogeny]. *Gazette hebdomadaire de Médecine et de Chirurgie,* 2e série, tome 19: 35–36, 53–55, 75–77, 105–107, 136–38.

————. 1884. Dynamogénie [Dynamogeny]. In *Dictionnaire encyclopédique des sciences médicales,* ed. J. Raige-Delorme and A. Dechambre, 756–60. Paris.

Bücher, K. 1896. *Arbeit und rhythmus* [Work and rhythm]. Leipzig.

Budinszky, K. 1884–85. A tornázás és az akarat fejlesztése [About gymnastic activity and the development of will]. *Tornaügy* [Gymnastics] 2 (4): 71–72; 2 (5): 87–88.

Burgerstein, L. 1920. Oker-Blom. *Zeitschrift für Schulgesundheitspflege* 33:33–37.

Carpenter, W. B. 1853. *Human physiology.* London.

————. [1876] 1993. *Principles of mental physiology.* 4th ed. London.

Cassel, R. H. 1950–51. The Oseretsky tests: Vineland adaptation. *American Journal of Mental Deficiency* 55:251–56.

Cattell, M. 1928. Early psychological laboratories. *Science* 67:543–48.

Chu, D. 1982. *Dimensions of sport studies.* New York.

Cohn, T. 1913. Sport bei nervenkranken [Sport for patients with nervous diseases]. *Zeitschrift für Balneologie, Klimatologie und Kurort-Hygiene* 6:153–59.

Cohnen, W. 1927. Einfluß der übung auf die wurfleistung von kindern

[The influence of practice on the throwing performance of children]. *Zeitschrift für angewandte Psychologie* 28:369–438.

Comité International Olympique. 1913. *Congrés international de psychologie et physiologie sportives* [International congress of pyschology and physiology of sport]. Lausanne.

Coubertin, P. de. 1900. La psychologie du sport [The psychology of sport]. *Revue des Deux Mondes* 4:160, 167–79.

———. 1913a. *Essais de psychologie sportive* [Essays about the psychology of sport]. Lausanne.

———. 1913b. Les congrès Olympiques. *Revue Olympique*, no. 86: 19–20.

———. 1913c. Les journées de Lausanne. *Revue Olympique*, no. 91: 103–12.

———. 1914. Critique du congrès de Lausanne. Parts 1–4. *Revue Olympique*, no. 97: 10–12; no. 98: 28–29; no. 99: 42–45; no. 100: 54–58.

Coué, E. 1913. *De la suggestion et de ses applications* [Concerning suggestion and its applications]. 3rd ed. Nancy.

———. 1922. *Self-mastery through conscious autosuggestion.* London.

Court, J. 2006. Konrad Koch: Die erziehung zum mute durch turnen, spiel und sport [Education of spirit through gymnastics, games, and sport]. In *Klassiker und wegbereiter der sportwissenschaft*, ed. J. Court and E. Meinberg, 37–42. Stuttgart.

Court, J., and J.-P. Janssen. 2003. Wilhelm Benary (1888–1955): Leben und werk [Wilhelm Benary (1888–1955): His life and works]. *Psychology Science* 45, Supplement 4: 1–84.

Court, J., and J. R. Nitsch. 2006. Alfred Peters: Psychologie des sports 1927 [Alfred Peters: The psychology of sports 1927]. In *Klassiker und wegbereiter der sportwissenschaft*, ed. J. Court and E. Meinberg, 167–77. Stuttgart.

Csikszentmihalyi, M. 1975. *Beyond boredom and anxiety.* San Francisco.

Debruyn, J. R. 1976. Thomas Hughes and Eduard Bertz. *Notes and Queries* 23:405–6.

Deon, B. 1997. *Légende centenaire Paris–Brest et retour* [The centenary legend of the Paris–Brest race and back again]. Rovieres.

Deutsch, H. 1925. Beitrag zur psychologie des sportes [Beitrag on the psychology of sports]. *Internationale Zeitschrift für Psychoanalyse* 11:222–26.

———. 1926. A contribution to the psychology of sport. *International Journal of Psycho-analysis* 7:223–27.

———. 1967. Some dynamic factors in sport. In *Motivations in play, games and sports*, ed. R. Slovenko and J. A. Knight, 91–94. Springfield IL.

Dewey, J. 1886. *Psychology*. New York.

Diem, C. 1922. *Zur neugestaltung der körpererziehung* [On the renovation of physical education]. Berlin.

———. 1923. Die Deutsche Hochschule für Leibesübungen [The German Academy of Physical Exercises]. In *Vereine und Verbände für leibesübungen (verwaltungswesen)*, ed. C. Diem, 151–54. Berlin.

Djakow, V. A., N. W. Petrowski, and P. A. Rudik. 1927. *Psychologie des schachspiels auf der grundlage psychotechnischer experimente an den teilnehmern des Internationalen Schachturniers zu Moskau 1925* [Psychology of chess based on psychotechnical experiments with the participants of the International Chess Tournament in Moscow 1925]. Berlin.

Dockeray, F. C., and S. Isaacs. 1921. Psychological research in aviation in Italy, France, England and the American expeditionary forces. *Journal of Comparative Psychology* 1:115–48.

Downey, J. 1923. *The will-temperament and its testing*. New York.

Du Bois-Reymond, E. 1881. *Über die übung* [About practice]. Berlin.

Du Pasquier, C. 1896. Le plaisir d'aller à bicyclette [The pleasure of riding a bicycle]. *Revue Scientifique*, 4e série, tome 6: 145–48.

Fechner, G. T. 1860. *Elemente der psychophysik* [Elements of psychophysics]. Leipzig.

Féré, C. 1885. Le mouvement considéré comme dynamogène [Movement considered with reference to dynamogeny]. *Comptes rendus hebdomadaires de la Societé de Biologie* 37:629–32.

———. 1887. *Sensation et mouvement* [Sensation and movement]. Paris.

———. 1892. *La pathologie des émotions* [The pathology of emotions]. Paris.

———. 1904. *Travail et plaisir* [Work and pleasure]. Paris.

Ferretti, L. 1951. *Angelo Mosso, apostolo dello sport* [Angelo Mosso, apostle of sport]. Milano.

Galton, F. [1869] 1892. *Hereditary genius: An inquiry into its laws and consequences.* 2nd ed. London.

———. 1902. The most suitable proportion between the values of first and second prizes (with a "Note on Francis Galton's problem" by Karl Pearson). *Biometrika* 1:385–99.

———. 1925. *Seul à travers l'Atlantique* [Sailing over the Atlantic]. Paris.

Giese, F. 1924. *Körperseele* [Body-mind]. München.

———. 1925. *Geist im sport* [Mind in sport]. München.

Griesbach, H. 1895. *Energetik und hygiene des nervensystems in der schule* [Energetics and hygiene of the nervous system]. München.

Groller, B. 1899. Zur psychologie des sportes [About the psychology of sport]. *Die Wage* 20:337–39; 24:411–13.

Gundlach, H., ed. 1994. *Arbeiten zu psychologiegeschichte* [Works about the history of psychology]. Göttingen.

———. 1996. Psychologie und psychotechnik bei den eisenbahnen [Psychology and psychotechnics of the railways]. In *Untersuchungen zur geschichte der psychologie und psychotechnik,* ed. H. Gundlach, 127–46. München.

Günther, D. 1959. In memoriam: Rudolf von Laban. *Leibeserziehung* 1:13–21.

Gurewitsch [Gourevitch], M., and N. J. Oseretzky. 1925. Zur methodik der untersuchung der motorischen funktionen [On the method of assessment of motor functions]. *Monatsschrift für Psychiatrie und Neurologie* 59:78–103.

Haak, R. 1996. Grundlagen und entwicklung der Berliner psychotechnik [The fundamentals and the development of the Berlin psychotechnics]. In *Untersuchungen zur geschichte der psychologie und der psychotechnik,* ed. H. Gundlach, 165–76. München.

Hartgenbusch, H. G. 1926. Beobachtungen und bemerkungen zur psychologie des sports [Observations and comments on the psychology of sport]. *Psychologische Forschung* 7:386–97.

———. 1927. Gestalt psychology in sport. *Psyche* 27:41–52.

Herlitzka, A. 1928. Methoden zur auswahl und kontrolle der

luftzeugfahrer [Methods of selection and surveillance of aviators].
In *Handbuch der biologischen arbeitsmethoden*, ed. E. Abderhalden,
813–69. Berlin.

Hirschlaff, L. 1911. Über ruheübungen und ruheübungsapparate
[About calmness exercises and calmness training apparatuses].
Münchener Medizinische Wochenschrift 58:251–54.

Hoske, H. 1922. Deutsche hochschule für leibesübungen, 9:
Monatsbericht [The ninth monthly report of the German Academy
of Physical Exercises]. *Monatsschrift für Turnen, Spiel und Sport*
2:101–107.

Howard, G. E. 1920–21. Compensations. *Alpine Journal* 33:61–69.

Hutchinson, A. 1977. *Labanotation or kinetography laban: The system
analyzing and recording movement.* 3rd rev. ed. New York.

Janet, P. 1889. *L'Automatisme psychologique* [The psychological
automatism]. Paris.

Janssen, J. P. 1986. Zur institutionalisierung der sportpsychologie
in der Weimarer Republik an der Universität Berlin [On the
institutionalization of sport psychology in the Weimar Republic at
the University of Berlin]. In *Psychologie mitte der 8oer jahre*, ed. A.
Schorr, 88–100. Bonn.

———. 1997. Deutsche sportpsychologie im wandel dreier epochen:
Von der Wilhelminischen epoche zum geteilten Deutschland
[German sport psychology during three epochs of political
change: From the Wilhelmian epoch to the partitioned Germany].
Psychologie und Sport 4:8–33.

———. 2006. Robert Werner Schulte: Eignungs- und leistungsprüfung im
sport (1925) [Robert Werner Schulte's "Aptitude and performance tests
in sport" (1925)]. In *Klassiker und wegbereiter der sportwissenschaft*,
ed. J. Court and E. Meinberg, 135–42. Stuttgart.

Jaques-Dalcroze, E. 1907. *Der rhythmus als erziehungsmittel für das
leben und die kunst* [Rhythm as a means to education for life and
arts]. Basel.

———. 1919. *Le rythme, la musique et l'éducation* [Rhythm, music, and
education]. Lausanne.

Jiel-Laval. 1891. Ma course de Paris–Brest et retour [My race from Paris to Brest and back again]. *Revue des Jeux scolaires*, no. 10: 61–63; no. 11: 67–69; no. 12: 73–76.

Jossmann, C. 1931. *Der sportgedanke im französischen geistesleben* [The idea of sport in the intellectual life of France]. PhD diss., University of Berlin.

Keller, R. 1894a. Pädagogisch-psychometrische studien 1: Vorläufige mitteilung [Pedagogic-psychometric studies: First preliminary communication]. *Biologisches Centralblatt* 14:24–32; 38–53.

———. 1894b. Pädagogisch-psychometrische studien 2: Vorläufige mitteilung [Pedagogic-psychometric studies: Second preliminary communication]. *Biologisches Centralblatt* 14:328–36.

———. 1897. Experimentelle untersuchungen über die ermüdung von schülern durch geistige arbeit [Experimental investigations into the fatigue of school children caused by mental work]. *Zeitschrift für Schulgesundheitspflege* 10:335–39; 404–5.

Klages, L. 1929. *Der geist als widersacher der seele* [Spirit as the opponent of the soul]. 3 vols. Leipzig.

Klecker, U., and G. Bäumler. 1995. Philippe Tissié — un protagoniste de la psychologie sportive [Philippe Tissié — a protagonist of sport psychology]. *Sportonomics* 1:35–40.

Klemm, O. 1929. Zufall oder geschicklichkeit [Chance or skill]. *Neue Psychologische Studien* 5 (1): 23–64.

———. 1930. Gedanken über leibesübungen [Thoughts about physical exercises]. *Neue Psychologische Studien* 5 (2): 145–67.

Knappe, W. 1925. Die eignung des fußballspielers [The aptitude of the football player]. In *Eignungs- und leistungsprüfung im sport*, ed. R. W. Schulte, 268–75. Berlin.

Koch, K. 1900. *Die erziehung zum mute durch turnen, spiel und sport: Die geistige seite der leibesübungen* [Education of spirit by gymnastics, games and sport: The mental aspect of physical exercise]. Berlin.

Kulinkovic, K. A. 1983. Das werk von P. F. Lesgaft und das system der körpererziehung in der UdSSR [The works of P. F. Lesgaft and the system of physical education in the Soviet Union]. *Theorie und Praxis der Körperkultur* 32:655–60.

Kunath, P. 1963. Vorwort zu P. A. Rudiks "Psychologie" [Preface to P. A.

Rudik's "Psychology"]. In *Psychologie: Ein lehrbuch für turnlehrer, sportlehrer und trainer,* by R. A. Rudik, 13–16. Berlin.

Küppers, J. 1891. *Das turnen ein mittel der charakterbildung* [Gymnastics as a means of character formation]. Bonn.

Laban, R. 1920. *Die welt des tänzers* [The world of the dancer]. Stuttgart.

———. 1926. *Gymnastik und tanz* [Gymnastics and dance]. Oldenburg.

———. 1975. *Laban's principles of dance and movement notation.* 2nd ed. London.

———. 1980. *The mastery of movement.* 4th ed. London.

Lagrange, F. 1888. *Physiologie des exercices du corps* [Physiology of the physical exercises]. Paris.

Lammer, G. E. 1893. Das älteste alpine problem am Groß-Venediger, 3673 m (nordwest-wand) [The oldest alpine problem at the Grossvenediger, 3673 m (northwest rock face)]. *Zeitschrift des deutschen und österreichischen Alpenvereins* 24:404–27.

Langneau, M. G. 1888. Du surmenage intellectuel et de la sédentarité dans les écoles [About intellectual overburden and sedentary work in the schools]. *Annales Médico-psychologiques,* 7e série, 46e année: 301–5.

Lasurski, A. 1913. *Über das studium der individualität* [On the study of individuality]. Leipzig.

Lesgaft, P. F. [1888–1901] 1951–52. [Guide for the physical education of school children]. 2 vols. Moscow.

———. 1912. *Pamyati Pyotra Frantsevicha Lesgafta* [Memories of Pyotr Frantsevich Lesgaft]. St. Petersburg.

Lobsien, M. 1903. Kinderideale [The ideals of children]. *Zeitschrift für Pädagogische Psychologie, Pathologie und Hygiene* 5:323–44; 457–94.

———. 1909. *Beliebtheit und unbeliebtheit der unterrichtsfächer* [On the popularity and unpopularity of the school subjects]. Langensalza.

Longstaff, J. S. 2000. Re-evaluating Rudolf Laban's choreutics. *Perceptual and Motor Skills* 91:191–210.

Loosch, E. 2008. *Otto Klemm (1884–1939) und das Psychologische Institut in Leipzig* [Otto Klemm (1884–1939) and the Psychological Institute at Leipzig]. Berlin.

Lück, H. E. 1994. ". . . und halte lust und leid und leben in meiner ausgestreckten hand": Zu leben und werk von Robert Werner

Schulte ["... and so I hold pleasure, pain, and life in my stretched-out hand": Concerning the life and works of Robert Werner Schulte]. In *Arbeiten zur psychologiegeschichte*, ed. H. Gundlach, 39–48. Göttingen.

———. 1998. Das experiment zum schrittmacherphänomen von Norman D. Triplett: Ein "klassiker" nach 100 jahren neu betrachtet [The experiment on the pacemaking effect of Norman D. Triplett: A new view of "classician" after 100 years]. *Sportonomics* 4:87–92.

———. 2006a. Eduard Spranger: Psychologie des jugendalters (1924) [About Eduard Spranger's "Psychology of youth" (1924)]. In *Klassiker und wegbereiter der sportwissenschaft*, ed. J. Court and E. Meinberg, 122–25. Stuttgart.

———. 2006b. Hanns Sippel: Körper-geist-seele (1926) [Hanns Sippel's "Body-mind-soul" (1926)]. In *Klassiker und wegbereiter der sportwissenschaft*, ed. J. Court and E. Meinberg, 143–47. Stuttgart.

Märtin, R.-P. 2006. Heinrich Steinitzer: Sport und kultur, mit besonderer berücksichtigung des bergsports (1910) [Heinrich Steinitzer's "Sport and culture," with special consideration of the alpine sports (1910)]. In *Klassiker und wegbereiter der sportwissenschaft*, ed. J. Court and E. Meinberg, 50–60. Stuttgart.

Meiring, J. 1925. *Über die psychischen einflüsse und bildungswerte von leibesübungen* [On the psychological effects and the educational values of physical exercises]. PhD diss., University of Leipzig.

Messner, R., and H. Höfler. 1999. *Eugen Guido Lammer: Durst nach todesgefahr* [Eugen Guido Lammer: A thirst for deadly peril]. Augsburg.

Meumann, E. 1907–14. *Vorlesungen zur einführung in die experimentelle pädagogik* [Lectures on introduction to experimental education]. 3 vols. Leipzig.

Moede, W. 1914. Der wetteifer, seine struktur und sein ausmaß [On the structure and extent of competition]. *Zeitschrift für pädagogische Psychologie* 15:353–68.

———. 1920. *Experimentelle massenpsychologie: Beiträge zur experimentalpsychologie der gruppe* [Experimental psychology of the masses]. Leipzig.

———. 1920–21. Einzel-und gruppenarbeit [Individual and group work]. *Praktische Psychologie* 2:71–81; 108–15.

Mosso, A. 1884. *La paura* [The fear]. Milano.

———. 1891. *La fatica* [The fatigue]. Milano.

———. 1892. *L'educatione fisica della gioventù* [The physical education of youth]. Milano.

———. 1897. *Fisiologia dell' uomo sulle Alpi* [Physiology of man in the Alps]. Milano.

———. 1903. *Mens sana in corpore sano* [A healthy mind in a healthy body]. 2nd ed. Milano.

———. 1904. *Les exercises physiques et le développement intellectuel* [The physical exercises and intellectual development]. Paris.

Münsterberg, H. 1914. *Grundzüge der psychotechnik* [Outlines of psychotechnics]. Leipzig.

Nolte, W. 1925. Die boxschnelligkeit [Rapidity in boxing]. In *Eignungs- und leistungsprüfung im sport*, ed. R. W. Schulte, 240–52. Berlin.

Oker-Blom, M. 1910. Untersuchungen über die entwicklung der geistigen leistungsfähigkeit bezw: Der ermüdung im laufe des schularbeitstages in den Helsingforser volksschulen [Investigations into the development of mental ability and fatigue during a school day at the Helsingfors elementary schools]. *Zeitschrift für experimentelle Pädagogik* 10:71–118; 153–88.

Orlob, S. 1992. *Professor Rudolf Arndt — leben und werk* [The life and works of Professor Rudolf Arndt]. PhD diss., University of Greifswald.

Oseretzky, N. I. 1923. [A metrical scale for the assessment of the motor abilities of children, with a preface by Prof. Gourevitch]. Moscow.

———. 1925. Eine metrische stufenleiter zur untersuchung der motorischen begabung bei kindern [A metrical scale for assessment of the motor ability of children]. *Zeitschrift für Kinderforschung* 30:300–314.

———. 1929. Zur methodik der untersuchung der motorischen komponenten [On the methodology of assessment of the motor components]. *Zeitschrift für angewandte Psychologie* 32:257–93.

———. 1931. *Psychomotorik: Methoden zur untersuchung der motorik*

[Psychomotorics: Methods of assessment of motor ability]. Leipzig. (Beihefte zur Zeitschrift für angewandte Psychologie, Nr. 57.)

Pear, T. H. 1924. *Skill in work and play*. London.

———. 1925. *Geschicklichkeit in sport und industrie* [Skill in sport and industry]. Trans. M. Isbert. Erlangen.

Pearson, K. 1902. Note on Francis Galton's problem. *Biometrika* 1:390–99.

———. 1904–5. On the inheritance of the mental and moral characters in man, and its comparison with the inheritance of the physical characters. *Biometrika* 3:131–90.

———. 1906–7. On the relationship of intelligence to size and shape of head, and to other physical and mental characters. *Biometrika* 5:105–46.

———. 1909–10. On the value of the teacher's opinion of the general intelligence of school children. *Biometrika* 7:542–48.

Peters, A. 1927. *Psychologie des sports: Seine konfrontierung mit spiel und kampf* [Psychology of sport: Its confrontation with play and fight]. Leipzig.

Preston-Dunlop V. 1998. *Rudolf Laban: An extraordinary life*. London.

Puni, A. Z. 1961. *Abriß der sportpsychologie* [Outlines of sport psychology]. Berlin.

Reaney, M. J. 1914a. The correlation between general intelligence and play ability as shown in organized group games. *British Journal of Psychology* 7:226–52.

———. 1914b. The psychology of the Boy Scout movement. *Pedagogical Seminary* 21:407–11.

———. 1916. *The psychology of the organized group game*. Cambridge.

Richter, E. 1903. Über die triebfedern der bergsteigerei [Concerning the motivating forces of mountain climbing]. *Mitteilungen des Deutschen und Österreichischen Alpenvereins*, no. 5: 53–55.

Riordan, J. 1977. Pyotr Franzevich Lesgaft (1837–1909), the founder of Russian physical education. *Journal of Sport History* 4:229–41.

———. 1987. Soviet muscular socialism: A Durkheimian analysis. *Sociology of Sport Journal* 4:376–93.

Roazen, P. 1985. *Helene Deutsch: A psychoanalyst's life*. New York.

Rókusfalvy, P. 1974. *Sportpszichológia* [Sport psychology]. Budapest.

Ruckmick, C. A. 1930. "Die psychologie der leibesübungen" by R. W. Schulte, 1928. *American Journal of Psychology* 42:496.

Rudik, P. A. 1925a. [The analysis of practice]. Works from the Central Institute of Physical Culture. Moscow.

———. 1925b. [The influence of muscle work on the reaction process]. Works from the Central Institute of Physical Culture. Moscow.

———. 1925c. [The investigation into the process of reaction in sport activity]. Works from the Central Institute of Physical Culture. Moscow.

———. 1963. *Psychologie: Ein lehrbuch für turnlehrer, sportlehrer und trainer* [Psychology: A textbook for physical educators, sport teachers, and trainers]. Berlin.

Rumiantsev, N. E. 1914. Neuere arbeiten aus dem gebiete der experimentellen pädagogik in Rußland [New works from experimental pedagogy in Russia]. *Archiv für Pädagogik, Teil II: Die pädagogische Forschung* 2:327–36; 417–29.

Ryba, T. V., N. B. Stambulova, and C. A. Wrisberg. 2005. The Russian origins of sport psychology: A translation of an early work of A. C. Puni. *Journal of Applied Sport Psychology* 17:157–69.

Sachsenberg, E. 1927. Ein beitrag zum problem arbeit und rhythmus [A contribution to the problem of work and rhythm]. *Zeitschrift für angewandte Psychologie* 28:462–77.

Saffiotti, F. U. 1920. La evolutione della psicologia sperimentale in Italia [The evolution of experimental psychology in Italy]. *Rivista di Psicologia* 16:128–53.

Scheler, M. 1927. Begleitwort zu Alfred Peters' "Psychologie des sports" [Explanatory remarks to "Psychology of sport" by Alfred Peters]. Leipzig.

Schenkel, E. 2006. Eduard Bertz: Philosophie des fahrrads (1900) [About Eduard Bertz's "Philosophy of the bicycle" (1900)]. In *Klassiker und wegbereiter der sportwissenschaft*, ed. J. Court and E. Meinberg, 31–36. Stuttgart.

Schuftan, W. 1929. Rudolf von Laban. *Hochschulblatt für Leibesübungen* 9:112–13.

Schulte, R. W. 1921. *Leib und seele im sport: Einführung in die psychologie der leibesübungen* [Body and mind in sport: Introduction to the psychology of physical exercise]. Charlottenburg.

———. 1924. Persönlichkeit in der psychologischen beratung [Personality in psychological advice]. *Zeitschrift für angewandte Psychologie* 23:325–56.

———. 1925a. Die psychologie des boxers [The psychology of the boxer]. In *Eignungs- und leistungsprüfung im sport*, ed. R. W. Schulte, 217–25. Berlin.

———, ed. 1925b. *Eignungs- und leistungsprüfung im sport: Die psychologische methodik der wissenschaft von den leibesübungen* [Aptitude- and performance-testing in sport]. Berlin.

———. 1925c. Körper und geist: Eine experimentelle studie [Body and mind: An experimental study]. In *Eignungs- und leistungsprüfung im sport*, ed. R. W. Schulte, 277–82. Berlin.

———. 1926. Die eignung zum sport-und verkehrsflieger [Concerning the aptitude to sport and civil aviation]. *Die Schönheit*, no. 11: 525–43.

———. 1927a. *Leistungssteigerung in turnen, spiel und sport: Grundlinien einer psychobiologie der leibesübungen* [Improvement of performance in gymnastics, games, and sport: Outlines of a psychobiology of sport]. 3rd ed. Oldenburg.

———. 1927b. Medizinisch-psychologische beobachtungen bei einem fallschirmabsprung [Medico-psychological observations during a parachute descent]. *Psychologie und Medizin* 2:222–25.

———. 1928. *Die psychologie der leibesübungen* [The psychology of physical education]. Berlin.

———. 1931. Psychologische erfahrungen als sportflieger und fallschirmspringer [Psychological experiences as a sport aviator and parachutist]. *Psychologie und Medizin* 4:277–89.

Schultz, J. H. 1927. Über rationalisiertes autosuggestives training (autogene organübungen) [On rationalized autosuggestive training]. *Bericht über den 2: Allgemeinen ärztlichen Kongreß der Psychotherapie in Bad Nauheim*, 27–30.4, 289–96.

———. 1928. Über autogenes training [On autogenic training]. *Deutsche Medizinische Wochenschrift* 54:1200–1201.

———. 1929. Gehobene aufgabenstufen im autogenen training [Elevated levels of tasks in autogenic training]. *Bericht über den 4:*

allgemeinen ärztlichen Kongreß für Psychotherapie in Bad Nauheim,
11–14, 106–13.

Schulz, H. 1887. Zur lehre von der arzneimittelwirkung [On the
efficacy of the pharmacological remedies]. *Archiv für pathologische
Anatomie und Physiologie und für klinische Medizin* 108:423–45.

———. 1918. *Rudolf Arndt und das biologische grundgesetz* [Rudolf
Arndt and the fundamental law of biology]. Greifswald.

Schüssler, H. 1915. Turnerische veranlagung und intellektuelle
begabung [Talent in gymnastics and the intellectual ability].
Zeitschrift für angewandte Psychologie 10:452–59.

Schuwalow, F. P. 1963. P. F. Lesgaft — gelehrter, pädagoge, patriot [P.
F. Lesgaft — scholar, pedagogue, patriot]. *Theorie und Praxis der
Körperkultur* 12:871–79.

Scripture, E. W. 1894. Tests of mental ability as exhibited in fencing.
Studies from the Yale Psychological Laboratory 2:122–24.

———. 1897. *The new psychology.* London.

Sergi, G. 1873–74. *Principi di psicologia sulla base delle scienze
sperimentali, parte I & II* [Principles of psychology on the basis of
experimental science, parts 1 and 2]. Messina.

Seybold-Brunnhuber, A. 1952. Rudolf von Laban und "The art of
movement" [Rudolf von Laban and "The art of movement"].
Leibeserziehung, no. 2: 18–20.

Sippel, H. 1923. *Der turnunterricht und die geistige arbeit des
schulkindes* [Gymnastics in school and the mental work of the
school child]. Berlin.

———. 1928. Vom sinn und wesen der leibesübungen [On the meaning
and essence of physical exercises]. In *Stadion,* ed. C. Diem,
H. Sippel, and F. Breithaupt, 13–20. Berlin.

Slovenko, R., and J. A. Knight. 1967. *Motivations in play, games and
sports.* Springfield IL.

Steinitzer, H. 1907–8. Zur psychologie des alpinisten [Psychology of
the alpinist]. *Graphologische Monatshefte* 9 (9/10): 73–88; (11/12):
89–107; 10 (3/4): 21–58.

———. 1910. *Sport und kultur: Mit besonderer berücksichtigung
des bergsports* [Sport and culture: With special reference to
mountaineering]. München.

———. 1910–11. Alpine pioniere und ihre handschriften [Pioneers of alpinism and their handwriting]. *Deutsche Alpenzeitung* 10 (2): 15–19.

Thibault, J. 1985. Le livre et le sport: Le docteur Philippe Tissié et ses oeuvres (1852–1935) [The book and the sport: Doctor Philippe Tissié and his works (1852–1935)]. *Revue francaise d'histoire du livre* 54 (49): 543–49.

Tissié, P. 1887. Notes sur quelques expériences faites dans l'ètat de suggestion: Dynamometre, sensibilité et mouvement [Notes on experiences in the state of suggestion: Dynamometry, sensibility, and movement]. *Bulletin de la Société d'Anthropologie de Bordeaux et du Sud-Quest* 4:86–97.

———. 1888. *L'hygiène du vélocipédiste* [The hygiene of the bicyclist]. Paris.

———. 1892. Influence du vélocipède sur quelques fonctions organiques: Présentée par d'Arsonval [The influence of the bicycle on some organic functions: Presented by d'Arsonval]. *Comptes rendus hebdomadaires des séances et mémoirs de la Société de Biologie*, 9e série, tome 4: 449–55.

———. 1894a. La fatigue nerveuse dans les exercices physiques et les sports [The nervous fatigue in physical exercises and sport]. Association francaise pur l'Avancement des sciences, Congrès des Caen.

———. 1894b. Observations physiologiques concernant un record vélocipédique [Physiological observations concerned with a cycling record]. *Archives de Physiologie*, 5e série, tome 6: 823–37.

———. 1894c. Psychologie de l'entraînement intensif [The psychology of intensive training]. *Revue Scientifique*, 31e année, 4e série, tome 2: 481–93.

———. 1894d. Un cas d'instabilité mentale avec impulsions morbides traité par la gymnastique médicale [Treatment of a case of mental instability together with morbid impulsions by medical gymnastics]. *Archives cliniques de Bordeaux*, 3e année: 1–13.

———. 1895. Traitement des phobies par la suggestion hypnotique (reves et parfums) et par la gymnastique médicale [On the treatment of phobias by hypnotic suggestion (dreams and perfumes) and medical gymnastics]. VI Congrès de médecins aliénistes et neurologistes, Bordeaux.

———. 1896a. L'Entraînement physique [On physical training]. *Revue Scientifique*, 4e série, tome 5: 514–20.

———. 1896b. Un cas d'impulsion sportive ou ludomanie: Pathologie de l'entrâinement [A case of sportive impulsion and ludomania: The pathology of training]. *Journal de médecine de Bordeaux*, no. 4: 35–39.

———. 1897. *La fatigue et l'entraînement physique* [Fatigue and physical training]. Paris.

———. 1901. L'Exercise physique au point de vue thérapeutique [Physical training from the view of therapy]. *Journal de médecine de Bordeaux*, no. 52: 818–22.

———. 1909. *Les jeux et les sports en thérapeutique* [Play and sports in therapy]. Bibliothèque de therapeutique. Paris: Gilbert and Carnot.

———. 1917. Jiel-Laval (nécrologie). *Revue des Jeux scolaires et d'Hygiene sociale*, année 27, nos. 4–6: 57–59.

Triplett, N. 1898. The dynamogenic factors in pacemaking and competition. *American Journal of Psychology* 9:507–33.

Tuke, D. H. 1872. *Illustrations of the influence of the mind upon the body in health and disease designed to elucidate the action of the imagination*. London.

Tytschino, N. N. 1908. Title unknown. *Wjestnik Psychologii* 5 (2).

———. 1910. [Correlations of the speed of different psychomotor processes]. Monographs of Pedagogical Psychology, no. 10, ed. A. Netchayev.

Vernon, P. E. 1928. The psychology of rowing. *British Journal of Psychology* 18:317–31.

———. 1929. Tests of temperament and personality. *British Journal of Psychology* 20:97–117.

Voigtländer, E. 1923. Zur phänomenologie und psychologie des "alpinen erlebnisses" [On the phenomenology and psychology of the "alpine adventure"]. *Zeitschrift für angewandte Psychologie* 22:258–70.

Wagner, L. 1898. *Unterricht und ermüdung* [School lessons and fatigue]. Berlin.

Wonneberger, G. 1952. P. F. Lesgaft — ein großer russischer

wissenschaftler und körpererzieher [P. F. Lesgaft—a great
Russian scientist and physical educator]. *Theorie und Praxis der
Körperkultur* 1 (8): 5–19.

Wundt, W. 1874: *Grundzüge der physiologischen psychologie* [Outlines
of physiological psychology]. Leipzig.

Zusne, L. 1984. *Biographical dictionary of psychology*. London.

2

E. W. SCRIPTURE

THE APPLICATION OF "NEW PSYCHOLOGY" METHODOLOGY TO ATHLETICS

C. James Goodwin

Edward Wheeler Scripture (1864–1945) was an enigmatic figure in psychology's history. He began his career with impeccable credentials — a PhD from the venerable Wilhelm Wundt at Leipzig in 1891, a year as resident fellow with G. Stanley Hall and Edmund Sanford at Clark University, and then a faculty appointment to Yale University by George Trumbull Ladd in 1892. At Yale he quickly developed a state-of-the-art psychology laboratory and founded the *Studies from the Yale Psychology Laboratory*, which he guided through ten volumes from 1893 to 1902. Also during the 1890s Scripture published two books celebrating and promoting the new laboratory-based psychology that he had first learned about during his time at Leipzig. In the first, *Thinking, Feeling, Doing* (1895c), he coined the phrase "armchair psychologist," which he used in a derogatory manner to identify all nonlaboratory psychologists and philosophers. It also popularized the label *new psychology* to characterize the emerging psychology of the laboratory (Boring 1965). This label became the title of his second book (Scripture 1897). Despite these accomplishments, Scripture left Yale in 1902 under less than auspicious circumstances, and he failed to make any subsequent impact on experimental psychology.

In this chapter I examine the life and work of Edward Scripture and show how his interest in applying the methods of the new psychology was part of a broader aim on the part of American experimental psychologists to show that their work had some relevance to everyday life in America. A special focus of the chapter will be Scripture's attempts to show that the methods of the new laboratory psychology, especially the measurement of reaction time, had something to offer those interested in athletics.

A Promising Start

Scripture was born in New Hampshire in 1864, spent his formative years living in New York City, and graduated from the City College of New York in 1884. He encountered and became intrigued by psychology sometime during his senior year at City College, although he later expressed some regret about his decision to pursue psychology, reporting that he did "not know why [he] became interested in psychology during the last year in college and foolishly refused an offer from [his] father to send [him] through medical school" (Scripture 1936, 231). At the time, however, psychology apparently provided sufficient interest to lure Scripture to Europe in order to examine the discipline further. He studied briefly in Berlin with Hermann Ebbinghaus, of nonsense syllable fame, in Zurich with the positivist philosopher Richard Avenarius, and finally, at the Mecca of the emerging new laboratory approach to psychology, Leipzig. Scripture spent three years with Wundt, earning a doctorate in 1891 for a dissertation on the process of association, and becoming a confirmed believer that the laboratory held the key to truth.

The major lesson that Scripture learned from his days in Leipzig was that it was possible to study mental processes with some precision through laboratory procedures involving strict measurement. With a characteristic tendency to overstate the case, he concluded that not only was it valuable to study psychological phenomena scientifically but that to do so was the *only* approach worth pursuing. As he put it, "Only statements based on measurements are reliable. The corollary is: statements without measurements are not worth listening to. . . . Publications on psychological topics that do not treat . . . mental phenomena in the form of indicator numbers have no meaning and no value" (Scripture 1936, 231–32).

Scripture's unshakable positivism and his belief in the necessity for precise measurement was strengthened during 1891–92 when he returned to America and spent an academic year at two-year-old Clark University working in the laboratory of Edmund Sanford. Before 1892, when financial difficulties and other problems darkened the bright promise of Clark, the psychology laboratory there was as well equipped as any in the United States or Europe (Goodwin 2006). Sanford had a very generous budget, and he was the beneficiary of the fact that G. Stanley Hall pilfered most of the psychological equipment from the Johns Hopkins laboratory when he left Hopkins to become Clark's first president in 1889 (Ross 1972). During his year at Clark Scripture conducted several studies on the relationship between the rate of stimulus change and the ability to detect slight changes (that is, psychophysics).

A prestigious PhD from Germany and a postdoctoral fellowship at Clark made Scripture highly marketable in 1892, and he quickly landed a position as instructor and laboratory director at Yale University. He was hired by Ladd, known at that time for his encyclopedic textbook *Elements of Physiological Psychology* (1887).

The first detailed description of Wundtian laboratory psychology to appear in English, Ladd's book provided an introduction to this new psychology for most English-speaking psychologists (Mills 1974). Although Ladd supported laboratory work, as evidenced by his hiring of Scripture and the funding of a lab, he was never personally suited to the detail and precision of the lab, preferring a brand of psychology that harkened to the pre-Wundtian days when psychology was taught as moral philosophy (Sokal 1980). Eventually Ladd's and Scripture's contrasting views of the value of laboratory research, along with disagreements over the authoritative control of the lab, would create a conflict that contributed to the demise of both their careers at Yale.

Once at Yale Scripture did not waste a minute in beginning his research program. Several graduate students were already in residence, including Carl Seashore (1866–1949), who became Scripture's best-known student and in 1895 the first person to be awarded a PhD in psychology from Yale. Within a year of his arrival Scripture (1894a) was able to report that, despite the "incredible difficulties and incessant labor in getting matters arranged" (66), several studies had been completed and published in *Studies from the Yale Psychological Laboratory*, an in-house journal that he created. In that first year Scripture reported studies on reaction time and attention (reaching one conclusion — that "introspection is not to be trusted in estimating results" [Scripture 1894a, 67]), visual accommodation (by Seashore), reaction time as a function of stimulus intensity and pitch, and the musical sensitivity of school children. He also reported the creation of several specialized pieces of apparatus. Like other first generation experimental psychologists, and out of necessity, Scripture had a high degree of mechanical aptitude and was talented at designing and building research apparatus. He ended his first annual report of the lab's activities with a glowing description of his workshop, which, he argued, had already paid for itself by saving money on equipment that would otherwise have had to be purchased. By the end of his first year at Yale, Scripture was well on his way to a promising career as an experimentalist. In his remaining nine years at Yale *Studies from the Yale Psychological Laboratory* appeared annually, largely featuring Scripture's research and that of his students, his notes on apparatus that he had created or adapted, and in one case an early argument for the use of the median instead of the mean as the preferred measure of central tendency (Scripture 1895a).

Promoting the New Psychology

Historian John O'Donnell (1985) has described Scripture's approach to psychology as uncompromising, "an authentic experimentalist prospectus" (38). Yet Scripture, like everyone else, was subject to historical context, and a powerful force in early American psychology was the pragmatism that was becoming part of the national character — experimentalists felt the need to show that their science had useful applications. What we now call basic research might have been an ideal activity for these pioneers, the one for which they had been trained, but they were living in a culture that rewarded practical application. Furthermore, the experimentalists worked at universities, usually within departments of philosophy, where they needed budgets to run their labs and where one way to obtain budget support over the skepticism of their philosophical colleagues was to argue that the results of the lab would not only contribute to the knowledge base but also be able to improve the lives of people.

Scripture's response to these pressures for application was to produce two books within the span of two years, *Thinking, Feeling, Doing* (1895c) and *The New Psychology* (1897). Both books explicitly tried to show (a) that the "new" psychology of the laboratory was vastly superior to the "old" psychology that was tied to philosophy and (b) that it could be put to practical use in any number of ways. Scripture's second book went into greater detail about the fine points of laboratory work; the first one was unabashedly promotional, and it will be the focus of the discussion here.

In *Thinking, Feeling, Doing* Scripture did not mince words. Concerning the advantage of the laboratory over philosophical analysis, he wrote dismissively that the typical philosopher "sits at his desk and writes volumes of vague observation, endless speculation, and flimsy guesswork. The psychologist of the new dispensation must see every statement proven by experiment and measurement before he will commit himself in regard to it" (1895c, 282).[1] In addition, whereas the new psychology could offer practical benefits, philosophy did not. Addressing philosophers directly, Scripture wrote: "When you have written your 500 or 1,000 pages on these subjects, is the world any better off? Have you contributed one single fact to the advance of science and humanity? . . . Have you no thought, no suggestion as to how we may grow better ourselves and educate our children to a better life?" (283).

Having offended philosophers, Scripture then slighted Ladd, the man who hired him, and the esteemed William James, author of the authoritative *Principles of Psychology* ([1890] 1950).[2] After opening his preface with a bow to Wundt's work, he wrote:

No one else has produced a book explaining the methods and results of the new psychology. This is my reason for writing one.

This is the first book on the *new*, or experimental, psychology written in the English language. That it has been written *expressly for the people* will, I hope, be taken as evidence of the attitude of the science in its desire to serve humanity. (Scripture 1895c, iii; italics in the original)

There is no record of how Ladd, whose famous text had appeared eight years earlier, reacted to this bold statement. As will be seen, however, their relationship became increasingly rancorous over the years. As for William James, whose monumental two-volume *Principles* is often considered psychology's most famous text, he was known to have dismissed Scripture as a "barbarian" and his in-house journal at Yale as a "little college tin-trumpet" (quoted in O'Donnell 1985, 38).

Thinking, Feeling, Doing includes 209 drawings and photographs. Many of them were designed to impress the reader with the precision of measurement to be found in the Yale lab. For example, there are photos of apparatus set up for experiments on such standard topics as reaction time, steadiness testing, grip strength, and psychophysics; there are photos of the lab and the workshop; and there are drawings such as kymograph records showing data from various experiments. But many of the photos and drawings are designed to show how laboratory methods can be adapted to topics of interest to the lay reader. Consider these figure captions:

Measuring the Simultaneity of Actions of a Piano-Player (31)

Time of Thought at Various Ages in School Children (61)

Fatiguing Attention Preparatory to Hypnosis (102)

An Experiment in Tickling (105)

Everybody is Somewhat Deaf. Finding the Threshold of Intensity (147)

Taking an Orchestra Leader's Record with the Electric Baton (Scripture 1895a, 260)

The last example above, about an orchestra leader, is a good illustration of Scripture's general strategy in the book. In a chapter called "Rhythmic Action," Scripture tried to show that making precise measurements could have direct practical application — in this case making judgments about the comparative quality of orchestra leaders. He designed an electric baton, connected to a kymograph in such a way as to measure time per beat. He was then able to calculate an "index of irregularity" (that is, the average deviation from the mean amount of time taken for each beat) and to argue that good orchestra leaders could be differentiated from poor ones by this irregularity index: "An essential qualification . . . for the success of an orchestra leader is his *regularity* in estimating intervals of time" (Scripture 1895c, 261; italics in the original). By implication scientific methods used by the new psychologists could be used to improve one's experience at the symphony, either by training conductors to reduce their index of irregularity or by selecting conductors with low indices.

More generally, Scripture argued that a thorough scientific analysis of mental activity had important implications for life. As he put it in his typical tendency for hyperbole, "Rapid thought and quick action sometimes make all the difference between success and failure. . . . A man who can think and act in one half of the time that another man can, will accumulate mental and material capital twice as fast" (Scripture 1895c, 62).

Applying Laboratory Methods to Athletics

The extent of Scripture's direct interest in athletic activities is unclear. There is no hint of it in his autobiographical chapter in the *History of Psychology in Autobiography* series (Scripture 1936). In fact, the chapter focuses almost entirely on his research and reveals very little about him as a person.[3] However, as part of his effort to show that experimental psychology had everyday relevance, it is clear that he saw athletics as a prime example, and he vigorously promoted the idea. For instance, he contributed a paper "Reaction-time and Time-memory in Gymnastic Work" to the ninth annual meeting of the American Association for the Advancement of Physical Education, which was hosted by Yale in April 1894 (Scripture 1894c). And *Thinking, Feeling, Doing* (Scripture 1895c) includes six different figures illustrating a variety of athletic activities:

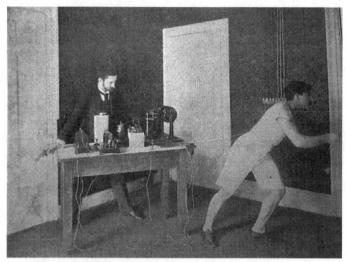

2.1. Reaction time for sprinters. Reprinted from Scripture 1895c.

Measuring a Runner's Reaction Time (46)

Measuring Mental and Muscular Time in Fencing (56)

Measuring How Rapidly a Pugilist Thinks and Acts (59)

Recording a Sportsman's Unsteadiness (69)

Walking with Pneumatic Shoes and Recording Drum (254)

Taking a Record with Electric Dumb Bells (262)

The latter two examples are in the chapter on rhythmic action, along with the orchestra leader example already described. A chapter on "Steadiness and Control" includes the sportsman photo — a man trying to remain still while aiming a rifle. The first three examples (runners, fencers, and pugilists) all involve reaction time and movement time, measurements that Scripture believed to have special relevance for athletics.

Scripture used simple reaction time measures when examining runners. Figure 2.1, with Scripture in the photo, shows the setup.

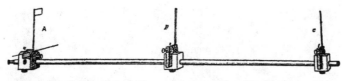

2.2. Apparatus for recording reaction and movement time. Reprinted from Scripture 1895c.

The experimenter fires a starter's pistol, and the runner lunges, breaking a thread attached to his pants. Electric circuits are broken at the instant of both actions, producing kymograph records that could be translated into reaction times. Scripture (1895c) reported that although he had not been able "to carry out an extended series of experiments on racers, the experiments made have shown a few facts" (45). First, he observed that sprinters had quicker reactions than long distance runners, a finding that he interpreted as meaning that "reaction time can be reduced by practice" (46) (ignoring the possibility that naturally quicker athletes would gravitate to the sprint events). Second, he noted that reaction time was slower when the whole body had to be moved than when just a part of the body such as a finger on a reaction key had to be moved. Arguing for a diagnostic function for reaction time, he pointed out that "if the youth has a long, simple reaction-time, you can select games and exercises that will make it shorter" (Scripture 1894c, 48). He did not provide examples of such games or exercises, however.

When examining boxers and fencers, Scripture looked at more than simple reaction time. With boxers, for instance, he created the apparatus shown in figure 2.2 for an experiment portrayed in figure 2.3. Point A in figure 2.2 holds a small flag, the movement of which signaled the start of a trial. The boxer would place one fist so that it was just touching the small vertical bamboo stick at point C. When the experimenter moved the flag, the boxer would throw a punch all the way to the bamboo stick at B, thereby deflecting both sticks. The time between the flag dropping and the move-

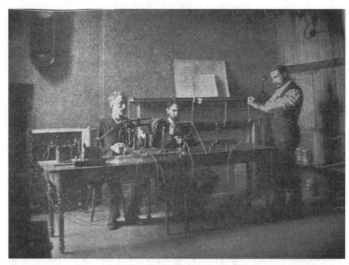

2.3. Reaction and movement time for boxers. Reprinted from Scripture 1895c.

ment of the stick at C yielded simple reaction time, whereas the time from movement of stick C to movement of stick B produced a measure of speed of punching (movement time). The process could be complicated by having the boxer move only when the flag fell in one direction rather than another. Thus the standard laboratory procedure of discrimination reaction time was incorporated into the application. Scripture did not report any specific results with boxers, but he used essentially the same apparatus with fencers, and he conducted a more elaborate experiment with them, complete with experimental and control groups.

Scripture described the study with fencers in both of his books, in an article in *Studies from the Yale Psychological Laboratory* (Scripture 1894b), and in one of his annual reports on work in the Yale lab (Scripture 1895b). The study came about when Yale was visited by a group of expert fencers. Scripture, never shy, evidently convinced them to come to the lab for some experiments.[4]

The experimental setup is shown in figure 2.4. In the first set of experiments the fencer started a trial with the tip of the foil against

2.4. Reaction and movement time for fencers. Reprinted from Scripture 1895c.

a small disk. When the experimenter on the left moved the flag, the fencer lunged with the foil to strike the large disk. The time between the flag movement and the initial movement of the foil against the small disk was simple reaction time; movement time was the time taken for the foil to reach the large disk (a distance of seventy-five centimeters). In the second set of experiments the flag was moved in different directions, and the movement of the foil had to correspond to those directions. The movement times now included a discrimination process. The third set of trials assessed accuracy — fencers had to hit the center of the large disk, with distance from center being recorded. For each subject in the study Scripture reported the average reaction time performance on "about 10 experiments [i.e., trials]" (Scripture 1894b, 123) and the average distance from center, on the accuracy trials, for the "seven best lunges" (123).

There were five fencers in the expert group, four who were regular competitors in national fencing tournaments and one who was "master of arms of the New York Athletic Club" (Scripture 1894b, 123).[5] The control group was comprised of two of Scripture's faculty colleagues — Ladd, said to be "formerly practiced in fencing" (123), and Professor Williams, said to have no experience in fencing. Scripture acknowledged that drawing firm conclusions would be difficult given the small sample, but as was the case with his other studies involving athletics, he made some summary statements about the results anyway.

With all the data combined for the two groups (reported in Bäumler 1996), Scripture found no difference between experts (.216 seconds) and novices (.206 seconds) in simple reaction time, but he found distinct advantage for experts (.302 seconds) over novices (.543 seconds) in movement time. As Scripture described it, the "average fencer is not quicker in simple reaction . . . than a trained scientist, . . . [but] once the mind is made up to execute a movement, fencers are far quicker in the actual execution. In rough figures, it takes them only half as long as the average individual. . . . The general conclusion seems to be that fencing does not develop mental quickness more than scientific pursuits, but it does develop to a high degree the rapidity of executing movements" (Scripture 1894b, 123–24).

On discrimination reaction time, that is, lunging in a specific direction as a function of the direction of the flag's movement, the average times for the scientists (.246 seconds) were actually faster than the fencers (.302 seconds), although a subsequent analysis by Bäumler (1996) found the difference not to be statistically significant. The fastest discrimination time of all, however, was by the best of the fencing masters, Graeme Hammond (see note 5), "whose mental quickness has probably been developed in some other way" (124). On the final measure, accuracy, the novices (28.5 mm off) were not quite as accurate as the experts (21.4 mm), but the difference was entirely due to the ineptness of Professor Williams, the only subject with zero experience in fencing. He was off by an average of 36 mm, whereas the error scores of all the others were between 18 mm and 24 mm; the overall difference was not significant (Bäumler 1996).

It would be easy to make too much of this study. Whether it is the first example of a sports psychology experiment or whether it is the first quasi experiment that used a control group, is not especially relevant or noteworthy. Rather, its importance lies in the fact that it reflects Scripture's unwavering faith in a scientific strategy and in his goal of showing how experimental psychology, with its apparent precision of measurement, could be relevant for the topics of interest (such as athletics) to the average American.

Fading into Obscurity

During his ten years at Yale Scripture remained dedicated to his laboratory, and he continued to be a vigorous advocate for experimental psychology. However, his advocacy and his visibility as an experimental psychologist came to an abrupt end shortly after the start of the twentieth century when he was told that he was no longer welcome at Yale.

The reasons for Scripture's demise are complicated and not entirely clear, but he was evidently quite skilled at annoying colleagues, both at Yale and within the emerging discipline of psychology (see Benjamin 2006). We have already seen the arrogance displayed in his books, the distain for those who might take a more philosophical approach to psychological issues, and his uncompromising faith in the laboratory and the truth-value of its empirical data. Thus well before his departure from American psychology, there were hints at problems with Scripture's character. Even his students, while generally supportive of his energy and enthusiasm for the lab, found him "nervously unstable" (Wallin 1955, 12).[6]

And there was a specific and serious problem that concerned

credible charges of plagiarism in Scripture's *Thinking, Feeling, Doing* (1895c). Any psychologist who writes for popular consumption is an easy target for charges of oversimplification and of making excessive and unsubstantiated claims. Indeed, reviews of *Thinking, Feeling, Doing* contained such criticism. Margaret Washburn (1895), for example, wrote that Scripture's effort "leaves unanswered the question whether experimental psychology can at the present time be popularized in a useful and dignified manner. It demonstrates without a doubt, however, its author's entire unfitness for such a task" (660). But the criticism went far beyond the quality of Scripture's effort. Both Washburn and, in another review, James Rowland Angell (1895) pointed out that long passages in the book, especially in a chapter on emotion, bore a striking resemblance to passages in a recent English translation of Wundt's *Lectures on Human and Animal Psychology*. Both reviewers specifically identified several examples of corresponding pages in the two books in which the passages were either virtually the same or in which Scripture's words were "a literal transcription" of words from the translation of Wundt's book (Washburn 1895, 661). One of the translators was the easily offended E. B. Titchener of Cornell, who attempted to have Scripture excommunicated from the American Psychological Association on ethical grounds (Goodwin 1985).[7] Cooler heads prevailed, however, and Titchener's Clark University friend Edmund Sanford wrote to him that perhaps Scripture had been punished enough by the reviews: "Scripture has had his dose, [and] the steal has been noticed elsewhere."[8]

The plagiarism issue probably contributed to Scripture's troubles at Yale. The details of his dismissal remain unclear, but the central issue appears to have been a gradual deterioration in his relationship with Ladd.[9] This deterioration was rooted in their opposing views of how psychology ought to be construed and in their differences over who should be in overall control of the lab (Mills 1969). As is clear by now, Scripture could accept no view other than his own — a psychology firmly grounded in the experimental laboratory. But as mentioned earlier, although appreciative of the value of laboratory psychology, Ladd was more philosophically inclined, being the kind of person that Scripture had in mind when referring sarcastically in *Thinking, Feeling, Doing* to armchair psychologists. These two worldviews about psychology were evidently irreconcilable, and tension between the two psychologists built during the 1890s. At one point Scripture wrote to James McKeen Cattell of Columbia that "I am convinced — as I should have been long ago — that there is little or no future for me at Yale" (quoted in Sokal 1980, 269).

Yale, under the leadership of a new president, apparently decided to resolve the conflict by ridding itself of both Ladd and Scripture. In 1902 Scripture was given a year's leave of absence but told not to return. Shortly thereafter, Ladd was named professor emeritus and forced to retire (Sokal 1980). After leaving Yale, Scripture went to Europe, where he earned an MD at the University of Munich in 1906 and became known, both in Europe and in the United States, for his work in the areas of phonetics and speech disorders.

Scripture, Experimental Psychology, and Athletics

Scripture has a place in the history of sport psychology. In his laboratory he attempted to show that the methods of experimental psychology could be beneficial to athletes. Apart from the laboratory, he even wrote about the relationship between athletics and character, arguing from case studies that felons who participated in athletic activities while in prison showed improvements in general attitude (Scripture 1900). Yet there is certainly no case for making Scripture the father of sports psychology. His primary goal was to promote the new laboratory psychology, not to found a new sub discipline. Hence it is not surprising that he did not develop a program of research into the application of psychological principles to sport — it would have been too narrow an interest for him.[10] Scripture's sports-related research comprised a very small proportion of his total work, and although he believed that it "would be important to determine if [the outcome of his fencing study] holds good for other sports and exercises, or if some of them are especially adapted to develop mental quickness" (Scripture 1894b, 124), there is no evidence that he pursued such a course of action.

Notes

1 Scripture has been credited with the creation of the term *armchair psychology*, a derogatory expression referring to those of a philosophical bent who speculate about psychological phenomena without basing conclusions on research. The attribution is based on this quote and at least three others in *Thinking, Feeling, Doing* (1895c). On page 24 there is a paragraph with the label "the arm-chair psychology" along with the sarcastic comment that "sitting at home in the arm chair is very pleasant but it is not the way to do business, and consequently psychology has been going backward." On page 28, during a discussion about the use of reaction time methods, he wrote that measuring mental events is "a knotty problem which all the discussion of a dozen arm-chair psychologists could not solve." And in the book's next-to-last paragraph, Scripture (1895c) wrote that "as long as psychology was an arm-chair science, anybody could teach it; today no one but a carefully trained man can do so" (295).

2 Another indication of Scripture's attitude toward philosophy is found in his chapter on attention in which he described a "disease" of attention that he called "metaphysical mania, where the patient cannot hear a word like 'good,' 'beautiful,' 'being,' etc., without irresistibly speculating on the problems of ethics, aesthetics, and metaphysics" (101).

3 Scripture (1936) recognized the absence of personal detail, as evidenced by this odd final comment: "I notice a paucity of personal details in my account. I have forgotten most of them and

I am not interested in the rest; I do not think the reader would be either" (261).

4 The purpose of the visit is not clear, but Yale established fencing as an intercollegiate sport in 1894, and the visit might have been related to this event. Fencing was a popular amateur sport at the time; it was regulated in the United States by the Amateur Athletic Union, which initiated national championships in 1888 and played a role in making fencing an Olympic sport in 1896. See Sports History: Fencing, Hickok Sports, http://www.hickoksports.com/history/fencing (last accessed December 22, 2008).

5 One of the fencers, Graeme Hammond was the U.S. champion in the épée (1889, 1891, and 1892), foil (1891), and saber (1893 and 1894), while another, Bernard O'Connor (mistakenly identified as P. F. O'Connor by Scripture), was champion in épée (1892) and foil (1889). See Sports History: Fencing, http://www.hickoksports.com/history/fencing.

6 According to Boring (1950), Scripture did not attract very many students to his lab, despite the quality of the facility. Only three of Scripture's students made names for themselves: Carl Seashore (as an experimental psychologist), J. E. Wallace Wallin (as a clinical psychologist), and Matataro Matsumoto (who became prominent in Japanese psychology).

7 Titchener was not prone to forgive and forget. Two years later, in a letter dated October 26, 1897, to former student Walter Pillsbury, Titchener solicited some further criticism of Scripture, writing, "Could you give me for *MIND*, very soon, a 1 and ½ or 2 pp. (small print) notice of Scripture, showing (1) his real merits & originality, (2) his absurd self-conceit, and (3) his curious backwardness in the matter of visual theory, as well as any other points you cared for?" (Titchener Papers, Cornell University Archives, Ithaca NY).

8 E. C. Sanford to E. B. Titchener, December 21, 1895, Titchener Papers. Scripture also did not hesitate to self-plagiarize. He wrote accounts of his fencing study in four different places using exactly the same phrasing in all four.

9 As is customary, the notice in *Psychological Review* simply noted

that Scripture had "resigned his position at Yale University" (Anonymous 1903, 620).

10 In this regard Scripture's contribution to sport psychology was similar to that of Walter Miles in the 1920s (see Baugh and Benjamin, this volume).

References

Angell, J. R. 1895. Review of *Thinking, feeling, doing. Psychological Review* 2:606–9.

Anonymous. 1903. Notes. *Psychological Review* 10:620.

Bäumler, G. 1995. The contributions to sports psychology by E. W. Scripture and his Yale group: Part I; E. W. Scripture as an experimental psychologist, and his paper read in 1894 before the American Association for Physical Education. *Sportonomics* 1:100–104.

———. 1996. The contributions to sports psychology by E. W. Scripture and his Yale group: Part II; Scripture's 1894 experiment on the reaction-time of fencers. *Sportonomics* 2:21–24.

Benjamin, L. T., Jr. 2006. Hugo Münsterberg's attack on the application of scientific psychology. *Journal of Applied Psychology* 91:414–25.

Boring, E. G. 1950. *A history of experimental psychology.* 2nd ed. Englewood Cliffs NJ: Prentice-Hall.

———. 1965. Edward Wheeler Scripture: 1864–1945. *American Journal of Psychology* 78:314–17.

Goodwin, C. J. 1985. The origins of Titchener's Experimentalists. *Journal of the History of the Behavioral Sciences* 21:383–89.

———. 2006. Edmund Clark Sanford and the consequences of loyalty. In *Portraits of pioneers in psychology,* ed. D. A. Dewsbury, L. T. Benjamin, Jr., and M. Wertheimer, 3–17. Vol. 6. Washington DC: American Psychological Association.

James, W. [1890] 1950. *Principles of psychology.* Vols. 1 and 2. New York: Dover.

Ladd, G. T. 1887. *Elements of physiological psychology.* New York: Scribner.

Mills, E. S. 1969. *George Trumbull Ladd: Pioneer American psychologist.* Cleveland: Case Western Reserve Press.

—————. 1974. George Trumbull Ladd: The great textbook writer. *Journal of the History of the Behavioral Sciences* 10:299–303.

O'Donnell, J. M. 1985. *The origins of behaviorism: American psychology, 1870–1920.* New York: New York University Press.

Ross, D. 1972. G. *Stanley Hall: The psychologist as prophet.* Chicago: University of Chicago Press.

Scripture, E. W. 1894a. Reaction-time and time-memory in gymnastic work. In *Ninth annual meeting of the American Association for the Advancement of Physical Education*, 44–49. New Haven CT: n.p.

—————. 1894b. Tests of mental ability as exhibited in fencing. *Studies from the Yale Psychological Laboratory* 2:122–24.

—————. 1894c. Work at the Yale laboratory. *Psychological Review* 1:66–69.

—————. 1895a. Practical computation of the median. *Psychological Review* 2:376–79.

—————. 1895b. The second year at the Yale laboratory. *Psychological Review* 2:379–81.

—————. 1895c. *Thinking, feeling, doing.* Meadville PA: Flood and Vincent.

—————. 1897. *The new psychology.* New York: Scribner.

—————. 1900. Cross-education. *Popular Science* 56:589–96.

—————. 1936. E. W. Scripture. In *A history of psychology in autobiography*, ed. C. Murchison, 231–61. Vol. 3. Worcester MA: Clark University Press.

Sokal, M. M. 1980. Biographical approach: The psychological career of Edward Wheeler Scripture. In *Historiography of modern psychology: Aims, resources, approaches*, ed. J. Brozek and L. J. Pongratz, 255–78. Toronto: Hogrefe.

Wallin, J. E. W. 1955. *The odyssey of a psychologist: Pioneering experiences in education, clinical psychology, and mental hygiene.* Wilmington DE: self-published.

Washburn, M. 1895. Review of *Thinking, feeling, doing. Philosophical Review* 4:659–61.

3

NORMAN TRIPLETT

RECOGNIZING THE IMPORTANCE OF COMPETITION

Stephen F. Davis, Matthew T. Huss, and Angela H. Becker

During the late 1800s and early 1900s the study of physiological-physical processes and abilities such as reaction time, threshold determination, attention, and feeling occupied the time and energies of such notables as Hermann von Helmholtz, Ernst Weber, and psychology's founding father Wilhelm Wundt (Schultz and Schultz 2008). As the new psychology spread from its German roots to take hold in the United States, these problems continued to be of interest. However, such interests were not limited just to the new psychologists. Researchers, especially those in physical education, were quick to adapt the new scientific research procedures to their own areas of interest. Sport, because of its emphasis on such issues as learning a motor skill, improving reaction times, and transferring skill learning between situations, was among these areas.

Early Studies of Motor Learning, Reaction Time, and Transfer of Training

One such early researcher who attempted to apply physiological-psychological processes to the field of education was George Wells Fitz (1860–1934) of Harvard University's Lawrence Scientific School. Fitz established what is believed to be the first physical education laboratory in North America and headed the Department of Anatomy, Physiology, and Physical Training at Harvard from 1891–99 (Wiggins 1984). In 1895 Fitz published the results of a study concerned with multiple reaction times in the *Psychological Review*. He constructed an apparatus that was designed to test "the power of an individual to touch an object suddenly disclosed to him in an unexpected position" (Fitz 1895, 37). The apparatus consisted of an arched horizontal strip of brass configured to signal when a subject made contact with the surface and then recording the reaction time via a chronoscope with a balanced pendulum. When the screen covering the apparatus fell, the subjects were to remove their finger from the tip of their nose and place their hand at the point on the blackened brass strip where a white spot was visible. As soon as the screen fell, the chronoscope began recording the subject's reaction time. Fitz believed that the test's ability to measure quickness would have applications to athletics. He summarized that those individuals who demonstrated quicker and more accurate times would be better at sports such as tennis and fencing.

Upon completion of the experiment, Fitz indicated that the full value of any direct application of the reaction time apparatus was not yet fully understood, but he did believe it would be an appropriate predictor of individual motor ability. Fitz (1895) concluded that (a) subjects who were quicker were not necessarily less accurate; (b) on an everyday basis time, not accuracy, demonstrated greatest variability; and (c) no relation could be found between accuracy and time. Although Fitz could not predict performance in athletic events based on reaction time, his study provided an early example of the application of scientific principles in this area.

In the late 1800s Walter Wells Davis of Iowa College also investigated the application of basic psychological principles to the world of sport. While working on his doctorate at Yale University, Davis published studies in two separate volumes of *Studies from the Yale Psychological Laboratory* (Kroll and Lewis 1970). Davis reported a surprising result from studies in which subjects raised a five-pound dumbbell by flexing the arm at the elbow. Initially subjects accomplished this task with both the right and left arms. For the ensuing two to four weeks they lifted the weights using only the right arm; then both arms were tested for changes. Not only did the right arms increase in size and strength, but the left arms also increased in both size and strength. This finding was interpreted as reflecting the effects of cross-education, or as it became known, transfer of training.

Another physical educator interested in transfer of muscle training was William G. Anderson, also of Yale University. In a series of experiments Anderson (1899) demonstrated that if muscles on one side of the body are strengthened either by squeezing an object or by balancing on a tight rope, comparable muscles on the other side of the body are strengthened without any exercise of those muscles.

S. G. Noble (1922) also conducted transfer-of-training research. He concluded that transfer occurred between similar activities such as shooting lay-ups and short push shots but not between dissimilar activities such as shooting lay-ups and free throws.

Research during this early period was not limited only to transfer of training. For example, Daniel Starch (1911) described a series of studies that demonstrated trial-and-error motor learning through the use of a mirror-tracing task. Similarly, Robert

A. Cummins (1914) of the University of Washington investigated the effects of basketball practice on motor reaction, attention, and suggestibility. Cummins concluded that the average college student should not practice basketball because it breaks up motor control. Herbert Hayes Murphy (1916) tested the effects of varying schedules of practice on the performance of javelin throwers and found that practice could be distributed by giving practices on alternate days or even weekly without any significant loss in learning.

Although many of these studies can be classified as simple motor learning research, others clearly provided direct applications to a variety of sports. Another group of early researchers was interested in the role of sports in the development of personality.

Studies Relating Personality Development and Sport: The Importance of Play

In contrast to the experimentally oriented studies of motor learning, reaction time, and transfer, a number of studies focused on the relationship of personality variables and sports. In fact, it became fashionable to create a theory to explain the need or desire for sport and play. Among these explanations were the Schiller-Spencer Theory (play is surplus energy), Pryor's Theory (play is inherently pleasurable), and the Imitation Theory (imitation is a fundamental human faculty) (see Hermann 1921). Few of these theories were based on sound scientific manipulations.

The most methodologically sound of these personality studies was conducted by Edward W. Scripture (1900), the director of the psychological laboratory at Yale University during the late 1800s and early 1900s. This research relied on a number of case studies. Scripture sought to uncover whether the long-held belief that participation in sports leads to an improvement in a variety of personality characteristics or character was correct. He attempted to examine this relationship by examining young felons in a program at Elmira Reformatory. Scripture reported remarkable success at improvements in self-control and general behavior in those individuals who participated in a program of athletics, calisthenics, and manual training. It was believed that such motor activity built character that was then transferred to everyday living. Though not meticulous by any standard and reporting anecdotal data, Scripture's attempt does represent one of the few personality studies from the early twentieth century with any methodological rigor.

Fitz (1897), Patrick (1903, 1914), and Hermann (1921) are much more representative of the literature of the time. Fitz (1897) made the claim that play was a means of preparing one for life by enabling the individual to develop (a) judgmental capabilities such as alertness, (b) the ability to perceive conditions correctly, and (c) the ability to react quickly to an ever-changing environment. Fitz (1897) believed that one should play "and as a result become an abler, nobler, and spiritually stronger man" (215).

Patrick (1903, 1914) developed a much more formalized theory for play. He felt that childhood play was a reflection of ancestral adult survival practices. For example, actions such as running, wrestling, and jumping were more popular to spectators because they allowed the spectators to return to basic instinctual levels and to rest higher brain functions that were constantly being utilized in a society increasing in complexity.

Hermann (1921) hypothesized that play enabled humans to develop *life-long habits* and that muscles were the mechanism by which one developed habituation, imitation, obedience, character, manners, and customs. He proposed that there was an indisputable interconnection between mind, body, and spirit and that through play an individual could apply ethical and other knowledge to real situations.

In addition, Kellor (1908) advocated for the inclusion of physical play as a means not only to build a strong body but also a strong mind. She argued that even though women were restricted to calisthenic-like activity, they should be regularly encouraged to participate in games of spirit and competition such as basketball, rowing, lacrosse, tennis, and handball. It was only through similar games that one is truly able to create the energy that allows one to "accomplish the same quantity and quality of intellectual work as men" (104). Hence she concluded that physical play allowed one to relieve the full tension of the mind, to create the inspiration that is essential for returning to intellectual activity, and to utilize intellectually relevant faculties such as reflection, memory, and reason in entirely different ways.

The studies conducted by the early researchers in these two disparate areas predated the more directed and scientific approach that was to characterize Coleman Griffith. Yet before Griffith's seminal work a single study from the creative mind of an Illinois school teacher was to point irrevocably in the direction that sport psychology was destined to take.

Norman Triplett and the Study of Competition

Although the early research on reaction time and motor learning and the musings about why individuals engage in sport provided a premonition of sport psychology, it was a research project conducted by Norman Triplett (1898) that cut to the heart of the interface between sport and psychology. This core was competition.

A life-long devotee of athletic competition, Triplett investigated the effects of the presence of other competitors on performance. In his article "The Dynamogenic Factors Involved in Pace-making and Competition" (1898), Triplett analyzed official records from the Racing Board of the League of American Wheelmen for bicycle racing performance under three conditions: (a) unpaced (no competitor or pacemaker present), (b) paced (a fresh team of three or four cyclists set the pace on each lap for the competitor), and (c) paced cycling against an actual competitor or competitors (each competitor was paced by a team). His review of these cycling data indicated that the presence of pacemakers and actual competition against other cyclists resulted in superior performance. Although one can appeal to several factors to account for these results, Triplett felt that the presence of the pacemakers or competitors served as a stimulus for the release of energy that remained latent under the unpaced and direct competition conditions. In addition to the release of this latent energy, Triplett also believed that the visual and auditory presence of the pacemakers or competitors served as an inspiration for increased effort.

In an attempt to generalize from cycling to a different form of behavior, these predictions were tested in a laboratory experiment in which subjects wound fishing line as rapidly as possible in order to move a toy flag around a course. As with the cycling data the most informative data came in the form of comparisons between times recorded by solitary individuals and those recorded when pairs of subjects competed; the quickest times were recorded when pairs of subjects competed. Triplett concluded that "from the . . . facts regarding the laboratory races we infer that the bodily presence of another contestant participating in the races serves to liberate latent energy not ordinarily available" (Triplett 1898, 533).

The importance of Triplett's article has stood the test of time exceptionally well. It is recognized as a timeless classic in social psychology as well as in sport psychology and as the initial demonstration of the phenomenon known as social facilitation. For example, Allport (1954) indicated that "the first experimental problem [in social psychology] — and indeed the only problem for the first three decades of experimental research — was formulated as follows: What changes in an individual's normal solitary performance occur when other people are present? The first laboratory answer to this question came from Triplett (1898)" (46). Thus

Triplett's research was a harbinger of the now-familiar topic of social psychological research, social facilitation (Holmes 2008). Likewise, Halberstadt and Ellyson (1990) chose Triplett's paper for inclusion in a book of readings covering the first century of research in social psychology.

Indeed, an examination of texts and chapters dealing with the history of sport psychology has yet to yield a single source that fails to acknowledge the importance of this pioneering work. For example, Iso-Ahola and Hatfield (1986) wrote that "the first scientific experiment of sport psychology was reported by Triplett in 1898. . . . One cannot help but feel awed by his scientific ingeniousness and rigorousness. It is ironic that only recently have psychologists issued calls for studies based upon field and laboratory data. Had they read Triplett's study, such an idea would have been self-evident. Needless to say, Triplett's is the study that all sport psychologists should read and learn the lessons provided by the pioneer" (16, 18–19). Likewise, Mahoney and Suinn (1986) indicated that "Norman Triplett (1898) of Indiana University is increasingly credited with the first technical publication in the area" (64). These acknowledgements notwithstanding, it is interesting to note that Scripture also conducted and published research on cycling that predated Triplett by four years (see Goodwin, this volume). Perhaps the greater visibility of Triplett's report resulted in his receiving this credit.

Because the boundaries and configuration of an entire discipline were being molded, the pressures faced by American psychologists in the early twentieth century were significantly different from those faced by contemporary academicians. In most instances psychology did not exist as a separate department or specialty. Additionally, there was no set curriculum, and specialty areas of programmatic research were unheard of. Thus turn-of-the-century psychologists were called on repeatedly to justify both the new discipline and their own existence. Such constraints effectively precluded the development of organized programs of research in sport psychology until the 1920s and the work of Coleman Griffith at the University of Illinois (see Green, this volume).

In many respects Norman Triplett might be cast as the prototypical example of these early researchers. Often their interest in sport, even though intense, was not sufficient to justify a concerted research program. Hence their interests were manifested in the occasional project and/or other relevant avenues. The pressures of that era were not conducive to the development of an extensive publication list, at least not extensive by current standards. In the case of Norman Triplett teaching was more highly prized than it appears to be today (see Benjamin 1991).

From Farm to University

Norman Triplett was born October 1, 1861, on a farm near Perry, Illinois.[1] He graduated from the Perry High School, and in 1889 his baccalaureate degree was awarded by Illinois College (Jacksonville, Illinois), where he served as valedictorian of his class. Following completion of his undergraduate training, Triplett served as the superintendent of schools in New Berlin, Illinois, from 1889 until 1891. Subsequently he taught science at Quincy (Illinois) High School from 1894 until 1897. The nature of his employment from 1891 to 1894 is not known.

Triplett did graduate work at Indiana University from which he received a master's degree in 1898, the "Dynamogenics" article being his master's thesis. The research for his thesis was conducted in the laboratory of William Lowe Bryan (1860–1955), who served as the twelfth president of the American Psychological Association in 1903 and who was G. Stanley Hall's second doctoral student. Hence it is little wonder that upon completion of the master's degree Triplett traveled to Worcester, Massachusetts, to study under Hall at Clark University. Triplett completed his PhD in 1900, becoming Hall's twenty-ninth doctoral student. His dissertation was "The Psychology of Conjuring Deceptions," whose topic was suggested by Hall. In addition to Hall, Triplett's dissertation committee consisted of Edmund C. Sanford and William Henry Burnham. As Goodwin (1987) has documented, Sanford is to be remembered for his development of laboratory equipment as well as for writing the first psychology laboratory manual in the United States. Burnham, an acknowledged authority on educational psychology and mental hygiene, headed the Department of Pedagogics at Clark University.

Publication of the dissertation in the *American Journal of Psychology* (Triplett 1900) established Triplett as an authority in this area. This eminence had not diminished three-quarters of a century later. For example, Rickard (1975) wrote that "the footnotes in Triplett's paper show a rather broad acquaintance with the literature of magic up to the date of the dissertation. It is quite evident that Triplett had studied the previous authorities, Binet, Dessoir, Jastrow, and Sidis" (6–7).

While at Clark University Triplett also performed an experiment in which fish served as his subjects (Triplett 1901). A two-chambered tank in which the chambers were separated by a removable glass partition was employed. Two perch were housed in one chamber while two minnows were housed in the other chamber. The perch initially tried to catch and eat the minnows but were unable to reach them because of the glass barrier. Following a month of such experiences, the partition was removed, and Triplett observed that the minnows swam unmolested with the perch. He concluded that "the perch's whole attitude is expressive of a desire to catch the minnow, a task which had become, however, hopeless" (Triplett 1901, 360).

Even though this paper was highly regarded by animal psychologists such as Robert M. Yerkes, whose lecture notes indicate that it was a standard reference in his courses through at least 1910, there were few dedicated animal researchers at this time.

Had this report been more widely read and discussed, Norman Triplett might have become known as the originator of the now-familiar *learned helplessness* paradigm (Seligman and Maier 1967). However, fame as a noted researcher was not in store for Norman Triplett. His career, and the careers of many of the early sport psychologists, were destined for the classroom and away from the laboratory. His first position in higher education was as an instructor in psychology and pedagogy at Mt. Holyoke College in Massachusetts. This one-year appointment was for the 1900–1901 academic year.

Triplett's Later Career

In 1901 Triplett accepted an appointment at Kansas State Normal School in Emporia, Kansas, as head of the Department of Child Study. Why he accepted a position at this teaching college is not known. At the turn of the century Emporia was a major center for the Santa Fe Railroad; it was a lively town that attracted many visitors. Triplett was an active and involved individual who would have appreciated and fit in well with this style of life. Perhaps Triplett's experiences with W. H. Burnham at Clark University and as a public school teacher in Illinois were sufficiently reinforcing to attract him to an institution at which teaching and teacher training were highly valued.

Some critics might characterize Triplett's KSN career as uneventful, possibly even pedestrian. Although uneventful might be an apt descriptor, Triplett's career was certainly not dull or boring. As was characteristic of many turn-of-the-century psychologists, Triplett was faced with the task of establishing a new department in a new discipline. Hence we find requests from Triplett in various editions of the Biennial Report to the Kansas Board of Regents for such items as (a) "a small yearly appropriation for the purchase of experimental apparatus for the psychology department, having in view the ultimate equipment of a modern psychological laboratory"; (b) additional funds to buy books for the department; and (c) a modification of the name of the department to reflect its psychological nature.

Triplett served as department head for thirty years from 1901 until his retirement in 1931. During the early years the psychology department was mostly a two-person operation with Triplett being the constant element. Apparently KSN was an excellent stepping stone or first position for many aspiring psychologists. Four of the twelve faculty hired by Triplett during this period had received their doctoral degrees from Clark University. Two additional faculty, James Bart Stroud and William H. Gray, had received their doctoral training at the University of Chicago and gave the department a definite functional flavor. Stroud (Harvey Carr's final PhD student) and Gray (who is remembered for developing the Gray Reading Readiness Test) joined the faculty in the late 1920s and were to become established fixtures as the department grew and prospered during the 1930s and 1940s. In recognition of Triplett's efforts in building a quality department, a 1935 yearbook memorial indicated that "he was instrumental in the development of a strong department of psychology, which included five instructors, all of whom held the doctor's degree when he retired from service in 1931." Kansas State Normal president Dr. Thomas W. Butcher also stated at the time of Triplett's retirement "that more psychology students . . . have gone on to receive master's and doctor of philosophy degrees in the universities of the country than students of any other department."[2]

As if the development of a separate department and a quality psychology program were not sufficiently demanding, Triplett assumed additional major roles and responsibilities during his career. For example, he served as the dean of men from 1913 to 1930.

Triplett's Athletic and Academic Interests

Triplett's intense interest in athletics and competition proved to be an enduring passion throughout his career. His influence was felt as early as 1903 when he and Professor J. M. Rhodes developed the plans for a grandstand for viewing athletic events at KSN. When the grandstand burned in 1923, Triplett was instrumental in the design and completion of a full-scale stadium. He even coached the track team for the 1909 season following the track coach's sudden resignation (Hawkins 1985). Triplett's habitual presence at practice sessions for *all* sports provided important encouragement for the student athletes. His daughter Dorothy summarized his importance by saying that "he was the patron saint of college athletics."[3]

Triplett was not without his own athletic prowess. He was one of the first men in the United States to win a gold medal for running the 100-yard dash in ten seconds. He also was a familiar fixture on the KSN faculty baseball team.

Despite such activities and accomplishments, it is clear that Norman Triplett's major contribution was in the teaching and training of students. A passionate interest in the intellectual growth of the KSN students was a Triplett hallmark. For example, in 1904 he was instrumental in founding an active psychology club, whose meetings were held a full decade before any other departmental club was organized at KSN. In reflecting on the psychology club, Triplett indicated in an article in the 1912 KSN yearbook that "when school was not so full of organizations, meetings of the Psychology Club, especially on nights when students discussed freedom of the will, were overflow meetings. The high water mark was 72, when students had to pile up on the floor of my little house."

Triplett's commitment to excellence and intellectual development did not begin and end with textbooks and club meetings.

He actively sought out and brought to campus well-known speakers. Among the notables that made the trip to Emporia were three former APA presidents: G. Stanley Hall, Joseph Jastrow, and Charles H. Judd.

In 1931 Norman Triplett retired from active service to KSN. Upon retirement he and his wife Laura traveled to California to visit a sister and to attend the 1932 Olympic Games. Following three years of retirement, Triplett passed away in 1934 in a Manhattan, Kansas, hospital. Norman and Laura Triplett are buried in the Maplewood Memorial Cemetery in Emporia, Kansas.

Triplett's Legacy

When he retired, the department that Triplett built had achieved national stature and was ranked on a par with departments in such schools as George Peabody College for Teachers in Nashville, Tennessee. The strength of the department resided in its students and their successes. More than 250 former students sent letters to acknowledge Triplett's retirement and their debt to him. Forty-three letters were from former students who were then faculty members at colleges and universities that ran the gamut from state teachers colleges to Ohio State University to the University of Chicago. Twelve protégés were public school principals, and another nineteen were public school superintendents. A variety of other educational positions, ranging from commissioner of education of the State of Indiana to the director of the Federal Board of Vocational Education, was represented by the occupations of an additional thirty-six former students. There were the letters from seven lawyers, a research physicist, two state senators, and others. Clearly Norman Triplett had influenced a *huge* number of students who had become most successful!

Praise of Triplett's teaching abilities and a clear indication that he had a lasting impact upon careers and lives was a central theme in these letters. For example, Byron Broom, a 1903 graduate, wrote that "I wish to express my appreciation of classroom contact and personal help extended by you to those of us who had the privilege of receiving your counsel and instruction." Triplett's profound influence was not a static and circumspect commodity; it persisted after students graduated. Amos H. Engle, a 1923 graduate who was on the faculty of the Texas College of Arts and Industries, remarked that "as the years increase their span, so, I believe, are there human influences that increase in their effectiveness after the direct contacts are made; many a young man and woman will vouch for this being especially true about you."

With the letter of A. B. Carlisle one comes full circle back to Triplett's experiment with the perch and the minnows. Carlisle, a faculty member at Butler University in Indianapolis, Indiana, wrote, "'So, even a fish may learn.' Again and again have these words, spoken by you one day when you were summarizing your learning experiment with the perch and minnows, been a source of encouragement to me. Especially has this been true when the progress of my students has seemed to be on a low level." Perhaps this massive testimonial and the impact of Triplett's career were best summed up by F. L. Pinet who wrote that "as I recall, you were not merely a professor of psychology but you were an institution."

Norman Triplett began his academic career with a study of cycling, a study that brought psychology and sport together on the question of improving athletic competition. That study as a graduate student earned him a place in sport psychology's history, but it was his lifelong role as a consummate master teacher that produced his greatest legacy — hundreds of students who used their start at Kansas State Normal School to pursue lives of great accomplishment.

Notes

1 Appreciation is expressed to the staff of the William Allen White Library at Emporia State University for providing access to the Normaliana Collection. Many of the details of Norman Triplett's life and career were gleaned from this collection.

2 Appreciation is extended to Dr. John Triplett, Norman Triplett's grandson, for making the entire collection of retirement letters available for study and use. Butcher's comments and those cited later come from this collection.

3 Telephone interview conducted with Dr. Dorothy Triplett Maxwell, June 21, 1989.

References

Allport, G. W. 1954. The historical background of modern social psychology. In *The handbook of social psychology*, ed. G. Lindzey, 3–56. Vol. 1. Reading MA: Addison-Wesley.

Anderson, W. G. 1899. Studies in the effects of physical training. *American Physical Education Review* 4:265–78.

Benjamin, L. T., Jr. 1991. *Harry Kirke Wolfe: Pioneer in psychology.* Lincoln: University of Nebraska Press.

Cummins, R. A. 1914. A study of the effect of basketball practice on motor reaction, attention, and suggestibility. *Psychological Review* 21:356–69.

Fitz, G. W. 1895. A location reaction apparatus. *Psychological Review* 2:37–42.

———. 1897. Play as a factor in development. *American Physical Education Review* 2:209–15.

Goodwin, C. J. 1987. In Hall's shadow: Edmund Clark Sanford (1859–1924). *Journal of the History of the Behavioral Sciences* 23:153–68.

Halberstadt, A. G., and E. L. Ellyson. 1990. *Social psychology readings: A century of research.* New York: McGraw-Hill.

Hawkins, S. A. 1985. A history of the track/field and cross country teams at Emporia State University, 1900–1984. Master's thesis, Emporia State University.

Hermann, E. 1921. The psychophysical significance of physical education. *American Physical Education Review* 26:283–89.

Holmes, J. 2008. Group processes. In *Twenty-first century psychology: A reference handbook*, ed. S. F. Davis and W. Buskist, 113–22. Vol. 2. Los Angeles: Sage.

Hyman, R. 1989. Psychology of deception. In *The annual review of psychology*, ed. M. R. Rosenzweig and L. W. Porter, 144–54. Palo Alto CA: Annual Reviews.

Iso-Ahola, S. E., and B. Hatfield. 1986. *Psychology of sports: A social psychological approach*. Dubuque IA: Brown.

Kellor, F. 1908. Psychological basis for physical culture. *Education* 19:100–104.

Kroll, W., and G. Lewis. 1970. America's first sports psychologist. *Quest* 13:1–4.

Mahoney, M. J., and R. M. Suinn. 1986. History and overview of modern sport psychology. *Clinical Psychologist* 39:64–68.

Murphy, H. H. 1916. Distribution of practice periods in learning. *Journal of Educational Psychology* 17:150–62.

Noble, S. G. 1922. The acquisition of skill in the throwing of basket-ball goals. *School and Society* 16:640–44.

Patrick, G. T. W. 1903. The psychology of football. *American Journal of Psychology* 14:104–17.

———. 1914. The psychology of play. *Journal of Genetic Psychology* 21:469–84.

Rickard, F. L. 1975. Norman Triplett and "The psychology of conjuring deceptions." *MAGICOL* 35:4–7.

Schultz, D. P., and S. E. Schultz. 2008. *A history of modern psychology*. 9th ed. Belmont CA: Wadsworth.

Scripture, E. W. 1900. Cross-education. *Popular Science* 56:589–96.

Seligman, M. E. P., and S. F. Maier. 1967. Failure to escape traumatic shock. *Journal of Experimental Psychology* 74:1–9.

Starch, D. 1911. *Experiments in educational psychology*. New York: Macmillan.

Triplett, N. L. 1898. Dynamogenic factors in pacemaking and competition. *American Journal of Psychology* 9:507–33.

————. 1900. The psychology of conjuring deceptions. *American Journal of Psychology* 11:1–72.

————. 1901. Educability of the perch. *American Journal of Psychology* 12:354–60.

Wiggins, D. K. 1984. The history of sports psychology in North America. In *Psychological foundations of sport*, ed. J. M. Silva and R. S. Weinberg, 9–22. Champaign IL: Human Kinetics.

Karl S. Lashley and John B. Watson

EARLY RESEARCH ON THE ACQUISITION OF SKILL IN ARCHERY

Donald A. Dewsbury

Among the earliest studies related to sport psychology was the research of psychologists Karl S. Lashley (1890–1958) and John B. Watson (1878–1958) on the acquisition of skill in archery. The work was published in a monograph, together with Watson and Lashley's "Homing and Related Activities of Birds," by the Carnegie Institution of Washington (Lashley 1915).

Alfred G. Mayer, director of the Carnegie Institution, provided Watson with funds to study the homing behavior of sooty terns and noddy terns to Bird Key in the Dry Tortugas Islands off the coast of South Florida. By the time Lashley joined him in 1913, Watson had already spent two summers on Bird Key and published several summaries (see Watson 1907, 1908, 1910). Watson's attempts to study homing had met with limited success until Lashley joined the project (Watson and Lashley

1915). In the preface to the publication Watson (1915) explained that Lashley's paper on the acquisition of skill in archery was included because the work had begun at the Tortugas under Carnegie auspices.

The archery research began with a preliminary study conducted by Watson on Loggerhead Key in the spring of 1913 (Watson and Lashley 1913). That summer, Lashley conducted a more extensive study in the Tortugas in which "he acted as subject and assisted in conducting this experiment" (108). A new testing range was then constructed at the Johns Hopkins University in Baltimore in the spring of 1914.

A Brief History of the Sport of Archery

Archery dates well back in the history of humanity. Hunters with bows and arrows are portrayed in the Valtorta Gorge rock paintings in Spain that date from 8000 to 3000 BC (Haywood and Lewis 1997). A variety of bows were devised so that hunters could kill at a distance in order to provide protein, hides, and bone to aid in the struggle for life. There were many subsequent improvements. Around 1800 BC the Assyrians perfected a shorter recurved bow that was better suited to use from horseback. The technology of the Middle East surpassed that of Europe for centuries. Later, the longbow perfected by the Normans was a factor in defeating the English at the Battle of Hastings in 1066 AD. The bow and arrow became a factor of less importance in warfare with the invention of firearms in the sixteenth century (Arlott 1975; Bear 1979; Haywood and Lewis 1997).

Sport archery gained prominence soon thereafter. King Henry VIII promoted archery and in 1537 directed Sir Christopher Morris to establish an archery society, the Guild of St. George. Roger Ascham published the classic book *Toxophilus* (1545), a treatise on the use of the longbow; he prescribed practice with the bow as the national exercise. The first competition was the Ancient

Scorton Silver Arrow Contest, which was first held in 1673 at Yorkshire, England. Women were first admitted to the society in 1787 (Haywood and Lewis 1997).

Although Native Americans utilized archery extensively, the first organized sport archery in the United States began with the founding of the Club of United Bowmen of Philadelphia by five young toxophilites (archery enthusiasts) in 1828 (Elmer 1946). In the post-Civil War South there was a revival of interest in archery when southerners were forbidden from using firearms. The National Archery Association was founded in 1879 and soon sponsored tournaments.

Archery was also included as an Olympic event from 1900 to 1908 and in 1920 and then was reintroduced in 1972 when a uniform set of rules was finally developed. Olympic competitions are now held in the summer Olympics (Men's Individual, Women's Individual, Men's Team, and Women's Team).

Today, there is a wide range of competitions sponsored by the National Field Archery Association and the Professional Archers Association. It is common for compound bows, far more elaborate than the longbows used by Lashley, to be used in many of these competitions (Haywood and Lewis 1997).

Earlier Research on Human Learning

At the dawn of the twentieth century interest in the study of human learning was growing as pressures to make psychology applicable to practical situations was increasing. The tasks studied varied greatly as no standardization had yet been developed nor had an ideal method been developed.

A number of issues were of concern. One was that there might be different kinds of human learning. Thorndike (1913) proposed four varieties of human learning: connection-forming of the animal type, connection-forming involving ideas, analysis or abstraction, and selective thinking or reasoning. He regarded learning to swim, skate, and hit a golf ball or baseball by trial and error as an example of the animal type. Book (1908) noted that as his subjects learned to type, they appeared to display different kinds of learning. Sometimes they appeared to adopt a new behavioral approach "unintentionally so far as the subjects were concerned" (171) and only later to purposely adopt it. Other examples were provided by Ruger (1910) in a study using mechanical puzzles.

One means of addressing the underlying processes involved in learning was to search for discontinuities in the learning curves. These were interpreted as suggesting the involvement of new mechanisms. For Thorndike a plateau in the rate of learning *"means that the lower-order habits are approaching their maximum development, but are not yet sufficiently automatic to leave the attention free to attack the higher-order habits"* (96). The classic study of Bryan and Harter (1897, 1899) on learning telegraphy, both sending and receiving, suggested just such a conclusion. Thorndike (1913) interpreted this learning as involving "mastery of the habits of all orders" (95). Swift (1903) used three tasks: ball throwing, shorthand, and control of the reflex wink. The ball-throwing task involved "keeping two balls going with one hand, receiving and throwing one while the other is in the air" (201). Swift too found that improvement occurred in spurts as new strategies were used and added, "In polo, golf, baseball or football good form is absolutely essential for reaching a high degree of skill" (215). Ruger (1910) made similar observations, writing of "the value of explicit control of consciousness of the assumptions made concerning a problem" (86) as subjects solved puzzles.

The issue of the optimal distribution of practice was also generating growing interest. Pyle (1913, 1914) studied typing, shorthand, and learning to write in arbitrary characters. Lyon (1914) studied the effects of various practice distribution patterns on learning nonsense syllables, digits, prose, and poetry. Starch (1912) studied number-letter associations on a simulated keyboard and produced systematic data showing that "the shorter and more numerous the periods of work are the more rapid is the improvement" (211). Applying the approach to the administration of intelligence tests, Whitley (1911) suggested that "fewer tests administered oftener would give a truer estimate of an individual and a better basis for comparison and correlations" (137).

It was not uncommon for studies to address both issues: distribution of practice and the irregularity of learning curves. Leuba and Hyde (1905) studied both in research on learning to read or write German script. They believed that fatigue was a factor interfering with learning when two training periods rather than one were given in a day. They also observed that "the irregularities observed by previous investigators who dealt with the acquisition of motor skill are in evidence in our curves: instead of ascending steadily they frequently show drops without any periodicity" (353). Munn (1909) found similar sporadic improvement in a task involving letter substitution; he also found that spaced practice was more effective than massed.

As the literature grew, there were similar studies using many different tasks including tossing shot into a glass, a kind of typing task, and others (Bair 1902); the ability of subjects to tap repeatedly as fast as possible on a telegraph key (Wells 1908); the ability of subjects to inhibit the reflex wink that occurred as an object struck a thick plate glass just in front of their faces (Partridge 1900); and the learning by grade-school children of skills in addition (Hahn and Thorndike 1914). Dearborn (1910) presented data from a number of tasks that might be used in classes in educational psychology: tracing an image shown in a mirror, learning a task involving associating numbers with letters on a reproduction of a scrambled typewriter keyboard, memory of French and German vocabulary, and transfer of training. With the lack of standardization of tasks and with the problems encountered with many of these tasks, selection of archery as a task for study appears quite reasonable as a way to address the issues of the day.

The Lashley-Watson Research

The Conceptual Background

Although the sole author of the primary publication on the archery research was Lashley, the impetus clearly came from Watson. Indeed, Watson was the senior author of the early note describing some of the research (Watson and Lashley 1913). In 1913 Watson had held his PhD degree for ten years and was an established psychologist; he was already the editor of the *Psychological Review* and would serve as the president of the American Psychological Association in 1915. By contrast, Lashley was a graduate student; in 1914 he completed his doctorate in zoology with H. S. Jennings on the inheritance of sexual reproduction in hydra. Watson's *Behavior: An Introduction to Comparative Psychology* (1914), his major early statement of behaviorism, was published in this same period.

Lashley (1915) placed the research in the context of "habit formation in man" (107) and cited many of the studies reviewed in the last section. He expressed no particular interest in sport or sport psychology, but rather, he was carrying out part of Watson's program on the study of habit formation.

As part of his behavioristic program Watson (1914) sought explanations of behavior that were free of consciousness. He regarded thought processes as "implicit behavior" (1914, 19). But Watson argued for continuity across all species in the primary learning processes: "No new principle is needed in passing from the unicellular organisms to man" (318). However, Watson believed that language habits, whether implicit or explicit behavior, were important in human learning and that they masked the primary learning mechanisms: "The moment the child forms the first language habit, he is forever differentiated from the beast and henceforth dwells apart in another world" (331). In effect, if Watson were to demonstrate this continuity, he believed that "the man and the animal should be placed as nearly as possible under the same experimental conditions" (14). He sought a task free of language habits and implicit behavior.

Watson was further concerned about problems of motivation. He apparently thought that learning curves ought to produce smooth functions. However, those in the literature for tasks such as those used by Book, Swift, and Bryan and Harter revealed annoying plateaus at various places. Such plateaus were rarely found in animal learning. Watson speculated that "it is probable that their explanation is to be found in the failure to control the incentives" (202). One needed a task for humans in which subjects would demonstrate more consistent motivation. It is interesting that at this point Watson mentioned the archery research, noting that "in the curve of archery which we have obtained the slope is very gradual" (202).

Lashley (1915) picked up the banner from there. He reviewed the available information on learning in humans but noted that "the great majority of experiments upon habit formation in man have dealt with functions involved in implicit behavior; functions connected chiefly with speech mechanisms have received most attention" (107). He suggested that with tasks such as addition, translation of codes, mechanical puzzles, and even writing and telegraphy the learning curve tends to be irregular because different implicit habits kick in at different stages of learning. This differential aspect of learning makes it difficult to dissect the nature of the different functions in improved learning. A more "simple, more direct sensory-motor" (107) task was needed. He sought a comparable task for humans.

Lashley argued further that such tasks as tossing shot into a glass (Bair 1902), tracing a smooth maze (Whitley 1911), tossing balls (Swift 1903), tapping (Wells 1908), and inhibiting the wink reflex (Partridge 1900) "call for the formation of relatively simple motor habits but have the disadvantage of giving little to interest the subjects and probably offer a weaker stimulus to learning than is provided by more complex activities" (107). In this context "Watson suggested archery as a means of studying habit formation in man which would in part avoid the complexity of language habits" (107). Presumably Watson also believed that the motivational level would be more consistent.

The primary issue addressed in the research concerned the effectiveness of different distributions of trials in producing efficient learning. Not only was this an issue of interest at the time, but it was of particular interest to Watson (1914), who wanted to make psychology a practical science. He asked, among other questions, "What is the most advantageous way to teach a problem to an animal? Should we allow him to work at it continuously? Shall we give him one trial a day? Three trials a day? Five trials a day?" (47). In addition, within this same time frame, 1911–13, another of Watson's graduate students, John Linck Ulrich (1915), was studying the distribution of trials in learning in rats.

Methods

Lashley wrote that "the equipment used in the Tortugas experiments consisted of bows, arrows, target, screen to mark the results of wild shots, and a shield for the experimenter near the target" (1915, 108). The bows were six feet long and made of lemon wood. They required 44 pounds to draw (see figure 4.1). This is a fairly large bow: "generally, young people shoot with bows 15–20 pounds in draw weight, adults shoot bows 20–25 pounds in draw weight, and stronger adults shoot bows 25–30 pounds in draw weight" (Haywood and Lewis 1989, 16). In introductory classes at the University of Florida recurved bows with draws of 25 to 35 pounds are used. Lashley used arrows "of good quality," twenty-eight inches long. Targets were of official sizes, forty-eight inches, with

4.1. Photographs of three archers illustrating both the bows used and individual differences in style of shooting employed in Lashley's studies of archery. Reprinted from Lashley 1915.

ten-inch painted bull's eyes, and made of rye straw covered with white canvas. The targets were mounted on a metal tripod with the center of the bull's-eye four feet above ground. The distance from archer to target was forty yards. For the Tortugas research the surrounding muslin screen was used to catch errant arrows and to enable calculation of magnitude of error.

For the first experiment, conducted in the Tortugas, instruction was provided by word and example of nocking (placing the arrow on the bowstring in preparation for shooting), drawing back the bowstring, and loosing the arrow, but no instruction was given for aiming or other actions. Thus the subjects had to figure out for themselves how to position the body, aim, prevent the bowstring from catching on the arm or clothing, counteract the kick of the bow, and work out assorted other details.

Subjects fired twelve arrows a day at two-minute intervals for thirty days. They could not see other subjects and were prohibited from discussing results with other subjects, though this effort was not wholly successful. In one group (B), a $5 reward was given to the man with the highest score on the greatest number of days.

For the studies in Baltimore (Homewood) two small buildings were constructed, one at each end of a forty-yard area. One building was for the archer and served to protect and isolate the subject, and the other was for targets (see figure 4.2). The target shed had an area fourteen by twenty-four feet to catch stray arrows. Paper bull's-eyes were used.

Lashley reported that "rifle practice was used as an index of the relative ability of the subjects under the same conditions of practice" (109). A single-shot air rifle was used at a range of forty yards. An observer watched the target through a telescope in order to give the shooter feedback.

Lashley used inches from the bull's-eye as his dependent variable. He calculated the mean score for each day but analyzed his data three ways: first half vs. second half or all shots, first five

4.2. Equipment used in Lashley's studies of archery in Baltimore. Reprinted from Lashley 1915.

shots vs. last five shots, and first forty shots vs. last forty shots. Lashley emphasized the difficulty of the task:

> At the moment of aim the extensor muscles of the bow arm are resisting the pull of about 40 pounds; the flexors are under no strain. When the bowstring is released the extensors are suddenly freed from strain and tend to throw the arm outward. The tonus of the flexors must be increased immediately to counteract this tendency. The bow-arm of a beginner frequently swings 4 inches out of position before the arrow leaves the string and the delayed tensing of the flexors then draws it a still greater distance in the opposite direction. This movement must be almost wholly overcome before accurate shooting is possible. Equally accurate and difficult movements of the loosing hand must be acquired. An average variation of 2° of arc in the relative position of the hands results in an average of 25 inches from the center of the bulls-eye. Some of the championship records . . . require an average variation of less than 30' of arc in the alignment of the arrows. (116)

Results

EXPERIMENT 1

The first experiment, conducted in Florida, was designed to compare two groups of subjects. Each of eight subjects daily shot twelve arrows under identical conditions: four were investigators working in the laboratory, and four were skilled laborers. Lashley himself was one of the four subjects in the former group, but he had to exclude his own data from the overall analysis because he did so much better than the others (see figure 4.3). He attributed this accomplishment to his reading and interactions with other subjects that helped him "through the preëxisting language habits" (112); thus he used a different kind of learning. There was little difference between the two groups with respect to either initial skill or progress in learning.

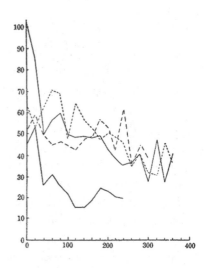

4.3. Data for several individuals learning archery in Florida. Lashley's own data are shown by the solid line. Note: Ordinate, the distance from the bull's-eye in inches, and abscissa, the successive shots arranged by twenties. Reprinted from Lashley 1915.

Experiment 2

The second experiment was conducted about one year later in Baltimore and was designed to test the effectiveness of different patterns of distribution of practice. Twenty-six subjects were distributed into four groups to shoot five, twenty, forty, and sixty arrows per day respectively; only nineteen subjects completed at least three hundred shots. All subjects were volunteers. None had any substantial experience shooting arrows or in other athletics. Although one woman was included in the five-shot group, Lashley believed that this inclusion had no real effect on the data.

Because it takes considerable strength and stamina to shoot sixty arrows a day, the sixty-shot group was composed of men nineteen to twenty-three years of age who were in good physical condition. They were studied after the other three groups had finished testing. This group was excluded from some analyses presumably because of bias in the sample. Data from the twelve-shot-a-day group from the Tortugas were included for comparison in some analyses.

Although Lashley wanted to conduct individual tests without interactions among his subjects, he could not, and consequently there was much viewing and possible imitation. Additionally, rivalry was encouraged by posting daily scores.

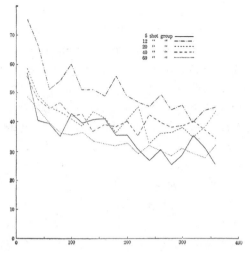

4.4. Learning curves for five groups learning archery. Note: Ordinate, the distance from the bull's-eye in inches, and abscissa, the successive shots arranged by twenties. Reprinted from Lashley 1915.

In addition to the archery, for comparison purposes, each subject fired twenty shots a day with a rifle. The data suggested to Lashley that the twenty-shot group was not quite as good with respect to the rate of improvement with the rifle as the five-shot and forty-shot groups.

Lashley analyzed the within-day data and concluded "that fatigue is much more severe after 40 shots than after 20" (118), a result that is hardly surprising. The evidence of changes after periods of no practice (that is, between test days) was mixed with some suggestion of a loss after practice was stopped.

Because different subjects used different methods in aiming, Lashley believed that imitation did not play a great role in improvement, even though the subjects were less isolated than had been those in the earlier experiment: "The great opportunity offered in the experiment for imitation and the small extent to which it seems to have been used raises the question of the real value of imitation in human learning" (119). He suggested further studies of archery as a means for studying of this issue.

With regard to the main point of the experiment, the effect of distribution of practice, because there were different numbers of total shots per group, Lashley analyzed only the first 360 shots. After examining the data, he concluded that "it appears that the 5-shot group is considerably superior to the others in final accuracy and in the amount of improvement, possibly excepting the 12-shot group" (1915, 120) (see figure 4.4). This result, however, is not especially apparent in the figure. Lashley believed that was because cold weather around the 320th shot resulted in a temporary decrement in accuracy. He noted that the result for the twelve-shot group was spurious because a slightly different method of scoring was used in the Tortugas and that "the 60-shot group shows a greater average accuracy but less improvement than the 5-shot group" (120). His conclusions are supported to some degree by data presented in tabular form. For example, if one considers the mean improvement in inches from the first-forty to the last-forty trials, the scores for the five-, twelve-, twenty-, forty-, and sixty-shot groups are 19.3, 26.0, 12.3, 15.5, and 15.7, respectively. After examining these and related data, Lashley concluded that "it appears from this that the rate of improvement per unit of practice is somewhat greater with [when?] the practice is distributed over many days than when it is concentrated into a few days" (121). Of course, there were no error bars or inferential statistics.

Lashley singled out the data from one subject who shot 1,300 arrows and had the opportunity to observe the five-shot group and work out some strategies before beginning trials. Lashley noted the slow rate of improvement with a plateau after about nine hundred shots. He believed that "the plateaus are the result either of the accidental formation of conflicting habits, or that they represent points where no improvement can be made until a new method of shooting is hit upon by the method of trial and error" (117). In general, improvement was greatest during the early stages of testing. Lashley wrote that "during the first part of practice improvement is made largely by a series of what Thorndike has called 'insights,' such as those found so constantly by Ruger in the solution of mechanical puzzles" (122). Even though the concept of plateaus in learning was an issue of the day and even though he had addressed it in his introduction, Lashley did not explore these plateaus further. Because the data presented were mainly from groups, the issue of plateaus in the curves of individual subjects cannot be addressed further.

Lashley used the data from rifle firing to support the view that the groups did not differ greatly in ability and thus that the differences in rate of improvement in archery were indeed due to distribution of practice. He noted that if the rifle data were to be trusted as an index of learning ability, the data from the twenty-shot group might underestimate their improvement in archery somewhat because they were slightly less able to learn than the other groups.

Lashley's Discussion

Lashley discussed his results in relation to a series of related phenomena from the literature. He noted the general agreement with most earlier results that showed that distributed practice was generally more effective than massed practice. He found reasons to dismiss the contradictory results of Leuba and Hyde (1905), Lyon (1914), and Hahn and Thorndike (1914). Although most investigators attributed the inferiority of massed practice to fatigue effects, Lashley sought other factors. Lashley grouped three of these under the heading of "Trial and Error":

> *Variety of Proprioceptive Set:* Within a session subjects might get fixed with a stereotyped reaction. Between sessions these sets may be broken up and lead to new and sometimes more effective approaches.

Loss of Conflicting Habits: Ineffective habits may be eliminated during intervals without practice, as suggested by Book (1908).

Change in the Primary Stimulus: Lashley appeared to suggest that effective external stimuli and internal motivation can vary during different blocks of trials.

Lashley also discussed a second set under the heading of "Direct Effects of Fatigue":

Neurone Patterns: In order to improve, different patterns of neurones would have to be used. This would be facilitated with rest periods.

Muscle Changes: There may be greater muscular development between sessions.

Lashley's third category was "Practice Between Practice Periods." Here he followed up a suggestion of Thorndike regarding an earlier study noting that subjects might sometimes engage in unscheduled between-session practice.

"Fixation of the Neural Arc" was listed as a fourth possible reason for the distribution effect and followed the suggestion of Starch (1912). This interpretation was essentially one of trace-consolidation theory. Activation of a neural arc activates a process of fixation that persists for a time; this process is not facilitated by input that follows immediately.

Lashley's final category was titled "The Time Relation of Practice to the Changes in the Primary Stimulus Resulting from Successful Activities" (126). In this category Lashley followed Ladd and Woodworth (1911, 551–52), whom he quoted at length. In essence, Lashley's interpretation appears to suggest that the reward value of performance in a given situation undergoes a short-term enhancement, weaker postresponse inhibition, and quicker fixation of the habit with success. This interpretation would predict an advantage to massed practice — the opposite of the results obtained.

Lashley was unable to discriminate among these possible interpretations. His main, and rather disappointing, conclusion was that "the effects of fatigue probably should not be emphasized too much" (127).

Archery Research in Sport Psychology after Lashley

As far as can be determined, neither Lashley nor Watson conducted any more research on archery after that reported in the 1915 monograph. However, Lashley did retain an interest in the problem of massed versus distributed practice and returned to it on two later occasions (Bruce 1986; Lashley 1917, 1918).

Citations of Lashley

One can gain some indication of the impact of a study from the citations it engenders. Lashley's study of archery was not widely cited and appears to have had little impact in the literature.

CITATION INDEX

A search of *ISI Citation Indices* for 1945 to the time of this writing yielded just eight citations. Not all dealt with the substance of the research. Two were historical studies. Todd and Morris (1986) cited the study in an article on the early research of John B. Watson. Bruce (1986) discussed the research in a treatment of Lashley's shift from bacteriology to neuropsychology.

Annett (1993) cited Lashley's article in a review of the common origins of the study on the learning of motor skills in ergonomics and sports science. He used Watson's suggestion to Lashley that learning archery does not involve language habits as a springboard for his review — a springboard that Annett later criticized.

The remaining five citations dealt with aspects of motor learning and the distribution of practice. With regard to distribution of practice, Massey (1959) cited Lashley's work in a study of stabilimeter learning. Sanderson (1983) cited the work in a brief review of the length and spacing of practice sessions in learning sport skills. Mohr (1960) cited Lashley's work in a review of skill learning, noting that forty of forty-five studies she located found spaced practice to be more advantageous than massed practice in skill learning. A slightly more complicated citation is that of Iran-Nejad and Homaifar (2000), who discussed Lashley's work on the distribution of practice but who listed his 1915 study of noddy and sooty terns rather than the archery study in their reference section.

Several authors, especially Annett (1971), emphasized Lashley's finding that there were different improvement patterns at different stages of acquisition (see also Massey 1959; Sanderson 1983). As noted, this result was not emphasized in Lashley's report, although it was an issue in the literature of the time.

OTHER CITATIONS

In addition to those discussed above, I searched for other citations and found but a few. Because the *Citation Index* begins in 1945, I searched volumes 1 through 16 (1930–45) of the *Research Quarterly of the American Physical Education Association*, probably the leading journal in the field at the time but found no citations. I located just two studies of archery; they dealt with the development of an achievement scale (Hyde 1936, 1937). Although she did not cite Lashley in these articles, she did so in an earlier, related article (Hyde 1934). Young (1954) also cited the work in a study of the effect of the spacing of practice periods on learning archery.

I also searched for citations in various books dealing with experimental psychology, sport psychology, motor learning, and skill acquisition. Lashley's article was not widely cited. It was discussed by Magill (1993) in a *Handbook of Research on Sport Psychology*, by Oxendine (1968) in *Psychology of Motor Learning*, and by Singer (1968) in *Motor Learning and Human Performance*.

A few citations appeared in handbooks of experimental psychology (Crozier and Hoagland 1934; Hovland 1951; Woodworth 1938). In all I located sixteen citations over a ninety-one-year period. Thus overall, the study appears to have been either unknown or ignored by most researchers in the field.

Later Studies of Skill Acquisition in Archery

A number of subsequent studies in the psychological literature, like Lashley's, were concerned with the acquisition of skill in archery. Hyde (1934) was concerned with developing norms in acquisition and reported a clear practice effect, no effect of interval between practices, and high correlations among scores at different distances. Young (1954) varied between-session intervals and found a slight advantage to a group with shorter intervals between practice sessions; the amount of practice per session appears not to have been varied. Singer (1966) was concerned with effects of initial success and satisfaction but found no effect of conducting initial training with the target at ten, twenty-five, or forty yards. An operant training procedure developed by Fred S. Keller was found effective by Davis, Hersh, and Nevitt (1976) in the acquisition of archery skill. Virgilio (1979) studied the effects of different styles of teaching upon acquisition. Beverley (1973) found that instant videotape feedback facilitated the acquisition of skill. Ishee and Shannon (1983) found male college students better than women at learning archery skills, Ishee and Titlow (1993) tried to develop norms for a pass-fail criterion for students undertaking archery instruction.

Studies of Factors Affecting Performance

Although the number of studies is not large, the array of variables potentially affecting performance levels that have been studied is impressive. In general, archery is regarded as a closed sport in that the conditions under which it is performed are relatively constant as compared with an open sport such as soccer. As there is comparatively little physical exertion, it is possible to study effects just before and after a shot with some precision.

The emphasis in archery studies seems to be on relaxation during aiming and has been approached in several ways. A series of studies was conducted at Arizona State University; some of this work was supported by the Sports Medicine Council of the United States Olympic Committee. Wang (1987) emphasized the advantages of archery as a task because of the importance of attention during aiming. He found effects on EEG lateralization and heart rate. During aiming, beta waves were prominent in the EEG, with greater activity in the right hemisphere than in the left, and there was a decelerated heart rate. Skilled subjects showed a greater response than the unskilled. Salazar et al. (1990) found no heart rate deceleration and greater alpha EEG activity in the left hemisphere. They concluded that there was hemispheric asymmetry, with performance more closely associated with left than right hemispheric changes. Landers et al. (1994) studied the effects of archery training on these measures to see if they were the result of preexisting patterns or of training. There was no heart rate deceleration or hemispheric asymmetry during the pretests. However, after training both heart rate deceleration and EEG asymmetry were present. They concluded that "HR deceleration and EEG asymmetries are learned patterns that can serve as unobstructive markers of focused attention during the brief period immediately preceding performance" (313).

Norlander and Bergman (1999) studied the effects of a Restricted Environmental Stimulation Technique (REST), in which an individual is immersed in a water tank filled with saltwater with an extremely high salt concentration as a means of relaxation just before shooting. Those in the REST condition experienced reduced perceived exertion, but marksmanship was not improved. The authors believed that the procedure might help to shift from left hemisphere secondary process dominance to right hemisphere primary or more instinctive processes.

Zervas and Kakkos (1991) found no effect of a specially designed program of "relaxation conditions and imagery rehearsal" on shooting scores or self reports of anxiety and confidence. The program did produce an effect on a tense-relaxed scale. Reilly and Halliday (1985) noted that although banned in Olympic competition, small doses of alcohol are often used before other competitions in archery to improve aiming and shooting skills. They broke archery down into its component skills and found that alcohol decreased arm steadiness and increased variability. Reaction time was slowed; other measures were not affected. Later, Robazza and Bartoli (1995) reported that a single archer's shooting performance was improved by hypnotic mental training.

Some approaches utilize Eastern methods. In a widely distributed book, Herrigel (1953) applied principles from Zen Buddhism to the art of archery. In doing so, he deemphasized the importance of hitting the target and stressed a Zen state in which bow, archer, and target come together as one in a kind of "instinctive" action. This Western author described his struggles in adapting this Eastern technique. Kerr et al. (1997) applied a "reversal theory" in which four separate pairs of metamotivational states are thought to form the basis of human motivation and personality. They tried to manipulate the "telic-paratelic pair" in which telic refers to serious and goal-oriented motivation and paratelic is spontaneous and impulsive. Metamotivational states were manipulated with verbal instructions, but few significant differences were obtained.

In another study at Arizona State University Landers, Boutcher, and Wang (1986) used a hierarchical linear regression model to predict success in archery performance. They found that "relative leg strength, reaction time, depth perception, endomorphy, imagery usage, confidence, and focus on past mistakes were variables associated with archery performance" (236). In a study of children and adults Beer, Fleming, and Knorr (1989) found no effect of eye color but determined that boys did better than girls.

Two articles were detailed studies of the interactions between archers and their coaches during practice sessions or competition. Van der Mars and Darst (1991) used audiotape recordings to analyze how time was spent during practice sessions between elite archers and their coaches in an effort to develop optimal management patterns during these sessions. D'Arripe-Longueville, Fournier, Saury, and Durand (2001) used frameworks from ergonomics and videotape to analyze the situated and constructed nature of the coach-athlete interaction in elite archery competition.

Karl S. Lashley and John B. Watson did not set out to develop sport psychology. Indeed, there is little evidence that either was especially interested in athletic competition. Rather, they were interested in the conditions affecting human learning — especially the effects of the distribution of practice. It was Watson, the faculty member, who appears to have provided the primary impetus for this research and Lashley, the graduate student, who became interested in it and contributed the bulk of the effort. Be that as it may, this study does represent one of the early examples of research in the field of sport psychology, whether it was deliberate or not.

Watson and Lashley considered the issues of the day in the study of learning. For practical reasons the issue of the distribution of practice was an important one. Watson already had one graduate student, John Linck Ulrich (1915), working on the problem in rats. It was logical to initiate similar research with humans as subjects. Seeking a task for which they believed there to be little effect of language habits but that would be sufficiently interesting to motivate human subjects, they settled upon archery as a task. Others have followed the path they blazed of studying archery as sport psychology, even if Watson and Lashley had no intention of blazing such paths and even if their work was not always cited in later research.

One might wonder why the work appears to have had so little influence. At least three possible reasons stand out. First, the results were frankly less than spectacular. Second, the location of publication was not prominent. As the report appeared in the *Papers from the Department of Marine Biology of the Carnegie Institution of Washington* and as it was buried in a field study of homing in terns, it is likely that few researchers interested in sport psychology in general or archery in particular would have seen it. Finally, Lashley and Watson neither promoted nor continued the research. Both had other paths to travel. To them the archery project appears to have been something of a diversion from their main journeys. However, their attitude does nothing to diminish the importance of the research.

References

Annett, J. 1971. Acquisition of skill. *British Medical Journal* 27:266–71.

———. 1993. The learning of motor skills: Sports science and ergonomics perspectives. *Ergonomics* 37:5–16.

Arlott, J., ed. 1975. *The Oxford companion to sports and games.* London: Oxford University Press.

Bair, J. H. 1902. The practice curve: A study in the formation of habits. *Psychological Review Monograph Supplement* 5 (19): 1–70.

Bear, F. 1979. *Fred Bear's world of archery.* Garden City NY: Doubleday.

Beer, J., P. Fleming, and W. Knorr. 1989. Effects of eye color and sex on accuracy in archery. *Perceptual and Motor Skills* 68:389–90.

Beverley, L. 1973. The effects of instant videotape feedback in learning target archery. PhD diss., University of Southern Mississippi.

Book, W. F. 1908. The psychology of skill with special reference to its acquisition in typewriting. *University of Montana Publications in Psychology* 53:1–188.

Bruce, D. 1986. Lashley's shift from bacteriology to neuropsychology, 1910–1917, and the influence of Jennings, Watson, and Franz. *Journal of the History of the Behavioral Sciences* 22:27–44.

Bryan, W. L., and N. Harter. 1897. Studies in the physiology and psychology of the telegraphic language. *Psychological Review* 4:27–53.

———. 1899. Studies on the telegraphic language: The acquisition of a hierarchy of habits. *Psychological Review* 6:345–75.

Crozier, W. J., and H. Hoagland. 1934. The study of living organisms. In *A handbook of general experimental psychology*, ed. C. Murchison, 3–108. Worcester MA: Clark University Press.

D'Arripe-Longueville, F., J. Fournier, J. Saury, and M. Durand. 2001. Coach-athlete interaction during elite archery competitions: An application of methodological frameworks used in ergonomics research to sport psychology. *Journal of Applied Sport Psychology* 13:275–99.

Davis, S., L. Hersh, and J. Nevitt. 1976. Behavior shaping techniques and personalized instruction in an archery class. *Perceptual and Motor Skills* 43:913–14.

Dearborn, W. F. 1910. Experiments in learning. *Journal of Educational Psychology* 1:373–88.

Elmer, R. P. 1946. *Target archery, with a history of the sport in America.* New York: Knopf.

Hahn, H. H., and E. L. Thorndike. 1914. Some results of practice in addition under school conditions. *Journal of Educational Psychology* 5:65–84.

Haywood, K. M., and C. F. Lewis. 1989. *Teaching archery: Steps to success.* Champaign IL: Leisure Press.

———. 1997. *Archery: Steps to success.* Champaign IL: Human Kinetics.

Herrigel, E. 1953. *Zen in the art of archery.* New York: Vintage.

Hovland, C. I. 1951. Human learning and retention. In *Handbook of experimental psychology*, ed. S. S. Stevens, 613–89. New York: Wiley.

Hyde, E. I. 1934. The measurement of achievement in archery. *Journal of Educational Research* 27:673–86.

———. 1936. National research study in archery: Report submitted to the National Association of the Directors of Physical Education for College Women. *Research Quarterly of the American Physical Education Association* 7 (4): 67–71.

———. 1937. An achievement scale in archery. *Research Quarterly of the American Physical Education Association* 8 (2): 109–16.

Iran-Nejad, A., and A. Homaifar. 2000. The nature of distributed learning and remembering. *Journal of Mind and Behavior* 21:153–84.

Ishee, J. H., and J. L. Shannon. 1983. Scoring collegiate archery. *Perceptual and Motor Skills* 57:525–26.

Ishee, J. H., and L. W. Titlow. 1993. Validation of criterion-referenced archery cutting scores. *Perceptual and Motor Skills* 76:643–46.

Kerr, J. H., H. Yoshida, C. Hirata, K. Takai, and F. Yamazaki. 1997. Effects on archery performance of manipulating metamotivational state and felt arousal. *Perceptual and Motor Skills* 84:819–28.

Ladd, G. T., and R. S. Woodworth. 1911. *Elements of physiological psychology: A treatise of the activities and nature of the mind from the physical and experimental points of view.* New York: Scribner.

Landers, D. M., M. Han, W. Salazar, S. J. Petruzello, K. A. Kubitz, and T. L. Gannon. 1994. Effects of learning on electroencephalographic and electrocardiological patterns in novice archers. *International Journal of Sport Psychology* 25:313–30.

Landers, D. M., S. M. Boutcher, and M. Q. Wang. 1986. A psychobiological study of archery performance. *Research Quarterly* 57:236–44.

Lashley, K. S. 1915. The acquisition of skill in archery. *Papers from the Department of Marine Biology of the Carnegie Institution of Washington* 7 (211): 105–28.

———. 1917. A causal factor in the relation of the distribution of practice to the rate of learning. *Journal of Animal Behavior* 7:139–42.

———. 1918. A simple maze: With data on the relation of the distribution of practice to the rate of learning. *Psychobiology* 1:353–67.

Leuba, J. H., and W. Hyde. 1905. Studies from the Bryn Mawr College Psychological Laboratory: An experiment in learning to make hand movements. *Psychological Review* 12:351–69.

Lyon, D. O. 1914. The relation of length of material to time taken for learning. *Journal of Educational Psychology* 5:1–9, 85–91, 155–63.

Magill, R. 1993. In *Handbook of research on sport psychology*, ed. R. N. Singer, M. Murphey, and L. K. Tennant, 193–241. New York: Macmillan.

Massey, M. D. 1959. The significance of interpolated time intervals on motor learning. *Research Quarterly* 30:189–201.

Mohr, D. R. 1960. The contributions of physical-activity to skill learning. *Research Quarterly* 31:321–50.

Munn, A. F. 1909. The curve of learning. *Archives of Psychology*, no. 12: 36–52.

Norlander, T., and H. Bergman. 1999. Primary process in competitive archery performance. *Journal of Applied Sport Psychology* 11:194–209.

Oxendine, J. B. 1968. *Psychology of motor learning*. New York: Appleton-Century-Crofts.

Partridge, G. E. 1900. Experiments upon the control of the reflex wink. *American Journal of Psychology* 11:244–50.

Pyle, W. H. 1913. Economical learning. *Psychological Bulletin* 10:73.

———. 1914. Concentrated versus distributed practice. *Journal of Educational Psychology* 5:247–58.

Reilly, T., and F. Halliday. 1985. Influence of alcohol ingestion on tasks related to archery. *Journal of Human Ergology* 14:99–104.

Robazza, C., and L. Bartoli. 1995. A case study of improved performance in archery using hypnosis. *Perceptual and Motor Skills* 81:1364–66.

Ruger, H. A. 1910. The psychology of efficiency: An experimental study of the processes involved in the solution of mechanical puzzles and in the acquisition of skill in their manipulation. *Archives of Psychology* 19 (2): 1–88.

Salazar, W., D. M. Landers, S. J. Petruzzelo, M. Han, D. J. Crews, and K. A. Kubitz. 1990. Hemispheric asymmetry, cardiac response, and performance in elite archers. *Research Quarterly* 61:351–59.

Sanderson, F. H. 1983. Length and spacing of practice sessions in sport skills. *International Journal of Sport Psychology* 14:116–22.

Singer, R. N. 1966. Transfer effects and ultimate success in archery due to degree of difficulty in initial learning. *Research Quarterly* 37:532–39.

———. 1968. *Motor learning and human performance: An application to physical education skills*. New York: Macmillan.

Starch, D. 1912. Periods of work in learning. *Journal of Educational Psychology* 3:209–13.

Swift, E. J. 1903. Studies in the psychology and physiology of learning. *American Journal of Psychology* 14:201–251.

Thorndike, E. L. 1913. *The psychology of learning*. Vol. 2. New York: Teachers College, Columbia University.

Todd, J. T., and E. K. Morris. 1986. The early research of John B. Watson: Before the behavioral revolution. *Behavior Analyst* 9:71–88.

Ulrich, J. L. 1915. Distribution of effort in learning in the white rat. *Behavior Monographs* 2, no. 5, serial no. 10: 51.

van der Mars, H., and P. Darst. 1991. Practice behaviors of elite archers and their coaches. *Journal of Sport Behavior* 14:103–12.

Virgilio, S. J. 1979. The effects of direct and reciprocal teaching strategies on the cognitive, affective, and psychomotor behavior of fifth grade pupils in beginning archery. PhD diss., Florida State University.

Wang, M. Q. 1987. A psychophysiological investigation of attention during archery performance. PhD diss., Arizona State University.

Watson, J. B. 1907. Report of John B. Watson on the condition of the noddy and sooty tern colony Bird Key, Tortugas, Florida. *Bird Lore* 9:307–16.

———. 1908. The behavior of noddy and sooty terns. *Papers from the Tortugas Laboratory of the Carnegie Institution of Washington* 2 (103): 187–255.

———. 1910. Further data on the homing sense of noddy and sooty terns. *Science* 32:470–73.

———. 1914. *Behavior: An introduction to comparative psychology.* New York: Holt.

———. 1915. Preface. *Papers from the Department of Marine Biology of the Carnegie Institution of Washington* 7 (211): 5–6.

Watson, J. B., and K. S. Lashley. 1913. The effect of the amount and frequency of practice in learning archery. *Carnegie Institution of Washington Yearbook* 12:180–81.

———. 1915. Homing and related activities of birds. *Papers from the Department of Marine Biology of the Carnegie Institution of Washington* 7 (211): 1–104.

Wells, F. L. 1908. Normal performance in the tapping test: Before and during practice, with special reference to fatigue phenomena. *American Journal of Psychology* 19:437–83.

Whitley, M. T. 1911. An empirical study of certain tests for individual differences. *Archives of Psychology* 3 (19): 146.

Woodworth, R. S. 1938. *Experimental psychology.* New York: Holt.

Young, O. G. 1954. Rate of learning in relation to spacing of practice periods in archery and badminton. *Research Quarterly* 25:231–43.

Zervas, Y., and V. Kakkos. 1991. Visuomotor behavior rehearsal in archery shooting performance. *Perceptual and Motor Skills* 73:1183–90.

5

Psychology and Baseball

THE TESTING OF BABE RUTH

Alfred H. Fuchs

In 1921, after playing a baseball game for the New York Yankees, George Herman "Babe" Ruth went with famed sportswriter Hugh S. Fullerton to the Columbia University Psychological Laboratory. The laboratory was in Schermerhorn Hall on the university's Morningside Heights campus (Woodworth 1942) and was a short distance from the Polo Grounds, the home of the New York Giants and the stadium in which the Yankees then played their home games until the construction of Yankee Stadium, the House that Ruth Built. Fullerton hoped to determine the basis for Ruth's success at hitting home runs by having him perform laboratory tests developed by psychologists to study sensory-motor performance.

Both baseball and psychology were rooted in the nation's cultural history. Baseball had evolved from games of bat and ball played in Britain and elsewhere and transplanted to colonial America to grow as an amateur and professional sport (Block 2005). Like baseball, psychology had entered the colonies of North America in the guise of British mental philosophy and, subsequently influenced by infusions of continental philosophies, had been established in the curricula of American colleges and universities. Although the psychology of 1921 was heir to that tradition, it was significantly transformed by the new experimental psychology that originated in Germany in the last quarter of the nineteenth century and that was brought to North America by those who studied the new science in European laboratories (Fuchs 2000; Fuchs and Milar 2003).

By 1921 baseball and psychology were on the verge of dramatic growth and change. The convergence of a sportswriter eager to bring science to bear on the analysis of a physical skill and a baseball player willing to participate in tests in a psychological laboratory reflect the changes that were taking place in baseball and in psychology in the decades following the end of World War I. The developing maturity of the natural sciences in the twentieth century helped to encourage the public's growing belief that science was the path to answering questions about the natural world.

Baseball

By the first two decades of the twentieth century, baseball was a popular sport played by amateurs and professionals alike in many parts of the United States. The National League of professional baseball teams, formed in 1876, had resolved its conflicts with the newer upstart American League over competition for fan attendance in cities in which both leagues had teams. The National Agreement that joined the leagues together in 1903 was designed to "protect property rights and assign territory as well as to prevent competitive bidding for the services of players" (Fullerton 1912a, 199). Organized baseball had entered the modern era.

The loud participation of fans (short for fanatics) in the grand-stands came to be as much a part of the game as the play itself (Fullerton 1912b). To satisfy the appetites of fans for game analyses, sports writers competed to offer lively reports of the games that supplemented the printed box scores appearing in the sports sections of the newspapers.

Baseball in the pre–World War I era was played with strategies that emphasized strong pitching and solid defense, in which "the real value of hitting lies in advancing runners who are already on base: the sacrifice bunt, the bunt and run, the hit and run and hitting as the runner starts" (Fullerton 1912c, 300). Those strategies, together with positioning players to take advantage of the pitches thrown to a hitter and of game situations, were considered to be part of the "science" of baseball (Douglas 1922). The spitball (often from a pitcher chewing tobacco) was legal; fielders might further discolor a ball to make it more difficult for a batter to see. The few baseballs used in a game (often only two or three) became not only discolored but also deformed from being hit. As a consequence home runs were hit infrequently. For example, the powerful third baseman of the Athletics and later Yankees, Frank "Home-Run" Baker, never hit more than twelve home runs in a full season; he earned his nickname by hitting two home runs in the 1911 World Series (Berg 1941). Under these conditions pitching and defense, advancing the runner one base at a time, and seeking any other small advantage on the bases were sensible strategies for victory.

By the end of the second decade of the twentieth century, however, the game and its strategies were changing. One con-tributing change was the construction of the ball. During World War I foreign yarn was not available; to compensate for the infe-rior domestic product, manufacturers of baseballs adjusted their machines to wind the yarn tighter. Berg writes that "when the war was over, the foreign yarn was again available, but the same

machines were used. The improved technique, the foreign ingredients, Babe Ruth and bat, conspired to revolutionize baseball"
(1941, 282).

With the aid of the new more lively ball, Ruth became "the
primary agent" and the most visible cause of the revolution in game
strategy: "Scrappy, one-run, slap-hit, grab-a-base-at-a-time-play
retreated and home run power became the name of the game"
(Gould 2003, 38). As Christy Mathewson, a star pitcher of the
dead ball era, phrased it, "The inside game is of little avail when a
batter knocks a home run with the bases full" (Mathewson [1912]
1977, 281). Moreover, as the prosperity of the Roaring Twenties
brought more fans to baseball games, seats added in the stands
bordering the outfields shortened the distances that a ball would
have to travel for a home run. Fans who attended games became
enamored of the increased offense, even while proponents of the
earlier strategies of the game lamented their loss.

Babe Ruth

Ruth's ability to hit home runs and his exploits in eating, drinking,
and womanizing made him a larger than life figure who provided
copy for sportswriters throughout his Major League career. He
began as a pitcher for the Boston Red Sox in 1914 when "he was
6′2″ and weighed 198 pounds, all of it muscle. He had a slim waist
[and] huge biceps" (Honig 1990, 57). His won-lost record as a
pitcher from 1914 to 1919 consisted of eighty-nine wins and forty-
one losses (a winning percentage of .685), with an earned run
average of 2.55.[1] He pitched and won three World Series games,
one in 1916 and two in 1918, with an ERA of 0.87 (that is, less than
one run per game). In the pennant-winning year of 1916 Ruth led
the American League in ERA with a 1.75 average, in shutouts (9),
in the lowest average of hits per nine innings (6.40), was third in
number of wins (23), was second in winning percentage (.657),
and was third in number of strikeouts (170). His pitching was

a key ingredient of the powerful Red Sox teams of those years, winners of the World Series in 1915, 1916, and 1918.

On the days that he pitched, Ruth demonstrated his ability to hit, with the result that he began to be used as a pinch-hitter and in the field between pitching starts. In his fifth season with the team (1918) he appeared in ninety-five games, twenty as a pitcher and the remainder as an outfielder or a first baseman. He was already being called the Home Run King (Holtzman 2005, 179) because of his impressive achievements in that season of the dead ball era: eleven home runs and a slugging percentage of .555.[2] In the 1919 season his achievements were even more extraordinary for the time. He played in 130 games (only 17 as a pitcher) and hit twenty-nine home runs, a new record and more than each of eight of the sixteen *teams* in the two leagues combined, while compiling a slugging percentage of .657. For those exploits, "Ruth was the talk of baseball" (Montville 2006, 90) and "acclaimed throughout the country as the greatest batsman the game has ever known" (Wagenheim 1974, 49).

Despite his hitting and pitching in 1919 (he won nine games and lost five), the Red Sox finished in sixth place in the league of eight teams. Ruth's personal success, however, prompted him to demand publicly that his salary be raised from $10,000 to $20,000 for each of the remaining two years of the contract that he had signed at the start of the 1919 season. He threatened to quit baseball for other pursuits if the Red Sox failed to meet his demands (Wood 2000). In the same season the New York Yankees had finished third, their best showing in years, and the players and team management believed that the addition of Ruth to their team would win them the 1920 American League pennant.

The owners of the Yankees were cash rich, with Jacob Ruppert, one of the team's owners, being a successful brewer. The Red Sox owner, Harry Frazee, had earned his money as a theatrical producer and was in 1919 cash poor. Both owners were residents of New York City and knew each other and the needs of their teams. The Red Sox had sold or traded players to the Yankees since Ruppert had become an owner in 1914. A deal was reached: Babe Ruth was sold to the Yankees for the then unheard of sum of $125,000, more than twice the amount previously paid for any player, and an undisclosed (at the time) $300,000 loan to the Red Sox owner. The collateral for the loan was a mortgage that the Yankees were to hold on Fenway Park in Boston, the stadium in which the Red Sox played (Montville 2006).

The Yankees did not win the pennant in 1920, Ruth's first year, but they received their money's worth from him. Playing the outfield (excluding two games at first base and one in which he pitched and won), Ruth hit fifty-four home runs, more than *fourteen* of the sixteen teams in both leagues combined. He also drove in 137 runs (RBI). His slugging percentage of .847 is still a single-season Major League record. Moreover, the attendance for the Yankees in the 1920 season doubled their previous high of 619,000 to 1,289,000, "the first time a big league team had drawn more than a million. It was nearly 30 percent better than the old Major League record" (Whitman as cited by Holtzman 2005, 80). Ruth capitalized on his growing fame in many ways, including publishing a novel under his name titled *The Home Run King* (Ruth 1920); the actual author is unknown (Smelser 1975). The book's dust jacket saluted the putative author as "the greatest batter our national game has ever known."

In the 1921 season Ruth led the Yankees to the pennant, their first ever, by hitting fifty-nine home runs, one in every 10.9 at bats; by driving in 171 runs; and by establishing the second-highest season slugging percentage on record, .846, second only to his own .847 of 1920. His seasons of 1920 and 1921 constitute one of the most remarkable pairs of seasons in the history of the game. His Major League batting records for the single season of 1921 have withstood the test of time: most runs scored since 1900 (177), most extra-base hits (119), and highest total bases (457) are still all-time season records (Siwoff 2007). It was during that grand season of 1921 that the Babe entered the Columbia laboratory after an afternoon game in which he had hit a home run.

Hugh S. Fullerton

Hugh Fullerton reported on baseball for newspapers in several cities and wrote on baseball for popular magazines during a long and venerable career. He was a founding member of the Base Ball Writers Association (BBWAA) and is credited with discovering and encouraging a number of successful sportswriters (Ring Lardner among them). He was a pioneer in publishing interviews with ball players and well known for his keen analysis of the strategies of baseball. His careful attention to the play of the Chicago White Sox in the 1919 World Series led him to identify the complicity of some of their players in purposely losing the Series to the Cincinnati Reds.

His analytic approach to inside baseball was evident in published magazine articles and in a coauthored book (Fullerton and Evers [1910] 2004). He earned the sobriquet "The Great Prognosticator" (Holtzman 2005, ch. 19) for his remarkable success at analyzing team play in order to predict the outcome of a game. For example, he correctly predicted that the Chicago White Sox would defeat the Chicago Cubs, a 3–1 favorite, in the 1906 World Series, through his analysis of their respective team strengths (Holtzman 2005).

In 1910 Fullerton described the geometry of baseball infields. He measured the distances covered by the infielders, the "grooves" between infielders in which a ground ball might result in a safe hit, and he used stop watches to determine that the average speed of fifty balls hit on the ground were calculated to travel "100 feet in one and three-twentieth seconds" (Fullerton 1910, 1). Data gathered from games in leagues of different levels of play led him to determine the ratio of safe hits on ground balls to ground outs: about one of eight ground balls were safe hits in college games, one in ten in Minor League games, but only one in fifteen in the Major League. The differences, he concluded, did not depend on the speed of fielders but rather depended on their adjustments in positioning in game situations, a skill more evident with more experienced players (Fullerton 1910).

Fullerton's interest in analysis extended to speculating on the physics of baseball. He considered the effects of atmospheric pressure, the nature of the composition of the ball, and the effects of the resilience of an ash bat on the distance a fly ball would travel. Fullerton (1912d, 756) asked, "A ball, weighing five and an eighth ounces and with a circumference of 9 inches, pitched at an approximate velocity of 280 feet per second, will travel how far?" An answer would come years later from a physicist who took into account similar factors and estimated that the longest distance a baseball might be hit at about 450 feet (Adair 1990).

Taking Babe Ruth to the Columbia psychological laboratory to measure the skills that were the basis of the ballplayer's success as a hitter fit Fullerton's analytic approach to baseball. He was willing to add psychology, the new science, to his explorations of the geometry and physics of the game in order to discover the secrets of Ruth's ability to hit home runs. That ability was making less relevant the game strategies that Fullerton had come to analyze and explain to his readers.

The Columbia Laboratory

Although James McKeen Cattell would not be involved in the testing of Ruth, his laboratory would be the site of the ballplayer's assessment. Cattell, trained in the Leipzig laboratory of Wilhelm Wundt, was the first to hold the title of professor of psychology in an American university (University of Pennsylvania, 1887). He joined Columbia University's faculty as professor of psychology in 1891 and established a laboratory for teaching and research (Cattell 1947). He was a leader among the first generation of American psychologists who sought answers to psychological questions through experiments performed in psychological laboratories in which students were trained and in which research was conducted in the new scientific psychology.

Psychologists did not neglect to inform the larger public of their excitement over their new discipline, which they coordinated with other, more established, sciences and of its promise of useful applications to many areas of life. William James, for example, wrote "on a variety of psychological topics for magazines such as the *Nation* and *Atlantic Monthly*" (Viney, Michaels, and Ganong 1981, 270). The presence of the new laboratories of psychology in colleges and universities and the work being done there came to the attention of Albert Spalding, who was a baseball pitcher in the late nineteenth century as well as a founder of professional teams, an organizer of the National League, and an entrepreneur who established a successful sporting goods business. In 1910 he observed in an interview that "they have now, in colleges, a course which they call experimental psychology. The relation between thought and action is recorded by delicate instruments. These instruments . . . show that the mental reactions of the athletes are quicker than those of any other students."[3] Unfortunately Spalding offered no data on his assertion that the mental reactions of the athlete were faster than those of the nonathlete, but the idea that instruments in the laboratories of psychologists might shed some light on the foundations of athletic performance embodied the expectations of psychologists themselves that their new science would prove to be of practical use.

Psychologists' promotion of their discipline as both a pure science that stood with physics, chemistry, and biology and as an applied science of use in a variety of fields was evidenced by textbooks of the period (see Münsterberg 1913; Hollingworth and

Poffenberger 1923). Attempts to apply psychology to matters of practical concern had received impetus from the involvement of psychologists in World War I, during which they developed tests of the intelligence and the special abilities of recruits in order to identify those most likely to be easily trainable for complex jobs. Tests simulated dimensions of specialized tasks such as aiming and firing a gun from a battleship or piloting an airplane and successfully aiming its guns at a target (Thorndike 1919). Although public claims for the success of these military contributions may have exceeded the actual success in some areas, particularly in intelligence testing (Samelson 1975), psychology had nevertheless left the ivy covered walls of academe and entered the larger marketplace. In 1919 Walter Dill Scott established the first psychological consulting firm, an outgrowth of his work in the psychology of advertising, and in 1920 James McKeen Cattell formed the Psychological Corporation to develop and sell tests to business and industry.

During the years in which Cattell directed the laboratory at Columbia, he utilized laboratory tasks as components of a test to assess the intellectual capacities of Columbia students. The laboratory tasks included measuring the speed of response to a light or sound, determining the number of letters that could be recalled after one hearing, and scoring performance on a variety of sensory-motor and mental tasks that he believed, when taken together, would provide a measure of an individual's intelligence (Cattell 1890).

Cattell was no longer a member of the Columbia University faculty when the tests on Ruth were conducted. He had been fired in 1917, ostensibly for his opposition to conscription during World War I (Gruber 1975). Robert S. Woodworth became chair of the Psychology Department and director of the laboratory. Woodworth received his PhD under Cattell in 1899 (Woodworth 1942) and was the author of the "Columbia Bible," a textbook of experimental psychology that defined the nature of the psychology experiment for generations of students (Winston 1990).

The laboratory when Babe Ruth entered it was well equipped with apparatus designed to test the physical and mental capacities that could be presumed to underlie skilled hitting performance. The psychologists called upon to conduct the tests were Albert Johanson and Joseph Holmes, both with MAs from Columbia and both trained and experienced in the methods and procedures of experimental psychology. Johanson would earn his PhD in 1922 with a dissertation on reaction time, an area of research in which Holmes (PhD, 1923) also published. Fullerton could be confident that the laboratory and the practitioners in it would be up to the challenge of assessing the mental and motor skills of the premier home run hitter of the time.

Testing in the Laboratory

Fullerton had two goals in pursuing the tests of Ruth. The first was to reveal the secrets of the latter's ability to hit home runs with the power needed to drive the ball great distances with significant frequency. The second was to provide baseball scouts, known as ivory hunters, with a scientific basis for determining "whether or not other Ruths exist" (Fullerton 1921, 19). Apparatus was devised to measure the power of his swing; other tasks, common to the teaching and research laboratories of the time, were selected to measure his reaction time, attention, memory, and motor skills.

The Power of His Swing

The baseball world was fascinated with the length of Ruth's home run drives as well as with their frequency. The number of his home runs as a percentage of his times at bat was 11.8 in 1920, still the Major League record. He is both second on the list with 11.1 percent in 1927 and third with 10.9 percent in 1921. The number of home runs contributed substantially to his Major League record slugging percentage of .847 in 1920. In 1921, the year of his testing, Ruth led the league in total bases with 457 and extra-base hits with 119, both single-season Major League records.

While the number and frequency of home runs was well documented, the distance that some of them traveled, although never accurately measured, was part of the awe that the home run inspired among fans and sportswriters alike. Newspaper accounts did not fail to mention a prodigious clout when one occurred; for example, his forty-fifth home run in 1921 (tying his 1920 season record) was noted to have been the longest home run ever hit in Shibe Park, Philadelphia, when it went over the grandstand roof (Smelser 1975, 217). Similar feats were recorded in other stadiums (see Smelser 1975, 214, 216). The longest distance traveled by a home run hit by Ruth was one in 1921 that was *estimated* to have gone 550 feet (Smelser 1975, 214). A 1923 clout was said to have traveled at least 450 feet.[4] Another in 1927 was calculated to have been hit a distance of 474 feet (Smelser 1975, 353). Few players could claim similar feats, although Josh Gibson, the "Black Babe Ruth" of the Negro Leagues, was reputed to have hit a home run in the late 1930s that traveled a measured 512 feet (Peterson [1970] 1999). In a game in Yankee Stadium Gibson was said to have hit a ball that "hit the wall just two feet from the top of the stadium wall circling the bleachers in center field, about 580 feet from home plate" (Peterson [1970] 1999, 160); observers suggested that the ball would have traveled 700 feet had the wall not intervened.

The fascination with power and distance by fans and sportswriters along with Fullerton's personal interest in the physics of baseball (1912d) prompted the first two laboratory tests. The distance a batted ball can be hit is determined by several factors, including the speed of the pitched ball, the speed with which the bat is swung, the weight of the bat, and the resilience of the ball, among other factors. Accordingly, a test was arranged in which

Popular
Science
FOUNDED **MONTHLY** 1 8

Actual Photo
Babe Ruth
erve
e Tests
n Laboratory

ıbe Ruth's Home Run Secrets
Solved by Science
SEE HUGH S. FULLERTON'S ARTICLE ON PAGE 19

5.1. Babe Ruth in the laboratory, where the speed at which he swung a bat was measured. Reprinted from Fullerton 1921.

Ruth would swing at a ball suspended at an optimal height for his swing, with the bat connected to wires and a timer to measure the speed of the bat (see figure 5.1). The weight of the bat was fifty-four ounces, which Fullerton claimed to be the weight of the bats that Ruth used in games played that season. In the test Ruth swung the bat at a rate of 110 feet per second (75 mph) and hit a standard baseball weighing 4.25 ounces four inches from the end of the bat.

For the sake of calculations Fullerton assumed that a pitched ball traveling at the rate of 60 feet per second (about 41 mph) hit by Ruth could achieve a distance of 450 to 500 feet (Fullerton 1921).[5] This range encompassed most of the estimates of the hitter's longest home runs and one that coincides with the more recent estimate of the maximum distance a batted baseball might be hit (Adair 1990, 75). As Fullerton (1921) acknowledged, other factors, such as the resilience of the ball and the nature of the pitch, could affect his estimate as would atmospheric conditions and a bat of a different weight and made of a different density of wood (see Adair 1990, 74–77). There is no reason to doubt Fullerton's report that Ruth used a fifty-four-ounce bat for the test, but Smelser contends that Ruth did not use a bat that heavy after 1920. Although he did order some bats of that weight for the 1920 season, Ruth's usual model in 1920 weighed forty-four ounces, with his heaviest useful bat weighing only forty-seven ounces (1975, 187). Both would be heavy bats by modern standards.

A second test measured the changes in Ruth's breathing as he swung at an imaginary pitched ball (see figure 5.2). Fullerton (1921) reported that "as a baseball is pitched to him, Babe draws in his breath sharply as he makes the backswing with his bat, and really 'holds his breath' . . . until after the ball is hit" (21). Holding his breath in this way, Fullerton contended, tensed muscles that, if relaxed, would allow Ruth to hit with even greater force and achieve greater distances.

5.2. The breathing of Ruth was assessed as he swung at a simulated pitched ball. Reprinted from Fullerton 1921.

Assessing the Basis of His Power: Psychological Tests

The tests employed were adapted from experiments common to the laboratories of the period. They included tests designed to aid in employee selection for various jobs that required manual skill. The first of these tests measured Ruth's coordination by requiring him to insert a stylus into each of three holes of a triangular board, left to right, as quickly as possible. The number of times that a sequence of insertions was completed within one minute was recorded, for the left and right hands: 132 insertions for the left hand and 122 for the right (Ruth was left handed). The standard against which his performance was compared was an average of 82 that was derived from "hundreds of persons who have taken the test" (Fullerton 1921, 21). Ruth's coordination was judged therefore to be superior to the average of the general population.

In a similar test he tapped a metal plate that recorded the number of taps that could be made with a stylus in one minute. In this test he scored 193 taps per minute with his right hand and 176 taps with his left; an "average score for right handed persons undergoing this wrist-wracking experiment is 180" (Fullerton 1921, 160). No averages were available for right-handed individuals using the left hand, but Fullerton (1921) concluded nevertheless "that Ruth's record is much above the average" (160).

A test of steadiness, defined as the absence of tremor or irrelevant movement, was accomplished by having Ruth insert a narrow stylus into holes that varied in their diameter; touching the sides of the holes indicated tremor, or movement. On this task Ruth's score for control was determined to surpass 499 out of 500 individuals for whom scores were available. Once again, his scores were superior to the average of an unknown population, but as in the other tests no comparisons were made with averages for baseball players or athletes in other sports. Such averages were unlikely to have been available.

Reaction Time

Coordination and speed of responding were tested because they are components, or characteristics, of skilled performance. Perhaps most critical, however, to the act of hitting a baseball is the speed with which the batter reacts to a pitched ball. Reaction time was an early and critical focus of study in early psychological laboratories as an indicator of the time a mental process takes between the appearance of a stimulus and the production of a response to it.

Ruth was seated in the dark and was asked to press a key when he detected a flash of light. His average time for responding was 160 thousandths of a second, compared to the "average man" who required 180 thousandths of a second. In like fashion, his reaction time to sound was 140 thousandths of a second compared to 150 thousandths of a second for the average person. As Fullerton (1921) noted, the differences between Ruth and the average man "are so small that they seem inexpressive; yet a difference of twenty or ten one thousandth of a second indicates a superiority of the highest importance" (110). The significance to Fullerton was that pitchers would have to throw the ball faster to Babe than to an average person in order to fool him. Put another way, Ruth could presumably respond faster to a pitch than the average person who was not a baseball player. Fullerton did not, however, provide the source for the data on the average man; it is possible that he used data or estimates based on results of tests conducted on Columbia students.

To supplement these conclusions regarding Ruth's superiority in speed of responding, he was asked to identify letters of the alphabet flashed for 50 thousandths of a second in groups of four, five, and six, all of which he identified correctly. With a group of eight letters, he identified six correctly, compared with an average of four-and-a-half for the average individual. He was also asked to identify the number of dots flashed in the same fashion; he could identify the number correctly in groups up to twelve as compared to the average person's eight. In a task requiring him to write an assigned number to each of five different symbols, he equaled the performance of the average of those who had performed the task but performed at one-and-a-half times the average when asked to cross out all the instances of the letter *a* on a printed card.

Fullerton was in no doubt about how to interpret these tests. They revealed to him the secret of Babe Ruth's success: "His eye, his ear, his brain, his nerves all function more rapidly than do those of the average person. Further, the coordination of eye, ear, brain, and muscle is much nearer perfection than that of the normal healthy man" (Fullerton 1921, 110). The psychologists whose tests revealed the secrets of Babe Ruth's success as a batter were for Fullerton scientific ivory hunters, whose success in testing Ruth demonstrated that the science of psychology could contribute to baseball's quest for the means to identify that neophyte baseball player who might become the Babe Ruth of the future.

Reaction to Ruth's Testing

The results of Fullerton's 1921 tests of Ruth were reported in a front-page article for the *New York Times* (September 1921) but received little subsequent attention. Ruth's biographers referred to it briefly, if at all. In one of the few references to this episode in accounts of baseball's history, the purpose of the tests was misinterpreted by Lieb (1977) as an attempt to assess Ruth's intelligence. No report of Ruth's participation in the Columbia laboratory appeared in the psychological literature. Ruth's testing then went essentially unnoticed in the histories of psychology and baseball for a little more than seventy-five years when an account of the tests appeared in a psychological journal (Fuchs 1998), cited years later in a biography of Ruth (Montville 2006).

The 1921 tests were publicized anew when Albert Pujols, a talented hitter for the St. Louis Cardinals, was brought to the psychological laboratories of Washington University of St. Louis to participate in tests similar to those that Ruth had taken (Penn 2006). Like Fullerton, Penn thought that such tests might prove to be useful in selecting future stars of the game, and he was curious to see how a modern player would compare with the great Babe.

Pujols, with five years of Major League experience in 2006, was approximately at the same stage of his Major League career as was Ruth in 1921. His credentials include his unanimous choice for the National League's Rookie of the Year Award in 2001, his 2003 Major League–leading performance with a batting average of .359, 394 total bases, 137 runs scored, and 51 doubles. In 2004 he again led the Major Leagues in total bases (389) and in runs scored (133). In 2005 he led the Major Leagues once more in runs scored with 129 and was the National League's Most Valuable Player for that year (Siwoff 2007).

The results of Pujols's laboratory tests were comparable to those of the Babe. For example, the speed with which he swung his 35.5-ounce bat was measured at "86.99 miles per hour, generating the equivalent of nineteen horsepower" (Penn 2006, 300) as compared with Ruth's 75 miles per hour with a 54-ounce bat. Both results suggest that a baseball when hit would travel the maximum distance possible under comparable sets of conditions, Babe Ruth by swinging a heavier bat and Albert Pujols by swinging a lighter bat more quickly. But many players might, if similarly tested, match the bat speeds and power numbers in the laboratory. Hitting a baseball for any distance is a difficult feat and owes more to the mechanics of the swing than simply the force generated by it (Penn 2006).

The other tests to which Pujols was subjected also produced results to suggest his superiority but, like Ruth, without appropriate comparative norms, if any at all. In the letter-crossing test, Pujols crossed out all instances of the letter *a* on a sheet of jumbled text in sixty-one seconds, seven seconds faster than Penn, the writer who observed the tests (Penn 2006, 300). Placing pegs in the holes on a board placed Pujols in the seventy-ninth percentile, and he performed in the ninety-ninth percentile on a finger-tapping test. Like Ruth, he was average on the digit substitution test but "off the charts" when asked to copy the symbols quickly (Penn 2006, 300).

Hugh Fullerton's faith in the potential of psychology to identify early in their careers those baseball players who might achieve the same success in batting as Babe Ruth was not apparently shared by others. Baseball teams have not initiated a program of laboratory testing in the selection and development of players: indeed, according to Marcus Elliott, "the Babe Ruth testing was more appropriate and more intensive than any professional team is doing right now" (as quoted by Penn 2006). Neither have psychologists pursued the promise of laboratory tests for selecting the Babe Ruth of the future. The psychologists who conducted the tests had not initiated the testing of Ruth and did not publish their findings in a professional journal. Fullerton continued his career as a baseball writer but did not challenge baseball teams to follow his lead in using laboratory tests to identify the stars of the future. In 1964, nineteen years after his death in 1945, Fullerton received the J. G. Taylor Spink Award from the National Baseball Hall of Fame in recognition of his distinguished career and contributions to his profession.

Babe Ruth went on to set career Major League records: a lifetime slugging percentage of .690, the most seasons (thirteen) with a slugging percentage greater than .600, the most seasons (eleven) leading the Major Leagues in home runs, and the most seasons (fourteen) in runs batted in (Siwoff 2007). If not the greatest batsman of all time, he was at least among the greatest. He established a standard of performance on the baseball diamond against which subsequent generations of baseball players have been measured.

Both psychology and baseball have prospered since 1921. The number of teams in the Major Leagues has grown from sixteen to thirty, and new records for fan attendance have been set in a number of cities. Home runs continue to dominate the sport, even as controversy over the role that performance-enhancing drugs have played in setting or pursuing home run records. Psychologists have expanded their research into new fields and specializations, including sports. However, the testing that brought Ruth and Fullerton together in the Columbia psychological laboratory became not the beginning of the field of sport psychology but an isolated episode in its prehistory.

As in 1921 the limitations of the later Pujols tests are unlikely to convince baseball scouts that the psychological laboratory offers a sound basis for evaluating talent. However, promising possibilities appear to exist: assessing binocular disparity for hitters may offer an avenue to predict hitting prowess; assessing personal characteristics may also help to predict baseball success (Penn 2006). As baseball teams continue to expend large sums of money on unproven talent, it might pay to develop tests to select those most worthy of their investment. If so, Hugh Fullerton may be vindicated, Babe Ruth may set another standard for baseball, and psychology may have one more area of research and testing in which to demonstrate its usefulness as an applied science.

Notes

This chapter is based on an earlier publication, A. H. Fuchs, "Psychology and the Babe," *Journal of the History of the Behavioral Sciences* 34 (1998): 153–65.

1 Earned run average (ERA) is the mean number of (earned) runs scored against a pitcher per nine innings, discounting those (unearned) runs that are due to fielding errors by other members of the pitcher's team: 9(ER/IP). Between 1914 and 1919 the average ERA in the American League was about 2.85, nearly a third of a run higher than Ruth's.

2 Slugging percentage (SLG) is the total number of bases of all of a batter's hits (that is, 1 for a single, 2 for a double, and so on) divided by the number of at bats. It is a measure of the extent to which a batter hits for extra-base hits: his "power."

3 E. Marshall, "The Psychology of Baseball Discussed by A. G. Spalding," *New York Times*, November 13, 1910, reprinted in Albert G. Spaulding, *America's National Game* (1910), revised and reedited by Samm Coombs and Bob West (San Francisco CA: Halo Books, 1991).

4 J. DeVries, "City Was Crazy for Bambino," *Herald & News*, April 29, 1923.

5 Fullerton's estimate of pitch speed is rather low. Although it is difficult to know the speed of an "average" Major League fastball in the 1920s with precision, today fastballs of ninety mph and higher are quite common. Assuming that the fastballs of Ruth's era had speeds of considerably more than half of today's, this speed would allow for possible home run distances longer than those Fullerton calculated.

References

Adair, R. K. 1990. *The physics of baseball*. New York: Harper and Row.

Berg, M. 1941. Pitchers and catchers. *Atlantic Monthly*, September.

Block, David. 2005. *Baseball before we knew it*. Lincoln: University of Nebraska Press.

Cattell, J. M. 1890. Mental tests and measurements. *Mind* 15:373–81.

———. 1947. *James McKeen Cattell: Man of science*. Vol. 2. Lancaster PA: Science Press.

Douglas, B. 1922. *The science of baseball*. New York: Wilson.

Fuchs, A. H. 1998. Psychology and the "Babe." *Journal of the History of the Behavioral Sciences* 34:153–65.

———. 2000. The contributions of American mental philosophers to psychology in the United States. *History of Psychology* 3:3–19.

Fuchs, A. H., and K. S. Milar. 2003. History of psychology as a science. In *History of psychology*, ed. D. K. Freedheim, 1–26. Vol. 1 of *Handbook of psychology*, ed. I. B. Weiner. New York: Wiley

Fullerton, H. 1910. The inside game. *American Magazine*, May.

———. 1912a. The baseball primer. *American Magazine*, June.

———. 1912b. Fans. *American Magazine*, August.

———. 1912c. How to win games. *American Magazine*, July.

———. 1912d. The physics of baseball. *American Magazine*, October.

———. 1921. Why Babe Ruth is greatest home run hitter. *Popular Science Monthly*, October.

Fullerton, H., and J. Evers. [1910] 2004. *Touching second*. New York: McFarland.

Gould, S. J. 2003. *Triumph and tragedy in Mudville*. New York: Norton.

Gruber, C. S. 1975. *Mars and Minerva*. Baton Rouge: Louisiana State University Press.

Hollingworth, H. L., and A. T. Poffenberger. 1923. *Applied psychology*. New York: Appleton.

Holtzman, J. 2005. *On baseball*. Champaign IL: Sports Publishing.

Honig, D. 1990. *The Boston Red Sox: An illustrated history*. New York: Prentice-Hall.

Lieb, F. 1977. *Baseball as I have known it*. New York: Coward, McCann, and Geohegan.

Mathewson, C. [1912] 1977. *Pitching in a pinch*. New York: Stein and Day.

Montville, L. 2006. *The big bam*. New York: Doubleday.

Münsterberg, H. 1913. *Psychology and industrial efficiency*. Boston: Houghton Mifflin.

Penn, N. 2006. How to build the perfect batter. *GQ*, September.

Peterson, R. [1970] 1999. *Only the ball was white*. New York: Gramercy.

Ruth, Babe. 1920. *The home run king*. New York: Burt.

Samelson, F. 1975. On the science and politics of the IQ. *Social Research* 42:467–88.

Smelser, M. 1975. *The life that Ruth built*. Lincoln: University of Nebraska Press.

Swioff, S., ed. 2007. *The Elias book of baseball records*. New York: Seymour Siwoff.

Thorndike, E. L. 1919. Scientific personnel work in the army. *Science*, n.s., 49: 53–61.

Viney, W., T. Michaels, and A. Ganong. 1981. A note on the history of psychology in magazines. *Journal of the History of the Behavioral Sciences* 17:270–72.

Wagenheim, K. 1974. *Babe Ruth*. New York: Holt.

Winston, A. 1990. Robert Sessions Woodworth and the "Columbia bible": How the psychological experiment was redefined. *American Journal of Psychology* 103:391–401.

Wood, A. 2000. *Babe Ruth and the 1918 Red Sox*. San Jose CA: Writers Club.

Woodworth, R. 1942. The Columbia University Psychological Laboratory: A fifty-year retrospect. New York: n.p.

An Offensive Advantage

THE FOOTBALL CHARGING STUDIES
AT STANFORD UNIVERSITY

Frank G. Baugh and Ludy T. Benjamin Jr.

Athletic competition has long been a fixture of the American landscape. Baseball, often acknowledged as America's national pastime, has seen its exclusive hold on the world of sport disappear, rivaled by a multitude of alternatives today from soccer to NASCAR, although perhaps none more popular than American-style football. The sport of football originated from the developing games of rugby and soccer that were popular among European and American college students during the late 1800s. The earliest form of American football was developed in 1880 largely through the efforts of Walter Camp, a student at Yale University. The regulations Camp worked to popularize among college teams were first introduced in an 1881 game between Princeton and Yale universities (Liss 1975; Perrin 1987). The popularity of the game spread quickly, and by 1900 intercollegiate football competition had become a staple among many colleges and universities.

Several football coaches of the era assumed a central role in shaping the new sport. Glenn S. "Pop" Warner, who began coaching at the University of Georgia in 1895 and later was at Carlisle, Cornell, Pittsburgh, and Stanford; Amos Alonzo Stagg, who began coaching at Springfield College in 1890 before moving to the University of Chicago in 1892; and John Heisman, who began his coaching career at Oberlin College in 1893 before moving to Buchtel College and then Auburn University all utilized their creativity to revolutionize the manner in which organized football was played (Liss 1975; Pope 1955).

The first college football game to be played on the West Coast was at the University of California in 1886. Two years later, the University of Southern California played its first game as the Southern California Methodists, defeating the Alliance Athletic Club 16–0 (Rappoport 1974). The head coach of the USC team was Henry Herbert Goddard, who was a recent graduate of Haverford College and who had played on its football team. In addition to his coaching duties, Goddard taught Latin, history, and botany at USC (Zenderland 1998). Goddard would later earn a doctorate in psychology from G. Stanley Hall at Clark University and achieve fame for his role in bringing the Binet intelligence test to America. His role as the first head football coach at USC and his record of two wins and no losses, making him the only undefeated head coach in USC football history (Pierson 1974; Rappoport 1974), has earned him a small place in USC sports history and as the subject of a question or two in a history of psychology trivia contest (Burtt and Pressey 1957).

Football in Crisis

The rapid spread of football across American college campuses at the end of the nineteenth century notwithstanding, all was not well with the sport. There were fiscal scandals involving payments to players and other misappropriations of university funds. Some teams fielded ineligible players, typically individuals who were not part of the student body. There was gambling and accusations of fixed games. But the central problem with the game was violence, both on the field and in the stands.

Violence had been a part of the game from its inception. The game between Harvard and Yale universities in 1894 was especially brutal and resulted in four players suffering serious injuries and causing the schools to suspend play against one another for three years. The Army-Navy series was cancelled in the same year for excessive brutality, a suspension that lasted for five years. Despite calls for rule changes that would reduce the level of violence, the brutal nature of the game continued. Watterson (2002) has described the situation as the twentieth century began: "The deaths of players in football led state legislatures to introduce laws banning the gridiron game. Players for big-time teams, critics charged, were coached to injure their opponents or 'put them out of business.' The nature of the game, with its mass formations and momentum plays, made football less an athletic contest than a collegiate version of wartime combat" (2).

In 1905 when nineteen football players died, the game reached a crisis point. President Theodore Roosevelt, a longtime advocate of college football, demanded that rule changes be made to end the violence, or he promised to take action to ban the game nationally. Approximately a dozen universities cancelled their football programs after the 1905 season including Columbia, Stanford, and the University of California. Harvard University's president Charles W. Eliot called for abolishing football at his university, but faculty and alumni supporters prevailed in keeping Harvard on the field. Instead, the university would lead the reform efforts in seeking to make the game less violent (Park 1984; Smith 1981). Yet violence seemed to be an indigenous part of the game, something that the spectators expected to see (Patrick 1903), and rooting it out was not easy. Indeed, the brutality continued, reaching a second crisis point in 1909–10 (Watterson 1981).

Stanford and the University of California continued their ban on football for about a decade. The California schools had replaced their football games with English rugby, and their presidents sought, largely unsuccessfully, to get other universities to follow their lead. Leading the charge on the Stanford campus to outlaw American football was psychologist Frank Angell, the faculty's athletic representative, who vehemently opposed football because of the cheating, deception, and violence that it encouraged. Angell had played rugby when he was a student at Oxford University, and he believed that game fostered better values in young men (Park 1984).

The West Coast universities were newer than their eastern counterparts and did not enjoy the prestige or political clout of the more established schools. California and Stanford sought to create athletic programs that would be seen as competitive with the eastern schools, but as American football continued to grow in popularity, it was clear that they would never gain parity without a return to that sport. Rugby had never proved popular with students or alumni. Eventually pressures from students, faculty, and alumni as well as the universities' desire for national recognition of their athletic programs led to the resumption of their football programs (Park 1984). In addition, rule changes, including the forward pass, and protective equipment had significantly reduced player injuries by 1916 (Watterson 2002).

The New Psychology and Sport

The growing popularity of football coincided with the emergence of the new psychology in America. Edward Scripture and Norman Triplett were two of the early psychologists who used the methods of their new science to investigate questions in sports such as fencing, running, and cycling (see Goodwin, this volume; Davis, Huss, and Becker, this volume). The origin of sport psychology, a growing research and applied specialty (see LeUnes 2009), is often traced to the 1890s, especially to the initial study of cycling by Norman Triplett (1898), a psychologist and cycling enthusiast. Yet the scattered studies of the 1890s should be regarded as anticipations and not foundations of sport psychology (Sarup 1978).

In the contemporary textbooks and articles that treat the history of sport psychology in America, it is common to see Coleman Griffith identified as the founder of the field. Griffith was a psychologist at the University of Illinois who from approximately 1918 to 1940 sought to use psychological methods and measurements to improve sport performance or athlete selection and who believed that athletic performance could be appreciably improved by the application of psychological methods (see Griffith 1925). Griffith is arguably the first sport psychologist in America in that, unlike his predecessors who conducted a few studies of athletes and then moved on to other fields, he pursued an organized program of research on the psychology of athletics for more than twenty years. However, to link him to the rise of sport psychology in America in the 1960s requires something of an origin myth. As Green (see this volume) has noted, there is no direct connection between Griffith and contemporary sport psychology research and practice.

During his tenure at the University of Illinois, Griffith established a sport psychology laboratory in the Department of Physical Welfare (education and athletics). His work was aided by the department's director, George Huff, who supported Griffith's psychological investigations, predicated on Huff's belief that coaches placed too much emphasis on physical abilities in athletics, thus ignoring mental aspects that Huff believed were of considerable, if not greater, influence.

Griffith's work was also aided by Robert Carl Zuppke, head

football coach at Illinois from 1913 to 1941. Zuppke allowed Griffith to observe football practices and to test football players for his research. Griffith, who published books on the *Psychology of Coaching* (1926) and *Psychology and Athletics* (1928), collaborated with Zuppke on a book tentatively titled *The Psychology of Football*, but it was never published (an incomplete draft of the book can be found in the Coleman Griffith Papers in the archives of the University of Illinois).

Whereas Griffith was interested in a number of sports, he favored team sports such as baseball, basketball, and football because of the life lessons learned therein from the competition and teamwork. He believed that the justification for athletic competition and why colleges in particular should be involved with athletics was that "the football field is a place where morale, spirit, courage, honor, sportsmanship, fair play, team work, and the like, are directly taught" (Griffith 1925, 198). He argued that those lessons could not be learned in the classroom.

Pop Warner and Stanford Football

Glenn Scobey Warner (1871–1954), better known in athletic circles as Pop Warner, shared Griffith's beliefs about the lessons learned in playing football, writing that the struggles with defeat and the quest for victory built character in those who played the game (Warner 1927). After graduating from Cornell University with a law degree, he began his coaching career, as noted earlier, at the University of Georgia in 1895. He next coached at his alma mater for several years before moving to the Carlisle School for Indians. There he coached Jim Thorpe, who many sports experts regard as the greatest athlete ever. In his next coaching job at the University of Pittsburgh, Warner's teams won thirty-three consecutive games and two national championships. In 1924 when Warner moved to Stanford University, the crises of college football were long forgotten. In the public euphoria of America in the 1920s, college football proved to be major entertainment, and nowhere more so than on New Year's Day in Pasadena, California, home of the fabled Rose Bowl. Warner would coach at Stanford for nine seasons, appearing in three Rose Bowls.

When he arrived at Stanford, Warner was a veteran coach, known not only for his winning records but also for his innovative football strategies. He has been credited with the invention of uniform equipment that reduced injury to players, the practice of putting numbers on players' jerseys, the huddle, plays such as the screen pass, and formations such as the single- and double-wing, which proved conducive to offenses that relied on the forward pass (Liss 1975; Watterson 2002). Not only did Warner introduce offensive formations and techniques that revolutionized football, he was not shy about implementing strategies developed by other coaches. Moreover, writings on the history of football paint a picture of Warner as a coach who constantly sought methods for gaining an edge on his competition (Liss 1975; Perrin 1987; Pope 1955). He may have believed that there was an edge to be gained from psychology.

The 1920s were a time of considerable popularity for psychology in America as evidenced by such markers as the growth of popular psychology magazines, psychology columns in newspapers, psychology articles in magazines, psychological self-help books for popular consumption, home-study courses on psychology, and classified newspaper advertisements for psychological services. In the public euphoria that followed victory in the Great War, the enfranchisement of women, and the growing economy, writers in the Roaring Twenties trumpeted the benefits of the science of psychology, not as an option but as a requirement for a life well lived. Echoing a popular sentiment, newspaper columnist Albert Wiggam (1928) wrote that "men and women never needed psychology so much as they need it today. . . . You cannot achieve [effectiveness and happiness] in the fullest measure without the new knowledge of your own mind and personality that the psychologists have given us" (13). Warner no doubt knew about psychology and about the interests of psychologists in sports in the 1920s.

Perhaps Warner had read some of the work of Coleman Griffith; or the studies by Harold Burtt and J. H. Nichols (1924), which assessed the intelligence of varsity athletes, including football players at Ohio State University; or the similar work by Vern Ruble (1928) on athletes at Indiana University; or perhaps the work of Charles Bean (1927), who applied a job-analysis technique to identifying the motor skills, perceptual abilities, intelligence, and other factors that appeared to be important to various athletic endeavors, including football positions; or the work of Donald Paterson and Emerick Peterson (1928), who examined the relationship between academic performance and participation in college athletics at the University of Minnesota. It seems likely that Warner was familiar with at least some of that research. So he may have been amenable to cooperate in a psychological study of his football players when approached by a member of the psychology department faculty at Stanford.

Walter Miles

Walter Richard Miles (1885–1978) was trained as a psychologist under Carl Seashore at the University of Iowa. He completed his doctoral degree in 1913 and initially secured a one-year teaching position at Wesleyan University. He was heavily influenced by the prominent experimental psychologist Raymond Dodge while at Wesleyan and later in his research position at the Carnegie Nutrition Laboratory in Boston. During this time period Miles assumed a central role in a series of experiments inspired by World War I; these studies investigated issues related to gas masks, airplane pilot aptitudes, and the psychological effects of undernutrition in draft-age male subjects.

Miles spent most of his professional career at Stanford University (ten years) and later at Yale University (twenty-two years). He is perhaps best known for a series of studies of human development in the later stages of life that began in 1930; this research with Lewis Terman and Catherine Cox Miles (his second wife) became known as the Stanford Later Maturity Studies. His honors included election in 1932 to the presidency of the American Psychological Association and in 1933 to membership in the prestigious National Academy of Sciences (Miles 1967).

In 1922 when Miles was still with the Carnegie Nutrition Laboratory, Frank Angell retired as head of the psychology department at Stanford, and Terman moved from the College of Education to fill Angell's chair. But Terman recognized that he needed someone with greater expertise in experimentation to head the psychology laboratory. After eight years in Boston and the Carnegie Laboratory, Miles moved to Palo Alto to join the Stanford faculty as professor of psychology and head of the psychology laboratory. Miles (1967) later indicated that the teaching opportunities available at Stanford were a decidedly important factor in his decision to leave his research position at Carnegie. He was also eager to be involved in research with graduate students.

What ensued was a very eclectic (some would say nonprogrammatic) period of research in which many of the articles published by Miles in his Stanford years were the result of student-initiated questions. Goodwin (2003) has written that Miles "never became a leading figure in any particular area of research in psychology . . . but drifted from one area to another, with the direction of the drift determined often by the presence of a particular type of apparatus or an apparatus-related problem that intrigued him" (58).

One of the student-generated questions that captured Miles's interest concerned the reaction time of football players. It was initiated by a graduate student working on his master's degree in psychology at Stanford in 1926–27. The student was Bernice Courtney Graves, a football coach from Texas, who for perhaps obvious reasons used the name B. C. Graves. Graves drew Miles into a complicated study involving construction of an ingenious apparatus to measure the effects of variations in signal calling on football charging, that is, the speed at which linemen moved in reaction to the signal for snapping the ball. The issue of what was the most effective starting signal to cue the offensive team to action was a subject of much debate in football strategy books written by coaches in the 1920s (Heisman 1922; Rockne 1925; Warner 1927; Zuppke 1924).

There seems no doubt that the idea for these studies came from Graves, although there is nothing in the published or unpublished record to confirm that. Miles's interest in the psychology of football certainly seems misplaced given the remainder of his considerable body of work. In his more than forty years of research, there are only these few studies, conducted in the span of less than two years, that are related to sport. Yet there is as least one hint that Miles had some interest in football prior to his association with Graves. In his autobiography Miles (1967) wrote of being able to keep up with his academic work while playing on the football team when he was enrolled in the Preparatory Department of Pacific College in Newburg, Oregon.

B. C. Graves

Bernice C. Graves (1899–1992) was an all-conference player in baseball, basketball, and football in high school and college and a star quarterback for the Buffaloes of West Texas State Normal College at Canyon, from which he graduated with his baccalaureate degree in 1923. His first job was at Sul Ross State Teachers College in Alpine, Texas, where he was hired to start a football program. The Sul Ross Lobos fared well in their first year, winning four of six games, and by 1928 Coach Graves had a winning percentage of better than seventy percent. In addition to coaching the football team, Graves coached the baseball, basketball, and track teams (Casey 1975).

After three years at Sul Ross, Graves took a leave of absence in 1926–27 to work on a master's degree (Anonymous 1926). He chose Stanford in large part because Pop Warner was there, and Graves wanted to work with him. Graves enrolled in the master's program in psychology in which he met Miles who would supervise his research on football signal calling. His thesis, titled "The Effect of Signal Variation on Speed and Uniformity of Football Charging" (Graves 1927), was defended and approved in September 1927. This study would be one of two that Miles would publish in four articles on football charging between 1928 and 1931.

The Stanford Football Charging Studies

When Graves arrived at Stanford in the summer of 1926, Warner was beginning his third year. He had winning records in his two previous seasons and in one had taken his championship team to the Rose Bowl, losing to Notre Dame. It is not known what kind of contact Graves had with Warner during that year, but it is likely that he was permitted to work with the team in some coaching or training capacity. One source reported that he served as a scout for the Stanford team, perhaps seeing some games of upcoming opponents (Anonymous 1973). In the records from the Sul Ross Archives Graves indicated on a handwritten résumé that he "studied under Pop Warner."[1]

There are no written records from Warner describing the two studies done by Miles and Graves. There are comments from him reported in several newspaper articles and statements made by Miles in some of his correspondence that suggest that Warner was quite interested in the psychological studies and their potential impact for improving the performance of his team. In essence, the studies emphasized measures of reaction time or in this case the speed of football charging. Players (linemen) would position themselves in the now traditional three-point stance (which some sources say Warner invented). An auditory signal would be given, indicating the snap of the ball, and the linemen would react as quickly as possible, meaning that they charged forward from their three-point stance. Their initial movement triggered the end of the timing interval and thus provided a measure of reaction time. Miles and Graves designed an apparatus, essentially a group chronoscope, that allowed the testing of as many as seven individuals simultaneously, recording a separate reaction time score for each lineman. Linemen were also tested individually in one study.

Graves's master's thesis was published in 1931, four years after he graduated from Stanford (Miles and Graves 1931). It is possible that Graves did not even know that his thesis had been published. He wrote to Miles in 1932 to ask for Miles's help on a football knowledge test that Graves had devised.[2] Miles replied that "sometime ago I tried to locate your address so as to send you some reprints of the study which resulted from your investigation. I am now sending them under separate cover and hope that you will be in agreement with the materials as printed in study number 3. When preparing this last year, I tried to locate you so as to get your OK on the manuscript but some way couldn't make the contact."[3] In 1932 Graves was still the football coach at Sul Ross, the same position he had held when he went to Stanford in 1926, so it seems odd that Miles would have had trouble locating him.

Miles refers to "study number 3," but there were only two studies. There were three articles in a numbered series titled "Studies in Physical Exertion" (the title of the first article was actually "Studies on Physical Exertion"). The first article (Miles 1928b) was wholly a description of the apparatus. The actual research was published as numbers 2 (Miles 1931) and 3 (Miles and Graves

1931) in the series. The other article that Miles (1928a) published on the football studies appeared in *Scientific American*; it provided a brief overview of the work but focused largely on a description of the apparatus.

Graves's study concerned several methods of calling signals and sought to determine whether one method was superior in producing the fastest charging times. In earlier years offensive linemen were coached to watch the ball and move when they saw the snap. But it was discovered that this prevented the linemen from seeing what their opponents were doing, so teams changed to a system whereby auditory signals from the quarterback indicated when the ball was snapped and thus when linemen could move. In this way linemen could continue to watch the positioning of their opponents across the line (Rockne 1925).

As noted by Miles (1928a), reaction time had been a topic of interest to scientists at least since the eighteenth century when English Astronomer Royal Nevil Maskelyne famously fired his assistant David Kinnebrook for "errors" in his measurements of stellar transits (see Boring 1950). Reaction time research was prominent in the beginnings of experimental psychology as well. For example, Hermann Helmholtz used it in his measures of the speed of nerve conduction in the 1850s, and James McKeen Cattell and Wilhelm Wundt used it to measure the speed of mental processes in the 1880s (see Cattell 1886). It was also the measure of choice in much of the sport psychology research that preceded Miles and Graves's investigations. Long before football coaches recognized the advantage of charging to an auditory cue versus a visual cue, Swiss astronomer Adolph Hirsch working in the 1860s had discovered that reaction times to an auditory cue were faster than responses to a visual cue. Hirsch did his research with the help of an engineering colleague, Matthäus Hipp, who invented a chronoscope that measured time in one thousandths of a second. Psychologists working at the end of the twentieth century, using the Hipp chronoscope, would confirm Hirsch's observations about the superiority of the auditory reaction time (Woodworth 1938).

The initial problem that Miles saw in answering the football charging questions posed by Graves was a chronoscope that could measure accurately the reaction times of a number of individuals at a single time. That was a challenge that Miles would have welcomed as evidenced by the fact that he often published articles describing apparatus he had developed for his psychological work. Indeed, Goodwin (2003) has described Miles's "fascination with apparatus" (61) and noted that his "penchant for apparatus is reflected in a portrait made for him in the early 1950s [that] shows him in the lab, surrounded by equipment" (58). Like Warner, Miles was an inventor and innovator, and he no doubt relished the creation of what he called his multiple chronograph. Miles also believed in testing in the field when possible, so it was his goal to devise a way to test football players on the practice field. Apparently Miles was so pleased with his invention that he described it in considerable detail in two publications, one of which, as noted above, was devoted solely to a description of the apparatus (Miles 1928a, 1928b).

The multiple chronograph was a combination chronoscope and kymograph. Its major component was a drum, eighty-six cm in length and one thousand mm in circumference. The drum served as the kymograph, rotating at a speed of one revolution per second such that a distance of one mm on the paper covering of the drum equaled .001 second. The device was made to accommodate seven lineman at once. In the three-point stance, each lineman's head rested against a trigger release that would activate the moment the lineman began to charge forward from his fixed position. The linemen were each represented by a golf ball suspended above the drum at a fixed distance. Pressure on the trigger caused the golf ball to fall, independently for each

6.1. Walter Miles examining the multiple chronograph. Courtesy of the Archives of the History of American Psychology, University of Akron, Akron OH.

lineman, striking the drum below and making a slight indentation in the paper because of the wire mesh underlying the paper. The reaction time was measured by making a pencil mark in the center of the circular impression made by the golf ball and measuring that distance from the starting point of the signal, factoring in the drop time of the golf ball. Thus seven different reaction times could be obtained in one trial (Miles 1928a, 1928b). The chronograph was portable but heavy, although Miles (1928a) remarked that "the entire unit may be easily carried by four men" (227) (see figures 6.1 and 6.2). Perhaps the only real difficulty was finding an extension cord long enough to operate the device on the field.

The problem of signals and their importance for football charging was described as follows in a paragraph almost certainly written by Miles (and not Graves) that emphasized the importance of a charge in unison:

6.2. Walter Miles testing members of the Stanford University football team.
Courtesy of the Archives of the History of American Psychology, University of
Akron, Akron OH.

The successful football team not only demonstrates speed but shows
unison of movement. Snappy, precise action in unity is the strength
objective toward which the coach works and the men train. The
effort is to make the eleven individual nervous systems into one well-
integrated, powerful machine. This has to be accomplished in large
part on a stimulus-response basis, and involves the use of signals.
These give character and sequence to action, and provide a means
for timing movement particularly in its initial phases. Therefore we
find that starting signals in football are generally regarded as particularly important, and form the basis for much discussion. While
coaches vary in their opinions and preferences, they all recognize
the desirable ends to be obtained by signals properly devised and
expertly called. (Miles and Graves 1931, 14)

Obviously all signal systems had a target number, or sound, or
position in the count that was the signal for movement. Beyond
the need for that signal, coaches differed widely on what they
believed about signals. Some believed that players should not know
when the signal was to be given so that they would not be likely
to anticipate the signal and move prematurely. Some believed
in equal intervals between each of the sounds in the signal call-

ing, whereas others felt the cadence of the signal calling should vary to foil the charging time of the defense. In Graves's thesis he sought to look at those issues by investigating the following factors (Graves 1927, 8):

1 The effect of rate of rhythm upon speed, uniformity, and offsides in football charging (from calling signals at various rhythm rates).

2 Comparison of anticipatory and nonanticipatory signals as starting devices. In the former the position of the snap signal in a series is known; in the latter the snap signal is known, but the linemen do not know its location in the sequence.

3 The effect of nonrhythm on speed, uniformity, and offsides in football charging and a comparison of results to that of rhythm.

The design of the study was impressive, using multiple independent and dependent variables, multiple trials, counterbalanced conditions, and several levels of each independent variable.

Graves found that with regard to rhythm rates, a rate of one hundred signals per minute was found to be optimal for anticipatory signals while a rate of sixty signals per minute (thus a slower cadence) for nonanticipatory signals. Thus speed off the ball was maximized when signals were called at those rates. Moreover, it was found that the fastest starting times under most conditions occurred when the signal was called within two to five seconds after the players had set, typically a number in the fourth or fifth position of the sequence. If the signal could not be anticipated, it produced greater uniformity in charging speeds and fewer offside penalties by thirty-three percent. But charging speeds were faster when the signal call could be anticipated. With regard to rhythm in the cadence of the signal count, a rhythmic count produced faster charging speeds whereas a nonrhythmic count produced greater uniformity of charging speeds. Offsides were slightly more common for rhythmic counts (Graves 1927).

It is clear that charging speed and uniformity (unison) of charge were differentially affected by different signal-calling methods. That left Graves in a difficult position in trying to recommend the best starting signal. In his summary he opted for anticipatory signals, which he found had a .10 second speed advantage over nonanticipatory signals (a sizeable advantage), indicating his belief that charging speed was more important than uniformity of charge, contrary to Miles's suggestion in the 1931 article. Graves also believed that his data were clear about the desirability of giving the snap signal within the first five seconds after the players set, typically on the fourth or fifth number of the count (Graves 1927; Miles and Graves 1931).

In late summer or early fall of 1927 Miles used the multiple chronograph for one more study on the Stanford football players. Graves was back at Sul Ross and thus not involved in this work. Instead, Miles indicated that he was assisted by Mr. Kirk Miles (Miles 1931, 6), who was his seventeen-year-old son. In this study Miles wanted to obtain group and individual reaction times of the football players by position. As might be expected, he found that running backs registered the quickest times followed by ends, guards, tackles, and centers.

Miles also was interested in comparing the football charging scores to a numeric ranking of a players' overall speed as subjectively determined by the coaches. In other words he wanted to see if the coaches' rankings of speed mirrored the measures of charging time. Complete data were obtained for a total of sixty-one athletes, both varsity and junior varsity players. Correlations were not reported by Miles but have been calculated here (using Spearman's rho) by using his tabular data: for centers, $r = -.30$ (n = 5); for guards, $r = .10$ (n = 9); for tackles, $r = .33$ (n = 9); for ends, $r = .36$ (n = 17); and for backs, $r = .01$ (n = 21). It would be unwise to make too much of these numbers, given that the sample sizes are small and the reaction time scores were based on a single trial. It is not known if Miles actually calculated the correlations, but even if he did not, just looking at the two sets of paired rankings would have told him that the correlations were low.

Apparently from eyeballing the discrepant rankings of his reaction time data and the coaches' subjective rankings of player speed, Miles concluded that quickness on one task did not indicate quickness on another. It is not known what criteria the coaches used in making their speed rankings. It could be argued that football charging has little to do with speed and much more to do with quickness. Thus low correlations between the two measures might have been expected.

Miles believed that his multiple chronograph was a valid instrument for determining charging speed of individual football players and also the uniformity of their charge. But he clearly recognized that there was much more involved in determining the quality of a lineman's play than those variables. Miles argued — in some ways similar to Bean's (1927) job analyses of athletes — that to measure successfully the ability of a player at any position, it would be necessary to understand the principal job components of that position and, if possible, to define them in ways that would allow them to be measured (Miles 1931). Miles, however, would not pursue such questions. The work with the 1927 Stanford team would be his final venture into sport psychology.

Reactions to the Stanford Studies

There is a meager record of Warner's reaction to the research of Miles and Graves. As noted earlier, Warner may have welcomed the research, believing that it might enhance his team in some way. The way in which psychology was being hyped to the American public in the 1920s might have led Warner to believe that psychology could be of help in football as well. If "welcome" is too strong a word, he at least permitted the research to be done.

During the course of the studies there were several newspaper articles that quoted Warner as supportive of the research and interested in its outcome.[4]

Further, incorporation of the research procedures into daily football practices indicated Warner's support for the psychologists' work. The description of the research procedure detailed in Miles and Graves (1931) indicates that the chronograph was located on the practice field and that measurements were facilitated by having the football players report to the apparatus in platoons during practice and lined up by a member of the coaching staff. Using precious practice time for data collection implies that Warner must have seen some potential value in the data. In a 1927 letter to Raymond Dodge Miles wrote that Warner was intrigued by the preliminary data he had collected on twenty-eight football players (from the study with Graves). He said that Warner "has insisted that I canvass and rate the whole fall squad in the same manner" and, commenting further about the work, added that "it is rather good fun, and I believe we can get some worth-while data."[5]

Whereas the data generated in Graves's thesis were very useful and certainly spoke to the arguments of the day on the nature of signal calling, the study conducted by Miles in 1927 proved to have very little value. Studying charging speed in relation to variations in signals made sense, but trying to use charging speed as a measure to rate other qualities of players had questionable validity. After the second study in 1927 Warner must have reached the conclusion that the data were not helpful to him. Perhaps he was concerned that Miles's data did not mesh with the evaluations of player speed made by his coaches. If he believed in the abilities of his coaches to evaluate players, then he might have viewed the discrepancies as evidence of the uselessness of Miles's measurements. Such an outcome is seen in other sport psychology research in which coaches and managers cooperated with eager psychologists only to lose interest when the results did not appear useful (Kroll 1971) or cooperated reluctantly or inconsistently with psychologists and then largely ignored their recommendations (Green 2003). There is no evidence that Miles was ever invited to work with the football team again.

After the publication of the two studies in 1931, Miles received letters of interest from football coaches, physical education faculty, graduate students interested in similar work, and others. Leo Harris, football coach at Fresno State College, inquired about the research.[6] Hugo Bezdek, football coach at Pennsylvania State College (as it was known then), also inquired about the studies.[7] (Bezdek is the only person ever to have served as manager of a Major League baseball team, the Pittsburgh Pirates, and head coach of a National Football League team, the Cleveland Rams.)

Some correspondents were especially interested in the multiple chronograph. Charles H. McCloy, a professor at the University of Iowa and a distinguished researcher in physical education (see English 1983; McCloy 1932), was interested in building the device.[8] Frank L. Kleeberger, director of physical education at the University of California–Berkeley, was interested in building the device and later apparently made Miles an offer to buy the one at Stanford.[9]

By the time much of this correspondence arrived on Miles's desk, he had moved from Stanford to Yale University, and all thoughts of pursuing any additional studies with his multiple chronograph were likely gone. Did anyone else take up the torch of football charging? A search of the literature in psychology and physical education turned up several studies that cited one or more of the Miles articles (see Keller 1942; Burley 1944). These were studies that principally dealt with reaction time in athletes and sometimes with measures of quickness. There were also two studies on football charging that referenced Miles, neither of which matched the complexity or sophistication of the Graves study (Elbel, Wilson, and French 1952; Thompson, Nagle, and Dobias 1958).

Even If You Build It, They May Not Come

Although Miles did not pursue further studies on the psychology of football after the 1927 research, there is evidence that he was not ready to be finished with his career in sport psychology, or at least he was not ready to store his football machine in the attic. In a 1928 letter to Thomas Storey, Director of Physical Education at Stanford, about his disappointment with the lack of further interest in his football studies, he wrote:

> I had hoped for something in the way of spontaneous cooperation on the part of the football men here at Stanford and I had the ambition that the use of such an outfit [the multiple chronograph] would give us some advantage in properly selecting men for teams and the like. . . . No request has come to me from any of the football men for advice or help or cooperation in making measurements. Please understand I am not criticising [sic] or complaining. I thought that if I developed an equipment suitable for field work, coaches might be keen for it. . . . Please consider this letter personal.[10]

Storey replied in a very supportive way, asking Miles to come visit with him. He wrote that "my interest in seeing you is to discuss with you some of our plans for the future. We expect to develop our own departmental program shortly in such a way that will probably lead to the development of research activities of our own."[11] Despite the apparent invitation, there is no record that Miles collaborated with Storey or anyone in his department in the four years that remained in his tenure at Stanford.

When Graves contacted Miles four years later, as Miles was preparing to move to Yale, Miles wrote about his attempts to get someone at Stanford interested in using the multiple chronograph:

During the summer I wrote Warner and hoped to locate someone who would be willing to make further studies with the football machine. However, it seemed impossible to discover any man who wanted to work out a thesis along those lines just a[t] present. Hence, the whole apparatus and project has been dormant practically since you were here . . . . So far, no member of the Physical Education Department here in Stanford has given any indication of wanting to carry through studies of this nature. I, personally, have only a few more months here at Stanford having accepted a Professorship at Yale.[12]

Pop Warner continued to have successful teams at Stanford. His 1926 team, which had worked with Miles and Graves, was undefeated with ten wins and tied Alabama in the Rose Bowl. The 1927 team that had worked with Miles, won the conference championship again and defeated Pittsburgh in the Rose Bowl. Indeed, Warner had a winning record every year in his tenure at Stanford. In 1933 he moved to Temple University where he coached until his retirement in 1938. He is perhaps best remembered today for the Pop Warner League, the youth football league that started in 1929 and was named for him in 1934. In 1997 the United States Postal Service issued a series of commemorative stamps honoring four legendary football coaches: George Halas, Bear Bryant, Vince Lombardi, and Pop Warner. Warner died in 1954 in Palo Alto, California.

B. C. Graves returned to Sul Ross in 1927 after completing his master's thesis. In 1932 in a letter to Miles he wrote about his desire for a position on a larger stage:

I suggested to Coach Pop Warner, last summer, the possibility of my returning to Stanford and doing some graduate work along the Football Test and under your direction and work under the Department of Psychology; that is, if some way might be worked out to meet my general expenses. I tried to point out my belief that such a test movement would enable Stanford to locate the best football material, and that my experience under Coach Warner within a year or two might enable me to locate some coaching job in a larger college than the one I am coaching in.[13]

He continued, saying that "my work in athletics since leaving Stanford has been on the whole fairly successful. With the exception of a year or two, my football teams and basketball teams have been champions and near champions; then on the other hand I have had my bad times. My main objective just now is to work into a coaching place in a larger college if I may so qualify."[14] But that was never to happen to Graves.

In 1940, after seventeen years as coach of the Lobos, Graves took a leave of absence from Sul Ross to establish a physical fitness program for the Army Air Force. When the United States entered World War II, he enlisted in the Navy and was discharged in 1946 as a Lieutenant Commander in the Naval Reserve. Upon his discharge he resigned from Sul Ross and accepted a position as a psychologist with the Veterans Administration (VA). He remained with the VA until 1958 when he returned to Sul Ross for one year to coach the football team. At the same time he completed his doctorate in clinical psychology at the University of Texas, receiving his PhD in 1959. He returned to work with the military, serving as chief psychologist with the Air Force in Amarillo, Texas. When the Air Force base closed there in 1967, Graves moved to a psychologist position with the Amarillo Hospital District, for whom he worked until his late seventies. In 1973 he was invited back to Sul Ross for the homecoming game in celebration of fifty years of football at the college. The welcoming crowd included many former players and teachers who were there to pay tribute to an individual who was evidently much admired for his work there (Casey 1975). Whether Graves ever pursued further development of his football test is unknown; we were not able to locate any published version of it or references to it (an unpublished version is located in the Miles Papers in Akron). He died in a nursing home in Amarillo in 1992.

Walter Miles retired from Yale University in 1953 when he reached the mandatory retirement age of sixty-eight. During his time at Yale he had made a number of research contributions, especially during World War II. One of his more important contributions was the recognition from his earlier studies on dark adaptation that red light did not interfere with such adaptation. Recalling that fact provided him with a crucial insight that led to the development of red goggles and the use of red lights in ready rooms, airplane cockpits, and lookout towers, where some measure of vision was needed in the workspace but maximal night vision could still be maintained.

After retirement from Yale Miles spent three years in Turkey establishing a psychological laboratory at the Turkish University in Istanbul. He concluded his career as Scientific Director of the Medical Research Laboratory at the U.S. Naval Submarine Base in Connecticut where he worked for eight years. There he investigated psychological problems associated with men being submerged for long periods of time in the new atomic submarines developed as part of the escalating Cold War (Miles 1967; Miller 1980). Assessing the morale of submariners was a long way from measuring football charging.

As noted earlier, Miles's interest in the psychology of football was stimulated wholly by Graves. The latter had spent three years coaching college football and another eight years or more playing that sport, most of that time as a quarterback. Both as quarterback and coach he would have been aware of the importance of players moving as quickly as possible on the snap signal. Indeed, signal calling was a prominent subject in the literature and locker room conversations on football in the 1920s. Our belief is that Graves went to Stanford in 1926 because Pop Warner was the coach.

Graves found Miles because he had planned to get his master's degree in psychology, and in Miles he found a psychologist who relished the kind of problem solving that Graves required. Nothing like the multiple chronograph had been devised before, and it is clear from both published and unpublished sources that Miles was especially proud of this invention.

It is doubtful that Miles knew the starting signal issues that were of interest to Graves — rhythm, anticipation, numbers versus words, single versus double digit numbers, and position in the signal-calling sequence. The plan for the study was probably worked out by Graves. Miles, as an experimental psychologist, devised the instrumentation and likely assisted in some of the design issues for the various signal conditions that Graves wanted to test. Graves's thesis was truly a rich study in terms of the number of independent and dependent variables studied (charging speed, uniformity of charge, and offside infractions), and the results offered some clear recommendations, depending on what a coach might want, that is, faster charging speeds, more uniformity of charge, and fewer offside penalties. In short, it was a very impressive study.

In that sense Graves's thesis stands in contrast to the football charging study that Miles conducted after the former left. Why is that? Miles was a better psychologist than demonstrated by the quality of his 1927 study. That would be evident to anyone who looks at much of his other research and is supported by his receipt of the Warren Medal from the Society of Experimental Psychologists and his election to the National Academy of Sciences. It is likely that Miles had very little interest in football charging. His interest was in building the elaborate and sophisticated piece of equipment that would allow Graves's questions to be answered. According to Goodwin (2003), Miles acquired "an aptitude for building apparatus [that] became a lifelong trait" (59). When Graves departed, Miles was left with the football machine that he had created. Although he valued the machine, he had little love for the work for which it was suited. And sadly he was unable to attract anyone else to use it.

Despite the fact that Miles was not committed as a sport psychologist, he would perhaps be surprised today at how his few contributions to that field have been ignored. We examined thirty-three sport psychology textbooks published between 1980 and 2002 looking for mentions of Coleman Griffith, Norman Triplett, and Walter Miles. The results were Griffith (twenty-two), Triplett (nineteen), and Miles (three).

These results are not surprising. Griffith spent about twenty years of his professional career as a sport psychologist, established a laboratory for that work, published much on the subject, and even consulted in the field of professional sports. Triplett has been given the title as the first psychologist to conduct research on sport, and virtually all mentions of him were in the context of that priority. Miles merely put his toe in the sport psychology water for a few minutes, and hardly anyone noticed. It is not the case, despite the claim of Gould and Pick (1995), that Miles attempted "to initiate a systematic research program in sport psychology . . . at Stanford University" (392). No such grand plan existed. Illustrative of Miles's further absence from the contemporary literature is an article that purports to be "a comprehensive [historical] review" of the sport psychology research on American football that makes no mention of Miles (Freudenberger and Bergandi 1994).

There is no mention of the football studies in an obituary of Miles by Neal Miller (1980); it is likely that Miller did not even know of the existence of the studies. Miles (1967) did write about them forty years later in his autobiographical chapter as follows: "B. Graves worked with me on research still mentioned in athletic circles. In this study we used a multiple chronograph on the football field for measuring the charging time of each of seven men in the line of players" (239). Notice that there was no mention of the signal-calling work. Moreover, there is certainly little evidence from the published record that the football studies were being talked about in the 1960s as the new field of sport psychology was emerging in America. Nor were they cited in subsequent years.

We examined 110 books on coaching football from 1947 to 2002, and only one included any mention of the Miles's or Graves's studies. That was a book — a booklet, really — titled *What Research Tells the Coach about Football* (1973), written by Roderick R. Paige, who served as President George W. Bush's secretary of education. Paige was formerly a coach at Texas Southern University at which the book was written. One of the sections in the book is on starting signals, and although several studies are cited, the bulk of the coverage is given to the Miles and Graves (1931) research. Paige (1973) cited his own doctoral dissertation (done in 1969) in this section; this dissertation was a study of "the effect of the length of time lineman are held at the ready position upon reaction" (1973, 21). Paige found that the optimum holding time for a lineman for the quickest reaction was two to four seconds. He wrote that "this finding concurs with that of Miles and Graves" (Paige 1973, 21).

In the other 109 books on football coaching, it was quite rare to find any references of any kind. Evidently football coaches pronounce; they do not reference others.

The issue of signal calling was not prominently featured in most of those coaching manuals. Instead, these books emphasized offensive and defensive formations and how to defend against particular offenses, particular plays, special teams, punt formations, quarterbacks reading defenses, and so forth.

Yet the topic was mentioned in many books, and it was given significant coverage in a few. For example, Charles "Bud" Wilkinson, who was the legendary coach at the University of Oklahoma from 1947 to 1963 and whose teams won three national championships and an incredible forty-seven games in a row, was unequivocal in his belief in the paramount importance of signal calling. Wilkinson (1952) wrote that "the *most important single fundamental* of offensive football, regardless of the system of play, is the starting count. One of the two basic advantages of the offense is knowing at *what instant* the ball will be snapped" (92). He was also quite clear on whether he valued speed off the ball or the unison of the charge: "If this advantage [of knowing the snap count] is to be utilized it is imperative that the members of the offensive team get away together by properly executing the starting count. A good start is achieved only if the entire offensive team moves as one man when the ball is snapped. The offensive team should be neither ahead of nor behind the ball. The play-ers must move *with* the ball. This requires constant practice and effective concentration" (92–93). Wilkinson (1952) believed that through practice, differential reaction times across players could be altered so that all players "develop nearly identical reaction times to a charge signal" (96). He concluded his chapter on the starting count by reminding the reader of the singular importance of signal calling: "We know of no other single fundamental of the game which will pay bigger dividends than proper execution of the starting count. It is worth many hours of practice time to the offensive team" (97).

That the 1927 study that Miles conducted on his own has been forgotten is no tragedy, yet the fact that the thesis study by Graves and Miles has also been forgotten is a different matter. It is one of the best pieces of research in the early history of sport psychol-ogy in America. It asked a very important question: what is the best system for calling signals? And it answered that question with an experimental design involving multiple independent and dependent variables that was sophisticated for its time. Further, it used a complicated and ingenious apparatus that illustrated the creativity of its designer, allowing not only the speed of the charge to be measured but the unison of the charge as well. Much of the richness of that study was clearly due to Graves, whose football background led him to understand the multiple issues inherent in signal calling. It was, however, also the product of involvement with a talented experimental psychologist. In that sense it represents the best of collaborative work between scientist and coach. It is a contribution that arguably merits a place in the history of sport psychology.

Notes

This chapter was adapted from F. G. Baugh and L. T. Benjamin, Jr., "Walter Miles, Pop Warner, B. C. Graves, and the Psychology of Football," *Journal of the History of the Behavioral Sciences* 42 (2006): 3–18.

1 B. C. Graves, n.d. (1973 or later), Archives of the Big Bend, Bryan Wildenthal Memorial Library, Sul Ross State University, Alpine TX.

2 Graves to W. R. Miles, February 3, 1932, Miles Papers, Archives of the History of American Psychology, University of Akron, Akron OH.

3 Miles to Graves, February 19, 1932, Miles Papers.

4 "Pop Warner Has New Pet: Machine Tabs Chargers," *San Francisco Chronicle*, September 28, 1927, and "This Machine Tells How Fast Grid Players Move," unidentified newspaper, n.d., Miles Papers.

5 Miles to R. Dodge, September 7, 1927, Miles Papers.

6 L. Harris to Miles, n.d. (Miles's reply is dated March 31, 1933), Miles Papers.

7 H. Bezdek to Miles, February 23, 1933, Miles Papers.

8 Miles to C. H. McCloy, March 31, 1933, Miles Papers.

9 Miles to T. A. Storey, December 14, 1928, and Miles to Graves, February 19, 1932, Miles Papers.

10 Miles to Storey, December 14, 1928, Miles Papers.

11 Storey to Miles, December 18, 1928, Miles Papers.

12 Miles to Graves, February 19, 1932, Miles Papers.

13 Graves to Miles, February 3, 1932, Miles Papers.
14 Graves to Miles, February 3, 1932, Miles Papers.

References

Anonymous. 1926. Coach Graves leaves an enviable record. *Sul Ross Skyline* 1.

————. 1973. Coach. *Sul Ross Alumni News* 4 (1): 2–3.

Bean, C. H. 1927. Job-analyzing athletes. *Journal of Applied Psychology* 11:369–80.

Boring, E. G. 1950. *A history of experimental psychology.* 2nd ed. New York: Appleton-Century-Crofts.

Burley, L. R. 1944. A study of the reaction time of physically trained men. *Research Quarterly of the American Association for Health, Physical Education, and Recreation* 15:232–39.

Burtt, H. E., and J. H. Nichols. 1924. Intelligence of varsity athletes. *American Physical Education Review* 29:125–28.

Burtt, H. E., and S. L. Pressey. 1957. Henry Herbert Goddard: 1866–1957. *American Journal of Psychology* 70:656–57.

Casey, C. B. 1975. *Sul Ross State University, the cultural center of trans-Pecos Texas: 1917–1975.* Seagraves TX: Pioneer.

Cattell, J. M. 1886. The time it takes to see and name objects. *Mind* 11:63–65.

Elbel, E. R., D. Wilson, and C. French. 1952. Measuring speed and force of charge of football players. *Research Quarterly of the American Association for Health, Physical Education, and Recreation* 23:295–300.

English, E. B. 1983. Charles H. McCloy: The research professor of physical education. *Journal of Physical Education, Recreation, and Dance* 54:16–18.

Freudenberger, L. F., and T. A. Bergandi. 1994. Sport psychology research in American football: A review of the literature. *International Journal of Sport Psychology* 25:425–34.

Goodwin, C. J. 2003. An insider's look at experimental psychology in America. In *Thick description and fine texture: Studies in the history of psychology,* ed. D. B. Baker, 57–75. Akron: University of Akron Press.

Gould, D., and S. Pick. 1995. Sport psychology: The Griffith era, 1920–1940. *Sport Psychologist* 9:391–405.

Graves, B. C. 1927. The effect of signal variation on speed and uniformity of football charging. Master's thesis, Stanford University.

Green, C. D. 2003. Psychology strikes out: Coleman R. Griffith and the Chicago Cubs. *History of Psychology* 6:267–83.

Griffith, C. R. 1925. Psychology and its relation to athletic competition. *American Physical Education Review* 30:193–99.

———. 1926. *Psychology of coaching.* New York: Scribner.

———. 1928. *Psychology and athletics: A general survey for athletes and coaches.* New York: Scribner.

Heisman, J. W. 1922. *Principles of football.* St. Louis: Sports Publishing Bureau.

Keller, L. F. 1942. The relation of "quickness of bodily movement" to success in athletics. *Research Quarterly of the American Association for Health, Physical Education and Recreation* 13:146–55.

Kroll, W. 1971. *Perspectives in physical education.* New York: Academic Press.

LeUnes, A. D. 2009. *Sport psychology.* 4th ed. New York: Francis and Taylor.

Liss, H. 1975. *They changed the game: Football's great coaches, players, and games.* New York: Lippincott.

McCloy, C. H. 1932. *The measurement of athletic power: Some achievement standards in track and field athletic events for boys from ten to twenty years of age.* New York: Barnes.

Miles, W. R. 1928a. How fast can you "get away"? *Scientific American,* March.

———. 1928b. Studies on physical exertion: I; A multiple chronograph for measuring groups of men. *American Physical Education Review* 33:379–87.

———. 1931. Studies in physical exertion: II; Individual and group reaction time in football charging. *Research Quarterly* 2 (3): 5–13.

———. 1967. Walter R. Miles. In *A history of psychology in autobiography,* ed. E. G. Boring and G. Lindzey, 223–52. Vol. 5. New York: Appleton-Century-Crofts.

Miles, W. R., and B. C. Graves. 1931. Studies in physical exertion: III; Effect of signal variation on football charging. *Research Quarterly* 2 (3): 14–31.

Miller, N. E. 1980. Obituary: Walter R. Miles (1885–1978). *American Psychologist* 35:595–96.

Paige, R. R. 1969. The effect of pre-foreperiod preparation and foreperiod duration upon the response time of football lineman. PhD diss., Indiana University.

————. 1973. *What research tells the coach about football.* Washington DC: American Association for Health, Physical Education, and Recreation.

Park, R. J. 1984. From football to rugby — and back, 1906–1919: The University of California–Stanford University response to the "football crisis of 1905." *Journal of Sport History* 11:5–40.

Paterson, D. G., and I. E. Peterson. 1928. Athletics and scholarship. *University of Minnesota Department of Physical Education Research Bulletin* 1:1–16.

Patrick, G. T. W. 1903. The psychology of football. *American Journal of Psychology* 14:104–17.

Perrin, T. 1987. *Football: A college history.* Jefferson NC: McFarland.

Pierson, D. 1974. *The Trojans: Southern California football.* Chicago: Regnery.

Pope, E. 1955. *Football's greatest coaches.* Atlanta: Tuffer and Love.

Rappoport, K. 1974. *The Trojans: A story of Southern California football.* Huntsville AL: Strode.

Rockne, K. 1925. *Coaching.* New York: Devin-Adair.

Ruble, V. W. 1928. A psychological study of athletes. *American Physical Education Review* 33:219–34.

Sarup, G. 1978. Historical antecedents of psychology: The recurrent issue of old wine in new bottles. *American Psychologist* 33:478–85.

Smith, R. A. 1981. Harvard and Columbia and a reconsideration of the 1905–06 football crisis. *Journal of Sport History* 8:5–19.

Thompson, C. W., F. J. Nagle, and R. Dobias. 1958. Football starting signals and movement times of high school and college football players. *Research Quarterly of the American Association for Health, Physical Education, and Recreation* 29:222–30.

Triplett, N. 1898. The dynamogenic factors in pacemaking and competition. *American Journal of Psychology* 9:507–33.

Warner, G. S. 1927. *Football for coaches and players*. Stanford CA: Stanford University.

Watterson, J. S. 1981. The football crisis of 1909–1910: The response of the eastern "big three." *Journal of Sport History* 7:33–49.

———. 2002. *College football: History, spectacle, controversy*. Baltimore MD: Johns Hopkins University Press.

Wiggam, A. E. 1928. *Exploring your mind with the psychologists*. New York: Bobbs Merrill.

Wilkinson, C. B. 1952. *Oklahoma split T football*. New York: Prentice-Hall.

Woodworth, R. S. 1938. *Experimental psychology*. New York: Holt.

Zenderland, L. 1998. *Measuring minds: Henry Herbert Goddard and the origins of American intelligence testing*. New York: Cambridge University Press.

Zuppke, R. C. 1924. *Football techniques and tactics*. 2nd ed. Champaign IL: Bailey and Himes.

7

COLEMAN ROBERTS GRIFFITH

"FATHER" OF NORTH AMERICAN SPORT PSYCHOLOGY

Christopher D. Green

Coleman Griffith is often described as the father of North American sports psychology. Like many historical fathers and firsts, however, the matter is complicated by the definitions and criteria one uses. Griffith was not directly connected to the self-conscious discipline of sport psychology that arose in the 1960s, although many of the leaders of that movement paid their respects to Griffith's work as they themselves assembled the institutional apparatus that a discipline needs in order to take its place in the academic community. Nevertheless, Griffith's contributions to the psychological study of sport were significant. They break into two broad phases. First is his establishment of a laboratory specifically for the study of the psychology of sport in the late 1920s and early 1930s. Second, after a break of several years, was his work as a paid psychologist with the Chicago Cubs baseball club in the late 1930s. These two phases of Griffith's long career are the main foci of this chapter.

Griffith's Early Life and Career

Griffith was born in Iowa, but his family moved widely during his childhood, including among their temporary homes California, South Dakota, and Illinois.[1] In 1911 he entered Greenville College in Illinois, graduating in 1915. He was devoted to athletics and outdoor activities.[2] A year after leaving Greenville, he began graduate school at the University of Illinois under the supervision of Madison Bentley (1870–1955).[3]

At the American entry into World War I, only a year after Griffith's arrival at Illinois, Bentley volunteered for the Air Corps, for which he conducted research on the vestibular organs of the ear. Naturally, much of Griffith's graduate research was in a similar area, although there is no evidence that he had an interest in balance prior to his arrival at Bentley's laboratory.

Griffith emerged as a significant scholar in his own right about 1920. In January he was elected a member of the American Association for the Advancement of Science. In May he defended his doctoral dissertation and over the course of the year produced six journal articles about the impact on rats' sense of balance when raising them on a rotating platform. Bentley, who edited the *Psychological Index*, appointed Griffith to the post of assistant editor, and the university promoted Griffith from an assistant to an instructor.[4]

Surviving letters from Griffith to his students show him to have been a man with a wry sense of humor, as he always prodded them to do better. To one he wrote that "someone is always taking the joy out of life. Your Mathematics 4 seems to be the offender this time. . . . Suppose you try an extra fifteen minutes a day."[5] To another he remarked that "I see by your report for the first six weeks that you have been applying the principles of economics to the time you spend studying Economics 8. I wonder if you couldn't spend a little more time on Economics and remove the only bad mark against you."[6]

The year 1922 saw the publication of Griffith's first book, *An Historical Survey of Vestibular Equilibration* (1922). He also showed his penchant for technological innovation by employing in his study of disequilibrated rats ultra-rapid moving pictures, a technique he would later bring to the field of sport. His reputation growing, Griffith was courted by a variety of midwestern universities. In order to keep him at Illinois, Griffith was promoted to assistant professor, was appointed to the graduate faculty, and was made acting head of the department during Bentley's sabbatical of 1922–23. In addition, Bentley appointed him acting editor of the *Psychological Index*. Griffith had written a textbook on psychology that had sold over one thousand copies in privately mimeographed form over the previous few years.[7] By the end of 1922 he found a publisher, and the book appeared the following year under the title *General Introduction to Psychology* (1923). According to Griffith, it was immediately adopted by 125 colleges and universities.

The Athletics Research Laboratory

Griffith was already developing a new research program that would occupy the next decade of his life. Since 1918 he had been conducting psychological research, still unpublished, on athletes. The exact nature of these studies is not clear, but Griffith would later write that he began with "problems of vision and shifting attention" and "passing notice . . . of those shifting moods and attitudes which go so far toward keeping men on a winning streak or beguiling them into an unexpected defeat" (Griffith 1930, 35). By 1920 he was lugging a "Sanborn reaction time outfit" to the football field to test players' quickness.[8] Perhaps not surprisingly, he found that when practice squads were organized around the results of these tests, the squads with lower reaction times were more successful on the field. Naturally this finding caught the attention of Illinois football coach Robert Zuppke and Director of Athletics George Huff. A special section of Griffith's introductory psychology course was soon organized exclusively for athletes. In late 1921 he gave what appears to have been his first public talk on psychology and athletics at a meeting of a local honorary psychology fraternity called Psi Xi.[9] By early 1922 Griffith's work on athletics had already begun to attract national attention, meriting a short piece in the *New York Times* (April 22, 1922). In 1923 he offered a new course called Psychology and Athletics (Griffith 1930). The material for this course soon became the basis of Griffith's third book, *Psychology of Coaching* (1926).

Late in 1924 Griffith began a correspondence with Knute Rockne about the psychological side of coaching. Among the psychologist's questions for Notre Dame's legendary football coach was: Do you "key up" players before games, or just select those who "play the game joyously for its own sake"?[10] This exchange seems to have prompted Griffith to write to college football coaches all over the midwestern and northeastern United States asking them similar questions.[11]

The year 1925 saw the appearance of Griffith's "Psychology and Its Relation to Athletic Competition," his first published article on the psychology of sport. Interestingly, the basis of Griffith's appeal to coaches — here and throughout his career — was essentially moral in character rather than psychological. Griffith's "fundamental proposition" was that "the more mind is made use of in athletic competition, the greater will be the skill of our athletes, the finer will be the contest, the higher will be the ideals of sportsmanship displayed, the longer will our games persist in our national life, and the more truly will they lead to those rich personal and social products which we ought to expect of them" (Griffith 1925, 193). Rather than simply laying out ways in which coaches could use psychological knowledge to improve their athletes' performance, Griffith placed the question of the justification of athletics in the college context frequently at the center of his message: "Competition does justify itself because the football field is the place where morale, spirit, courage, honor, sportsmanship, fair play, team work, and the like, are directly taught. We do not learn these things in our courses in mathematics, English, or history" (Griffith 1925, 198).

This approach was apparently much to the liking of the university's director of athletics, George Huff, who proposed the founding of a laboratory dedicated specifically to athletic research with Griffith as the director. The board of trustees approved his plan in September of 1925, and Griffith's laboratory, the first of its kind in North America, came into being. It is worth noting, however, that in this same year the university constructed an enormous new athletic complex of which Griffith's facility seems to have been just one part (White 1926). Griffith's lab was not the first in the world. About a year earlier Robert Werner Schulte, founded a laboratory in Berlin for the "psycho-technical study of gymnastics, games, and sports" (Schulte 1925, cited in Bäumler 1997, 488; see also Bäumler, this volume).[12]

Along with the directorship of the new laboratory, Griffith was promoted to associate professor, and his appointment assigned to the College of Education rather than to the Department of Psychology. Lists of many possible research programs for the laboratory were rapidly drawn up. The research was to involve everything from studies of general health and conditioning to habit learning and the effects of stress on athletic performance. The sports to be studied included basketball, soccer, gymnastics, baseball, football, track, golf, swimming, and diving. Before the lab had published any research results, however, Griffith won a prestigious Guggenheim Fellowship to study in Germany for a year. Although he initially won the award in 1925, he appears to have delayed taking the trip for a year in order to get the new laboratory up and running.[13] Griffith proposed an extensive and detailed itinerary for his German study trip. Interestingly, however, there is no indication that he attempted to meet Schulte or to visit the latter's sport laboratory while in Berlin.

Griffith returned to Illinois in 1927, but it was not until the following year that he began to publish again (except Griffith 1927). The most important of these new works was his fourth book, *Psychology and Athletics* (1928a), although it was not based on research done in his new laboratory. He had written it before the laboratory opened, and it had been circulating in mimeographed form since about 1924. Both Macmillan, the publisher of his general textbook, and Knopf had declined to publish it, expressing doubts that it would sell well.[14] It was ultimately published by Scribner's, who had brought out Griffith's book on coaching two years earlier. He also published a minor piece on high school pep sessions (Griffith 1928b).

In 1928 Griffith published the first of eight articles in the *Athletic Journal*, a periodical worthy of some attention. Founded by a midwesterner named John L. Griffith, the *Athletic Journal* described itself as a national magazine for coaches. Along with John Griffith's editorials, it was filled mainly with news of college athletic programs around the country and with articles by coaches about new types of plays and strategies in a variety of sports. No apparent relation to Coleman Griffith, John Griffith had been born in Illinois in 1880 and educated at Beloit College in Wisconsin, from which he graduated in 1902. In 1908 he became a history teacher, athletic director, and football and track coach at Drake University in Des Moines, Iowa. Here he became a vocal promoter of intercollegiate sports. After serving in World War I, he became athletic director at the University of Illinois, where in 1920 he started the *Athletic Journal*. In June 1922 John Griffith was invited to head the Big Ten intercollegiate athletic conference, a position he would hold until his death in 1944.[15] He left Urbana to take up his new duties in Chicago; he also took the journal with him.

The two Griffiths almost certainly knew each other well, and the younger Griffith contributed regularly to the older Griffith's journal in the role of scientist among coaches. None of Coleman Griffith's many contributions to *Athletic Journal* took the form of research reports. They seem, rather to have been attempts to bring the *conclusions* of his research and his psychological wisdom directly to coaches. Strangely, however, it does not appear that full scientific reports of Griffith's laboratory research were published anywhere.

Although Griffith's total publication output in these years was prodigious, the character of his publications showed a marked change from earlier in his career. Griffith's appearance in *scientific* journals shows a sharp decline in the late 1920s and early 1930s in favor of less academic magazines. Even when he did publish in scholarly journals, his contributions were usually literature reviews (Griffith 1929, 1932), book reviews (Griffith 1931b), or very short technical pieces (Griffith 1931a, 1931b; Griffith and Eddy 1931) rather than reports on original research. It is not clear whether this shift was the result of the scientific journals of the day being unwilling to publish his work on the psychology of sport or whether it reflected a conscious effort on Griffith's part to bring his ideas about athletics directly to the coaches. Griffith did do some scientific reporting as in 1930 when five two-page reports that seem to describe research conducted in the Athletics Research Laboratory appeared in the *Proceedings of the IXth International Congress of Psychology*, but none seems to have ultimately been developed into journal articles.[16]

One of the more striking aspects of the curriculum vitae contained in Griffith's papers is that no fewer than seven books were characterized by Griffith as "contracted for and undergoing final editing for the press," and another six were said to be "contracted for and in active preparation."[17] Of these thirteen book projects no more than four — two textbooks on applied psychology, another on educational psychology, and his major work on systematic psychology — ever made it into print. Four of the books listed were to have been on topics related to sport, including a book on football coauthored by Illinois football coach Robert Zuppke.[18] None of these ever appeared in print, however.

Although Griffith and his students seem to have been quite active — six MA theses had been completed by about 1931 and three more were in progress — there appears to have been some serious snag along the path to founding the new discipline of sport psychology.[19] Although Griffith published two books on the topic (1926, 1928a), few of his articles on the topic, as noted above, appeared in traditional academic journals. Nor were there any new doctorates to set up their own laboratories elsewhere, generate their own research, and graduate their own students.[20] Thus the critical mass necessary for the founding of a journal dedicated to the psychology of sport, often the sign that a discipline has arrived, did not occur until decades later, and it did so under the leadership of other individuals.

In 1932, just seven years after it had opened, Griffith's laboratory was closed by the university. There have been two stories told about why this closing occurred. One is that with the onset of the Great Depression shrinking revenues forced the university to cut back, and Griffith's laboratory was simply one of the victims (Seidler 1948, cited in Kroll and Lewis [1970] 1978). The other story is that his research program had lost the confidence of Coach Zuppke (Kroll 1971, cited in Gould and Pick 1995). Whatever the reason, Griffith was shifted to an administrative post, director of the Bureau of Institutional Research, who reported to the university president. Although Griffith seems to have taken to his new duties zealously, he continued to find the time to publish four more books over a nine-year period: *Introduction to Applied Psychology* (1934), *Introduction to Educational Psychology* (1935), *Psychology Applied to Teaching and Learning* (1939), and *Principles of Systematic Psychology* (1943). Over the course of these four books — nearly 2,700 published pages — one can see Griffith's interest in sport psychology waning.

The Chicago Cubs

There would be one more serious attempt by Griffith to bring psychological insight to the field of sport. The opportunity came when Philip Knight Wrigley, the gum magnate and owner of the Chicago Cubs Baseball Club, contracted Griffith in late 1937 to work with the Cubs during the 1938 season. Wrigley had long been an advocate of the application of technology and science to business. He was among the first to invest heavily in factory automation when he became president of his father's gum company in 1925. He would later be among the first to bring in computers for staff and accounting work (Furlong 1969, 29). In the 1940s he used the results of empirical research into the psychological benefits of gum chewing to convince the U.S. Army to include his gum in the K rations of every U.S. soldier sent overseas during World War II.[21] He labored as well to convince American business leaders that it was their patriotic duty to supply his gum to their workers.

It seems that Wrigley thought that science might be able to solve his problems with the Cubs as well, so he called upon Griffith. In 1932 Wrigley had inherited the Cubs upon the death of his father William Wrigley Jr. The Cubs had done well under the elder Wrigley's leadership and continued to do so for a few years under the son, going to the World Series in 1932 and 1935. The younger Wrigley was not, however, much of a baseball man. He believed that he could build a loyal following for the team by enhancing the experience of being at the ballpark rather than by investing in good players. In 1937 he installed the now famous ivy on the outfield wall of Wrigley Field, the Cubs' home park. He also tried to plant trees along the back of the bleachers as well, but they were quickly killed by the notorious winds of Chicago.

So, partly because of Wrigley's failure to acquire players that would make the Cubs a winner, the team faltered after 1935. Hiring Griffith was, of course, much less expensive than paying top-notch players. Unfortunately, for Griffith, Wrigley had a reputation as a bit of a crank. For instance, in the early 1930s he hired an "evil-eye" to lay curses on opposing teams (Veeck 1962, 40–46). This aspect of Wrigley's character may have undermined the team's confidence in Griffith from the outset.

Nevertheless, Griffith went right to work, dubbing the project Experimental Laboratories of the Chicago National League Ball Club and ordering over $1,500 worth of equipment. This sum included $350 for a chronoscope and almost $600 for a slow-motion movie setup. Griffith hired an assistant, John E. Sterrett (d. 1984), who had earned an MA from the University of Iowa Athletics Department in 1934 and then coached football and basketball at St. Thomas and Bemidji State universities, both in Minnesota.[22] The two men attended spring training with the team on Santa Catalina Island.

The clash of cultures between the players and the professor seems to have been almost immediate. Whatever success Griffith might have had with college athletes, it was not to be repeated with the Cubs. In the main during this period, professional baseball was not a sport played by college-educated men. Managers were often still players, not much older than those they managed. They had some authority to be sure, but there were rarely complex game plans. Practices were relatively haphazard affairs: running, slapping some fat pitches into the outfield, shagging some fly balls, and picking up some easy grounders. The use of carefully researched skill-development drills was almost unheard of, especially with the Cubs.

In particular, Charlie Grimm, the moody manager of the Cubs, would have little to do with the "headshrinker" from Urbana (Angle 1975, 65). Grimm had been with the Cubs as a player since 1925. He replaced future Hall-of-Famer Rogers Hornsby as manager in 1932. He retired from playing in 1936 but stayed on as manager. He was known for his good humor but 1937 had been a stressful year for him. Cubs player Phil Cavarretta said that Grimm "seemed to be losing his drive as far as the game was concerned" (cited in Golenbock 1996, 259). Indeed, Grimm's disposition deteriorated to the point that he was temporarily replaced by catcher Gabby Hartnett for the final few weeks of the season. Grimm returned in 1938, but he was no longer the "Jolly Cholly" of times past.

In the spring of 1938 Griffith and Sterrett took their measurements and shot their films. Unfortunately, neither the raw data nor the films still exist. What remains is a set of sixteen short reports that Griffith and Sterrett wrote over the course of the 1938 season; a 183-page General Report, reviewing the whole campaign, written by Griffith, and a set of detailed reports on the batting performances of nine players during the 1938 season.[23] The General Report includes many excerpts from a no-longer-extant series of confidential reports that Sterrett wrote to Griffith during the year. In addition, there are four short reports by Griffith from the 1939 season and one from the 1940 season.[24]

Griffith submitted his first report, "The Psychological Point of View," to Wrigley in March 1938. He asserted that "every human being . . . is a psychologist simply because [of] the adjustments he makes to other people and the adjustments they make to him."[25] Therefore, he continued, the baseball manager is a psychologist whether he knows it or not because it is his job to "handle men." The players are psychologists too in that they must interact with the manager, the coaches, and each other. The only question, according to Griffith, is whether the team members use psychology effectively or not. A professional psychologist differs only in that he makes it his business to "know more about human nature than other people know."[26] By learning a thing or two from the psychologist about how to interact with others, the members of a team can come to work better as a unit. It is interesting to note how little this appeal had to do with the perceptual and psychomotor aspects of the game implied by his use of the chronoscope and movie equipment. Instead, it was more about the social psychology of teams.

Whatever Griffith's motives may have been, his attempt to draw Grimm into the circle of "psychologists" did not take, and perhaps the attempt made Grimm defensive. On April 26 Sterrett wrote Griffith, "I am convinced that Grimm is knocking our work as much as he can. Everything we say or do is reported to him and these are, in turn, passed on to the players. Grimm said to one of the players that he was afraid we might say or do something worthwhile and that if the players or the head office knew about it, it would put him in a bad light."[27]

The Cubs got off to a terrible start in 1938, and there was talk of Grimm being replaced by one of the players. Morale on the team was low and factionalism was high as Hartnett tried to position himself to take over when Grimm's fall finally came. During the first week of May, however, Wrigley surprised everyone by purchasing the popular pitcher Dizzy Dean from the St. Louis Cardinals. Most insiders knew that Dean's best days were behind him, but he brought a certain star quality to the Cubs that lifted spirits for a time.

Griffith and Sterrett wrote four more reports during May. The first was about the difference between what Griffith called physiological and practical limits.[28] The main ideas here were drawn almost directly from a passage in *Psychology and Athletics* (Griffith 1928a, 86–90). Contrary to what coaches often assume, Griffith argued, Major League players have not reached the performance limits of the bodies. They have reached only the limits allowed by the regimen of practice in which they are currently engaged. A better practice regimen would enable players to achieve better performance. Griffith also recommended the use of charts, diagrams, and films to help the players measure their progress over time, a theme that would recur often in Griffith's reports.

In the second May report Griffith recommended ways to make morning practices more effective — by improving skills rather than simply maintaining them.[29] He made several recommendations: (a) the distance between batter and fielder when playing "pepper" should be gradually shortened in order to improve reaction times; (b) batting practice should be organized around complete at bats in order to practice anticipating what the next pitch will be in various ball-strike counts; (c) players should have to run out hits during batting practice in order to automatize the action of getting down the line to first base; (d) practice bunting should be done more often; and (e) a batter should be included in pitching practice to make the situation more realistic.[30]

In the third report Griffith argued that slowly practicing the correct form of an action such as swinging a bat yields little benefit if, once learned, it is not afterward also practiced repeatedly at full speed.[31] Finally, in the fourth May report, Griffith proposed the construction of an extensive series of achievement tests for measuring the speed, strength, coordination, accuracy, and visual judgment of players' basic skills.[32] In an additional mid-June report Griffith made recommendations for infield practice.[33] He argued that fielding errors in games can damage the confidence of the player involved by subconsciously affecting his performance for many days afterward.

Apparently none of this advice was implemented, and Griffith's frustration boiled over in a July 1 report in which he denounced the Catalina Island sessions for having been "aimless, disorganized, and unproductive." In one of the very few actual measurements to appear in the entire set of reports, he claimed that only 47.8 minutes per day were spent on practice "effective for the playing of baseball."[34] The rest ("2 hours, 47 minutes per man per day") was wasted on diversions such as "pepper games, side line watching and coaching, running, and similar activities."[35] Apparently attempting to appeal to Wrigley's business sense, he argued that productivity should be demanded in baseball as in any other business, such as the *gum business*, he pointedly noted. He made a number of recommendations for the 1939 spring training session, many of which employed the phrase "the manager should." Griffith's criticism of Grimm was becoming sharper.

Through May and June Sterrett's disapproval of Grimm grew as well. On May 19 Sterrett wrote to Griffith that "Grimm is not using the right method with [backup catcher Ken] O'Dea. . . . Grimm adds to [O'Dea's] worries by yelling at him."[36] On May 23 he reported that "Grimm does not understand his men" and on June 14 that "Charlie knows how to play the game and he would make a good manager if he would . . . spend less time mooning about the defeats."[37] Grimm fought back. On June 21 Sterrett wrote to Griffith that "Grimm has not been convinced by any of our work and is doing his best to undermine it" and on June 26 that Grimm would not let the players watch the films that had been taken of their performances.[38]

On July 10 Griffith filed two more reports with Wrigley, one on the improvement of pitching practice and one on ways to make the conditions that prevail during practices more similar to game conditions: "One of the best attitudes for the actual playing of the game is expressed by the phrase, 'the will to win.' . . . This phrase means, of course, different things to different men, but each man can find out what it means for him. . . . What is still more important, — he should make it a necessary feature of every practice period and of every game he plays. He must reduce it to a habit."[39] Taking yet another swipe at Grimm, Griffith quipped that "any manager who is any good at all will study situations of this sort. . . . [He must] find an attitude during practice that can be carried over into the game."[40]

As it turned out, Griffith and Sterrett were not the only ones unhappy with Grimm. In mid-July the Cubs were in fourth place, and before the end of the month Grimm was replaced by the catcher and future Hall-of-Famer Gabby Hartnett. There was an immediate improvement both in the team's performance and in the players' attitudes toward the researchers. Sterrett wrote to Griffith that "I thought I enjoyed the confidence of the players one hundred percent, but it was only one-tenth of what I am getting now. . . . None of the players wanted to be seen talking to me, if Grimm were around."[41] On July 30 he reported that, unlike Grimm, Hartnett met with him nearly every day to discuss instruction of the players.[42] In mid-August, however, Sterrett abruptly resigned from the project, apparently to take a position as basketball coach at St. Louis University, leaving Griffith to complete the season alone.[43]

Early in August Griffith filed two more reports, one on how to improve the fielding practice game pepper and one titled "Instinct in Baseball." The latter is interesting because it shows a strong behavioristic streak not apparent in Griffith's previous writings.[44] Because most players believe that skill is a matter of instinct rather than learning, he began, there is only a "small amount of teaching or learning in professional baseball."[45] Continuing, Griffith wrote that "the word 'instinct' has almost gone out of use by those whose business it is to know such things, for the simple reason that it doesn't mean anything."[46] He concluded that "to appeal to instinct or to heredity is, therefore, a lazy, unimaginative and ignorant man's way of evading the demands of his job."[47]

September saw three more reports: one on improving training setups, one on better batting practice, and one on revised scouting procedures based on tests and drills. September also saw dramatic improvement in the team's performance. Near the end of a whole month of good play, on the evening of September 28, with daylight fading at the end of a crucial game against the league-leading Pittsburgh Pirates, Hartnett hit the famous "Homer in the Gloamin'" to win the game and propel the Cubs into first place with only a few days left in the season. They would go on to win the National League pennant, but they then faced the powerful New York Yankees. Not unexpectedly, the Yankees swept the Cubs in four games. Hartnett remained a hero with the fans for having led the Cubs as far as he did, but on the train back from New York he reportedly undermined his position with his players by threatening to trade them all before the next season for having lost the championship.

In his year-end General Report to Wrigley, Griffith wrote that Hartnett "was not at all a smart man. . . . Not a teacher nor would he have the ability to adapt himself to any other style of training and coaching but that with which he had been familiar throughout his playing career."[48] Even if Wrigley had wanted to fire Hartnett, and there was some indication that he did, it would have been terribly unpopular with the fans.[49]

Griffith's year-end General Report reviewed the season as a whole in detail. It summarized individually the performance of each player and made recommendations about whether each should be kept or traded. Among the plethora of special problems touched on were the influence of gossip on morale, the dynamics of cliques among players, the effect that the presence of the players' wives at games had on the players' performances, and how the belief in "baseball magic" that was widespread among the players undermined Griffith's attempts to put the game on a more scientific footing. The General Report also made public relations recommendations, reporting on a survey of three hundred fans that was conducted to discover their reasons for following baseball and for attending Cubs games. Focusing on "deep" psychological aspects of the matter, Griffith began by explaining that "both men and women who, because of lack of time or lack of ability, cannot achieve success in their own work, will compensate for their failure or for their fatigue, by trying to associate themselves, either in direct friendship or in a remoter association, with someone who is successful."[50] He referred to this phenomenon as identification. Bringing this general analysis to bear on the matter of the Cubs' success with fans, he reported that "about 72% [of the Cubs fans surveyed] frankly confessed the motive of identification as the basis of their own preference for the Cubs."[51]

It is often reported that Griffith's project with the Cubs ended here, but this is not the case.[52] In February and March of 1939 Griffith submitted reports on the batting performances of nine players. Three had played with the Cubs in 1938, three had been acquired by the Cubs from other teams during the off-season, and three had been released by the Cubs. The level of detail presented in these reports, which totaled over two hundred typed pages, was extraordinary. For example Griffith wrote the following:

> During the 1938 season Cavarretta faced [New York Giants pitcher Harry] Gumbert 15 times in six games. Gumbert delivered 23 pitches to the strike area, 27 to the ball area, for an average of 3.3 pitches per time at bat. Thirty four of the pitches were fast, 16 were curves, and there were no slow balls. . . . Gumbert work[ed] Cavarretta around most of the pitching area. In the strike area low and inside Cavarretta hit two curves and a fast pitch for outs, hit a fast pitch for a safe hit, and let four fast pitches go for called strikes. In the ball area of this section he hit a fast pitch for a hit. He was hit by a curve ball and took seven other pitches for called balls. In the strike area low and outside.[53]

And the report continues in this fashion for each of the nine batters, crossed with every pitcher each of them faced during the entire season.

Here we find an obvious failure of Griffith's analysis of players.

In a number of places, including in the player reports, Griffith concluded that Phil Cavarretta was a player without very much potential whom the Cubs might do well to rid themselves of. Contrary to Griffith's prediction, however, Cavarretta would soon become a fixture on the Cubs, serving as a starting first baseman and outfielder though the 1940s. He was a National League All-Star every year from 1944 to 1947, and the National League's Most Valuable Player in 1945. He would later go on to manage the Cubs from 1951 to 1953. Thus, despite what Griffith claimed to be his chief area of expertise, it appears he was neither able to detect Cavarretta's underlying talent nor bring that potential to fruition through his various drills and training regimens.

Nevertheless, Wrigley was sufficiently impressed with the 1938 project that he offered Griffith a full-time position for the 1939 season. Griffith refused it so that he did not have to move his family to Chicago.[54] He stayed on part time with the Cubs, however. Some of the players seem to have come to appreciate Griffith's efforts as well. Pitcher Bill Lee, for instance, who led the National League in both wins (twenty-two) and earned run average (2.66) in 1938, bought Griffith a new set of golf clubs as thanks for the work he and Sterrett had done with Lee using the films of his pitching motion.[55]

As the 1939 season began, it soon became clear that the Cubs were not up for a repeat of their 1938 performance. They quickly settled into the middle of the pack in the standings and stayed there all season, finishing fourth. Tensions on the team began to build as Hartnett, not being able to stop the slide, began berating and punishing his players.

Griffith wrote four short reports during the 1939 season. His relationship with Hartnett deteriorated to the point that in June he wrote that "as far as the team and its management is concerned, we have met not only with failure but with a large amount of suspicion and distrust."[56] He proposed a "psychological clinic," a week-long retreat with the managers, coaches, and senior players at which he could hold forth on his ideas about the "psychological point of view." It appears to have come to nothing. In the first of two August reports he wrote bluntly that "the center of the whole problem is Hartnett. . . . Hartnett is a man who must satisfy his ego at all costs."[57] Finally, in the last 1939 report, pointedly titled "Some Qualifications of a Baseball Manager," Griffith began by distinguishing between managers who are "users of men" and those who are "makers of men." After waxing poetic about the qualities of the "good manager" for some thirteen pages, it was clear, if only implicitly, that Hartnett was not among those Griffith believed to have such qualities.

In August 1940 Griffith wrote one last report. In tone it was quite unlike the previous ones. Rather than advocating the "psychological point of view," it was full of straight baseball advice — some of it harsh. Among other things, he recommended that Wrigley cut the players' salaries and make them dependent on performance because, Griffith said, when men have high salaries they have little more to work for and become complacent. Although Griffith flattered Wrigley by telling him that he paid among the highest salaries in baseball, Wrigley was in fact widely known to be stingy.[58] Griffith contended that several of the players were lazy and not properly conditioned. Finally, he devoted an entire section of the report specifically to Hartnett, denouncing what Griffith called "his grandstanding, his super-egotism, and his stupidity" and plainly called Hartnett "a bad manager."[59]

With this report Griffith's interaction with the Cubs came to an end. Cubs Vice President Bill Veeck is reported to have jokingly said about the project as a whole that "we didn't find out too much about what goes into the five or ten per cent of boys who can make the major leagues, but we did find out what goes into the 90 or 95 per cent who cannot" (cited in Anonymous 1961).[60] The Cubs finished in fifth place in 1940, playing sub-.500 ball for the first time since 1925. Hartnett was replaced at season's end.

Griffith never conducted serious research on the psychology of sport again. In 1944 he was promoted to provost at the University of Illinois; he held the post until 1953. His son has reported that he was forced out of the position in a controversy involving an Illinois physiology professor, Andrew Ivy, who claimed to have discovered a miracle cure for cancer called krebiozen (Gould and Pick 1995, 401). Economic historians Winton Solberg and Robert Tomlinson (1997), however, paint a somewhat darker picture. According to them, Griffith as provost became entangled in a controversy over the 1950 appointment of a new dean of Commerce in which the McCarthyism of the day played a significant role. Griffith soon went on, however, to head the National Education Association's Office of Statistical Information. In 1962 he retired from the Illinois faculty and took a position in the Oregon State System of Higher Education. He passed away in 1966.

It is interesting to note that Griffith ended his work on sport more than a generation before the discipline of sport psychology began to take shape. At that time the framers of the new field looked for historical precedents in which they might ground their claims to academic legitimacy. Griffith, although he had no direct connection with any of them, filled the bill of father admirably, and so his reputation became elevated to a level it had never seen during his active career.

Notes

Many thanks to the University of Illinois Archives for giving me permission to use their extensive collection of documents pertaining to Coleman Griffith and especially to archivists Robert Chapel and William Maher for their generous assistance. Thanks to Tim Wiles and the National Baseball Hall of Fame in Cooperstown, New York. Thanks also to my graduate research assistant Cathy Faye.

1 C. R. Griffith, A Biographical Blurb for *Coleman R. Griffith*, 1945, Coleman Roberts Griffith Papers, box 1, CRG Personal, 1945–50, University of Illinois Archives, Urbana.

2 Gould and Pick (1995) published photographs of Griffith in his
   baseball uniform and in his hiking gear. The Griffith papers at the
   University of Illinois contain many letters about his fishing trips
   and vacations to wilderness areas. Griffith also mentions having
   purchased a shotgun, though it is unclear whether he became a
   regular sport hunter.
3 Bentley had studied under two of Wilhelm Wundt's American
   students — first H. K. Wolfe at Nebraska and later E. B. Titchener at
   Cornell — and received his doctorate in 1899. He taught at Cornell
   for more than a decade before being called to head the psychology
   department at Illinois in 1912. The psychological laboratory at
   Illinois was founded in 1892 by William O. Krohn and was the
   seventeenth in North America (Garvey 1929).
4 C. R. Griffith, Curriculum Vitae, ca. 1931, Coleman Roberts Griffith
   Papers, box 3, Experimental charts, etc., 1931–33.
5 C. R. Griffith to A. H. Alisky, March 30, 1922, Coleman Roberts
   Griffith Papers, box 1, General correspondence, 1921–22, A–K.
6 C. R. Griffith to H. E. Beane, March 29, 1922, Coleman Roberts
   Griffith Papers, box 1, General correspondence, 1921–22, A–K.
7 C. R. Griffith to E. Bros, December 22, 1922, Coleman Roberts
   Griffith Papers, box 1, General correspondence, 1922–24, C–F.
8 Griffith cites Titchener's *Experimental Psychology* (1910) at this
   point, leading me to believe that he meant a *Sanford* reaction time
   setup. The Sanborn apparatus came later and was used primarily as
   a polygraph rather than for taking reaction time. My thanks to Rand
   Evans and his expertise in early psychological instrumentation.
9 J. F. Wright to C. R. Griffith, December 12, 1921, Coleman Roberts
   Griffith Papers, box 1, General correspondence, 1921–22, L–Z. For
   basic information about Psi Xi, see Brown (1923, 677).
10 C. R. Griffith to K. Rockne, December 9, 1924, Coleman Roberts
   Griffith Papers, box 1, General correspondence, 1924–25, J–Z. For
   published excerpts of this letter, see Benjamin (1993, 149–50).
11 See C. R. Griffith to J. Hawley, December 19, 1924, Coleman
   Roberts Griffith Papers, box 1, General correspondence, 1924–25,
   A–I. There are identical letters from the same date (just six days
   after Rockne had written his first reply to Griffith) to the coaches

of Harvard, Dartmouth, Pennsylvania, Yale, Cornell, Minnesota, Princeton, Michigan, Indiana, Chicago, Iowa, Ohio State, Northwestern, Purdue, and Wisconsin.

12 Schulte had been a student of Wilhelm Wundt and of his successor, Wilhelm Wirth, at the Leipzig laboratory in the late 1910s. He was a pioneer of diagnoscopy, the effort to assess talent and character through the use of EEG and other electrophysiological measures (Borck 2001). He died in 1932 at the age of just thirty-five.

13 H. A. Moe to C. R. Griffith, June 4, 1925, Coleman Roberts Griffith Papers, box 1, General correspondence, 1924–25, A–I. Griffith was first granted a leave by the University of Illinois Board of Trustees on July 28, 1925, and then again on May 15, 1926; see University of Illinois Board of Trustees, Twenty-third Report (1924–26), 297, 591. Another factor in the delay may have been that Griffith's first and only child, Wayland Griffith, was born on June 26, 1925.

14 H. S. Latham to C. R. Griffith, September 2, 1924, and P. B. Thomas to C. R. Griffith, January 21, 1925, Coleman Roberts Griffith Papers, box 1, General correspondence, 1924–25, J–Z.

15 In 1922 the members of the Big Ten were Chicago, Illinois, Indiana, Iowa State, Michigan, Minnesota, Northwestern, Ohio State, Purdue, and Wisconsin. Chicago dropped out in 1946; Michigan State joined in 1949. See http://bigten.cstv.com/trads/big10-trads.html (last accessed December 21, 2008).

16 This meeting was held in early September 1929 at Yale University, the first ICP to be held in the United States.

17 C. R. Griffith, Curriculum Vitae, Coleman Roberts Griffith Papers.

18 Fragments of many of these works, some several hundred pages of typescript in length, are contained in Coleman Roberts Griffith Papers, boxes 13–17, 19.

19 C. R. Griffith, The Laboratories for Research in Athletics, ca. 1931, Coleman Roberts Griffith Papers, box 3, Experimental charts, etc., 1931–33.

20 At least one of Griffith's students completed a doctorate: Stephen Maxwell Corey, who had a successful academic career but in educational psychology rather than in the psychology of sport.

21. The story relayed by Golenbock (1996, 266) that Wrigley

commissioned Columbia psychologist Harry Hollingworth to write *The Psycho-Dynamics of Chewing* (1939) is not in accordance with fact. Letters in the Hollingworth collection at the Archives of the History of American Psychology in Akron, Ohio, show that it was Wrigley's competitors at Beech-Nut who commissioned Hollingworth's monograph, though no mention of this relation appears in the book itself. (Thanks to Ludy T. Benjamin Jr. of Texas A&M University for pointing this out to me.) The cause of the error is probably the *Fortune* magazine article that Golenbock used as his source; this article notes Hollingworth's book without naming its sponsor and then says that "this was nothing new to Phil Wrigley. Bringing science into chewing gum years ago, he aimed to show a relation not only between nervousness and gum [as Hollingworth had] but between saliva flow and gum" (Anonymous 1943, 126). One obvious interpretation of this juxtaposition of sentences is that Wrigley was somehow responsible for the Hollingworth study, but this is not correct.

22 Thanks to David McCartney of the University of Iowa, Ann Kenne of the University of St. Thomas, and Alan Kornspan of the University of Akron for assisting my investigations of Sterrett's past.

23 C. R. Griffith, Reports, Experimental laboratories, 1938–39, and General Report, 1939, Chicago National League Ball Club, Coleman Roberts Griffith Papers, box 13, Jan. 1, 1938–Jan. 1, 1939; C. R. Griffith, Player Reports, 1939, Chicago National League Ball Club Experimental Laboratories, box 1, folders 2–17, National Baseball Hall of Fame Library, Cooperstown NY.

24 C. R. Griffith, Reports, and C. R. Griffith, General Progress of the Club, 1940, Coleman Roberts Griffith Papers, box 13.

25 C. R. Griffith, Reports, Coleman Roberts Griffith Papers, no. 1, 3.

26 C. R. Griffith, Reports, Coleman Roberts Griffith Papers, no. 1, 4.

27 Cited in C. R. Griffith, General Report, Coleman Roberts Griffith Papers, 48.

28 C. R. Griffith, Reports, Coleman Roberts Griffith Papers, no. 10.

29 C. R. Griffith, Reports, Coleman Roberts Griffith Papers, no. 11.

30 There are many forms of pepper. All seem to involve propelling the

ball (whether by batting or throwing) at high speed over a short distance in order to test the reflexes of the receiver of the ball. The form mentioned here involved batting the ball at fielders at relatively close range. Griffith here proposed to turn this warm-up game into a skill-improvement drill.

31 C. R. Griffith, Reports, Coleman Roberts Griffith Papers, no. 14.

32 C. R. Griffith, Reports, Coleman Roberts Griffith Papers, no. 12.

33 C. R. Griffith, Reports, Coleman Roberts Griffith Papers, no. 6.

34 C. R. Griffith, Reports, Coleman Roberts Griffith Papers, no. 2, 4–5.

35 C. R. Griffith, Reports, Coleman Roberts Griffith Papers, no. 2, 5.

36 C. R. Griffith, General Report, Coleman Roberts Griffith Papers, 48.

37 C. R. Griffith, General Report, Coleman Roberts Griffith Papers, 50–51.

38 C. R. Griffith, General Report, Coleman Roberts Griffith Papers, 53, 56–57.

39 C. R. Griffith, Reports, Coleman Roberts Griffith Papers, no. 3, 7.

40 C. R. Griffith, Reports, Coleman Roberts Griffith Papers, no. 3, 8.

41 C. R. Griffith, General Report, Coleman Roberts Griffith Papers, 58.

42 C. R. Griffith, General Report, Coleman Roberts Griffith Papers, 58.

43 After a year at St. Louis Sterrett moved on to coach at the University of Tulsa. Thanks to Alan Kornspan of the University of Akron, Miriam Joseph of St. Louis University, and Don Tomkalski and Marc Carlson of the University of Tulsa for helping me to discover and confirm these facts.

44 Compare, for instance, the tone here with Griffith's less aggressive critique of instinct in *Psychology and Athletics* (1928a, 214–17).

45 C. R. Griffith, Reports, Coleman Roberts Griffith Papers, no. 15, 1.

46 C. R. Griffith, Reports, Coleman Roberts Griffith Papers, no. 15, 3–4.

47 C. R. Griffith, Reports, Coleman Roberts Griffith Papers, no, 15, 8.

48 C. R. Griffith, General Report, Coleman Roberts Griffith Papers, 90–91. The intelligence required of catchers had long been one of Griffith's concerns. The topic occupied one of the longest passages

devoted solely to baseball in the whole of *Psychology and Athletics* (1928a, 72–76).

49 I. Vaughan, "Wrigley Displeased; May Oust Hartnett," *Chicago Daily Tribune*, October 12, 1939.

50 C. R. Griffith, General Report, Coleman Roberts Griffith Papers, 174.

51 C. R. Griffith, General Report, Coleman Roberts Griffith Papers, 174–75.

52 Wrigley's biographer reported that the "crowning blow" came near the end of the 1938 season when a game was played between a team of Minor League players with whom the psychologists had been working throughout the summer and a team selected by the scouts. The scouts' team is said to have "clobbered" the psychologists' team. Bill Veeck is said to have reported that a number of the scouts' choices made it into the high Minors while none of the psychologists' choices did (Angle 1975, 65). The story is repeated by Swoap (1998). It is possible that such a game took place, but if it did, it was not the decisive moment Angle thought because Griffith continued to work for Wrigley through the next season.

53 C. R. Griffith, "*Cavarretta* against the Pitching of *Gumbert* of New York," in "Comments on the Play of Cavarretta of the Cubs during the 1938 Season," Phil Cavarretta 1939, Chicago Cubs Experimental Labs Collection, box 1, folder 2, National Baseball Hall of Fame Library, Cooperstown NY.

54 W. C. Griffith, personal communication, 2001.

55 W. C. Griffith, personal communication, 2001.

56 C. R. Griffith, Reports, Coleman Roberts Griffith Papers, no. 17, 3.

57 C. R. Griffith, Reports, Coleman Roberts Griffith Papers, no. 19, 26.

58 Records show that Wrigley had lowered even Grimm's and Hartnett's salaries from about $20,000 in 1936 to about $18,000 in 1937. All the other players made much less. No records exist for 1938. See D. Pappas, "Salary Highlights from the Thirties," Outside the Lines, 1995, http://roadsidephotos.com/baseball/1930SSALS .htm (last accessed December 21, 2008).

59 C. R. Griffith, General Progress, Coleman Roberts Griffith Papers, 8, 10.

60 Furlong (1969, 29) reports essentially the same comment, though he changes the "five or ten per cent" to "1 per cent," and the "90 or 95 per cent" to "99 per cent."

References

Angle, P. M. 1975. *Philip K. Wrigley: A memoir of a modest man.* Chicago: Rand McNally.

Anonymous. 1943. Chewing gum is a war material. *Fortune,* January.

———. 1961. Progressive Phil hired prof to measure skill of players. *Sporting News,* October 4.

Bäumler, G. 1997. Sports psychology. In *A pictorial history of psychology,* ed. W. G. Bringmann, H. E. Lück, R. Miller, and C. E. Early, 485–89. Carol Stream IL: Quintessence Books.

Benjamin, L. T. 1993. *A history of psychology in letters.* Boston: McGraw-Hill.

Borck, C. 2001. Electricity as a medium of psychic life: Electrotechnological adventures into psychodiagnosis in Weimar Germany. *Science in Context* 14:565–90.

Brown, J. T. 1923. *Baird's manual of American college fraternities.* New York: Brown.

Furlong, W. B. 1969. *Chicago Tribune Magazine,* October 12.

Garvey, C. R. 1929. List of American psychology laboratories. *Psychological Bulletin* 26:652–60.

Golenbock, P. 1996. *Wrigleyville: A magical history tour of the Chicago Cubs.* New York: St. Martin's.

Gould, D., and S. Pick. 1995. Sport psychology: The Griffith era, 1920–1940. *Sport Psychologist* 9:391–405.

Green, C. D. 2003. Psychology strikes out: Coleman Griffith and the Chicago Cubs. *History of Psychology* 6:267–83.

Griffith, C. R. 1921. Some neglected aspects of a history of psychology. *Psychological Monographs* 30:17–29.

———. 1922. *An historical survey of vestibular equilibration.* Urbana IL: University of Illinois Press.

———. 1923. *General introduction to psychology.* New York: Macmillan.

———. 1925. Psychology and its relation to athletic competition. *American Physical Education Review* 30:193–99.

———. 1926. *The psychology of coaching: A study of coaching methods from the point of psychology.* New York: Scribner.

———. 1927. Mental hygiene in everyday life. *Electric Journal* 24:100–107.

———. 1928a. *Psychology and athletics: A general survey for athletes and coaches.* New York: Scribner.

———. 1928b. The psychology of "pep" sessions. *High School Teacher* 4:366–67.

———. 1929. Vestibular sensation and the mechanism of balance. *Psychological Bulletin* 26:549–65.

———. 1930. A laboratory for research in athletics. *Research Quarterly* 1:34–40.

———. 1931a. A flexible form of the Carr slot maze. *American Journal of Psychology* 43:283–85.

———. 1931b. A new method for administering shock in animal experimentation. *American Journal of Psychology* 43:286–87.

———. 1931c. Review of L. Bretagnier, *L'activité psychique chez les animaux: Instinct et intelligence* [Psychological activity in animals: Instinct and intelligence]. *American Journal of Psychology* 43:422–24.

———. 1932. The perceptions and mechanisms of vestibular equilibration. *Psychological Bulletin* 29:279–303.

———. 1934. *Introduction to applied psychology.* New York: Macmillan.

———. 1935. *Introduction to educational psychology.* New York: Farrar and Rinehart.

———. 1939. *Psychology applied to teaching and learning: A first book in the field of educational psychology.* New York: Farrar and Rinehart.

———. 1943. *Principles of systematic psychology.* Urbana IL: University of Illinois Press.

Griffith, C. R., and J. R. D. Eddy. 1931. An improvement in the Seashore serial discriminator. *American Journal of Psychology* 43:435–37.

Kroll, W. 1971. *Perspectives in physical education.* New York: Academic Press.

Kroll, W., and G. Lewis. [1970] 1978. America's first sport psychologist. In *Sport psychology: An analysis of athlete behavior,* ed. W. F. Straub, 16–19. Ithaca NY: Movement Publications. Originally published in *Quest* 13:1–4.

Schulte, R. W. 1925. *Eignungs-und leistungssteigerung im sport* [Enhancement of ability and achievement in sport]. Berlin: Hackebeil.

Seidler, A. H. 1948. *A history of the professional training in physical education for men at the University of Illinois.* Master's thesis, University of Illinois.

Solberg, W. U., and R. W. Tomlinson. 1997. Academic McCarthyism and Keynesian economics: The Bowen controversy at the University of Illinois. *History of Political Economy* 29:55–81.

Swoap, R. A. 1998. *Coleman Griffith's kick-off of applied sport psychology in America.* Paper presented at the 106th meeting of the American Psychological Association, San Francisco CA.

Veeck, B. 1962. *Veeck as in wreck.* Chicago: University of Chicago Press.

White, J. M. 1926. The new gymnasium at Illinois. *Athletic Journal* 6 (9): 11–13.

Paul Brown

BRINGING PSYCHOLOGICAL
TESTING TO FOOTBALL

Stephen T. Graef, Alan S. Kornspan, and David Baker

As can be seen in previous chapters, during the 1920s and 1930s psychologists were becoming more seriously interested in how psychology could be applied to sport. At the same time coaching schools were being developed at universities to train athletic coaches, and not coincidently, psychology was one of the topics discussed and taught at some of the coaching schools in the 1920s and early 1930s.

A main topic of the early application of psychology that pertained to sport and that was most probably an important topic of discussion at these early coaching schools was a focus on various psychological skills such as reaction time. Additionally, professors of psychology were beginning to cover the topic of athletic psychology in applied psychology classes.[1] Moreover, psychologists were attending meetings and coaching conferences in which they were explaining to coaches and other psychologists how psychology could be effectively applied to the field of coaching and athletics (Bean 1927; Smith 1930). Further, well-known coaches such as Glenn "Pop" Warner were discussing the psychology of their sport at these coaching schools.[2]

As stated above, collaboration between psychologists and coaches appears to have been focused principally on reaction time and other types of experimental psychology laboratory tests during this early time period. For example, in the 1930s John Lawther, a basketball coach and psychology professor at Westminster College, conducted reaction-time studies and studies of the ability to control emotions in his athletes.[3] Thus by the beginning of the 1930s psychologists and coaches were thinking about athletes' personalities and about how some may be better than others at remaining calm under pressure.

As applied psychology expanded, coaches and psychologists began to use paper and pencil inventories to assess various psychological traits of athletes; these traits included intelligence and personality. The principal paper and pencil inventories given to athletes were used to measure intelligence. As Kornspan (2006) noted, there was disagreement in the scientific literature on the importance of intelligence for success in athletics. Common during this time period was research conducted to determine differences between athletes and nonathletes in terms of levels of intelligence as well as scholarly achievement based on grades and grade point averages. For example, a newspaper story reported that "intelligence tests of all Stanford students . . . revealed a rating of sixty-one per cent for all members of major sports teams, a mark which is ten points lower than the average student attains."[4] Some psychologists such as Charles Homer Bean (1927) believed that the relationship between IQ and athletic performance was strong enough that it could be used in recruitment and selection for athletic teams. Other studies looked at the grades of athletes compared to nonathletes (Paterson and Peterson 1928).

The result was that some college coaches began to use intelligence testing as part of their procedure for selecting football players. Unfortunately little specific information exists about how such testing was used for those purposes. A few interesting descriptions of these testing programs have been located in historical newspaper descriptions. For example, at the University of Montana in 1930 the athletic department and E. A. Atkinson of the psychology department collaborated to select the quarterback for the football team.[5] Interestingly, the advertisement that was placed in the university newspaper asking students to be tested sought individuals who were intelligent. In fact, the advertisement called for individuals who were in the top twenty-fifth percentile in their class. Other coaches also used intelligence tests to help in the selection of athletes. For example, it was reported that Al Sharpe, the football coach at Washington University, used intelligence testing to help select his athletes for the football team, particularly the quarterbacks.[6]

Why did these football coaches become interested in the selection of athletes through the use of psychology? One theory may be that coaches were beginning to be educated in the psychology of coaching. Coleman Griffith's books on the psychology of coaching and athletics were published during this time (Griffith 1926, 1928). Moreover, coaches were encountering the psychology of athletics in their clinics and coaching schools. In fact, at the University of Illinois Griffith's course on the Psychology of Athletics was a part of the coaching and physical education curriculum.

One individual who became well known for his use of intelligence testing and is known today in athletic circles as an innovator in the use of intelligence testing for professional football was Paul Brown. Although intelligence testing was used by other psychologists and coaches at the collegiate level, Paul Brown appears to have been one of the first football coaches to systematically use intelligence testing over a long period of time at the high school level, the college level, and the professional level. Because the use of psychological assessment, including intellectual, is widespread in professional sports today, it is important to understand how coaches and psychologists began their collaboration in the testing enterprise.

The emphasis of this chapter will be on the use of psychological testing in the sport of football, centering on the work of Paul Brown in intellectual and personality assessment. We explore Brown's use of psychological tests in player selection, focusing on the types of tests that were used and how they were used. We also offer several hypotheses about why Brown began using these tests. Additionally, the chapter will discuss other psychologists who were using psychological testing of athletes during this time.

Paul Brown, Football, and Psychological Testing

Every year, prior to the National Football League (NFL) draft, roughly three hundred college football players are invited to Indianapolis, Indiana, for the NFL Scouting Combine.[7] The Combine is a weekend-long opportunity for professional football teams to get a closer look at the talent of the upcoming class of potential draft picks. In addition, it provides NFL hopefuls with an opportunity to show off their skills and abilities for representatives from each NFL organization. The first two days consist of lengthy physical evaluations based on speed, strength, quickness, and health, while the third day focuses on a series of psychological tests.[8]

Although many teams provide their own tests, there is one psychological test that is used by all teams, the Wonderlic Personnel Test (WPT) (Kornspan 2006). The WPT was developed in 1937 by E. F. Wonderlic as part of his doctoral thesis at Northwestern University.[9] Participants who complete the WPT are given twelve minutes to answer fifty questions related to math, vocabulary, reasoning, logic, and more (Kornspan 2006). The overall goal is to assess the individual's ability to solve problems.[10] Problem-solving ability in turn is thought to predict the ease with which players can learn and retain critical information such as that contained in a typical NFL team playbook.[11]

Paul Brown is often regarded as the first NFL coach to use the WPT when he was head coach of the Cincinnati Bengals (1967–75).[12] Some sources, however, have credited Tom Landry, coach of the Dallas Cowboys (1960–88), with that priority. Gil Brandt, former vice-president of Player Personnel for the Dallas Cowboys from 1960–89, stated his belief that Paul Brown was the first to use the Wonderlic but that the Cowboys, and in particular Tom Landry, were first to use a battery of tests.[13] The Dallas Cowboys' use of psychological testing is discussed in more detail below.

Priority for the use of the WPT aside, there is agreement that Brown was the first professional football coach to use psychological testing in the NFL to aid in the selection of his players (Kornspan 2006).[14] His utilization of intelligence and other psychological tests for player selection originated in his days as a high school football coach in the 1930s (Kornspan 2006). His testing program was carried on into his collegiate and professional coaching experiences in the 1940s, 1950s, and 1960s.[15] Brown's use of psychological testing was essentially the genesis of the NFL testing program, which has become a vital part of player selection today.

Who Was Paul Brown?

In order to appreciate Paul Brown's utilization of intelligence testing, it is important to know something of his background. Brown was a person who attended to details, and he expected the same from others (Oliver 1998). He was a stern, yet respected individual who was described as a benevolent dictator. Donald Steinberg (1992), former Ohio State University football player and author of *Expanding Your Horizons: Collegiate Football's Greatest*

Team, wrote that Brown's dedication to football was remarkable. Steinberg said that Brown would keep his coaches every night for film study and meetings. Although Steinberg did not recall any use of psychological testing while at Ohio State, he acknowledged Brown's ability to select successful football players.[16] Former Ohio State football player Gene Fekete described Brown as a "psychologically minded person" and as "one of the best organizers [in that] he paid attention to every minute detail." Fekete called Brown a great recruiter. Although Fekete was never subjected to any intelligence tests, he knew that Brown wanted players with good common sense, a good family, and a decent IQ.[17] In general, Paul Brown had a system that governed his work both on and off the field. If players bought into his system, success was almost inevitable. If they did not, they likely received a one-way train or bus ticket home (Brown and Clary 1979).

Success was not a novel concept to Brown, nor was it accidental. Paul Brown was, and still is, considered one of the most successful and innovative individuals ever to coach the game of football.[18] His records and accolades speak volumes about his ability to coach and teach his players. His distinguished coaching career began in Massillon, Ohio, where he coached the Massillon Tiger high school football team to an 80-8-2 record and won six state championships from 1932–40. In addition, it was at Massillon that Brown implemented many of the innovations that he is best known for today, in particular intelligence testing. After his tenure with the Massillon Tigers, Brown coached collegiate football at Ohio State University, where he compiled an overall record of 18-8-1 and earned the Buckeyes a national championship in his third season. After a brief, yet successful stint as coach of the Great Lakes Naval Station football team during World War II, Brown assumed the position of head coach of the Cleveland Browns. From 1946 to 1952 Brown coached the Cleveland Browns to four American Association Football Conference (AAFC) championships and three NFL championships. After his years with the Cleveland Browns Brown became coach and eventually owner of the Cincinnati Bengals.[19]

It is evident that Paul Brown experienced incredible success throughout his years as a football coach and that that success was no accident. Brown brought many innovations to the game of football that proved to be vital to his success as both a head coach and owner. Some of his remarkable innovations include being the first to employ a year-round coaching staff, having players use a notebook-playbook, having players engage in film study, keeping the team together in a hotel the night before a game, calling plays through the use of substitutions, creating detailed pass patterns, viewing defense scientifically, using "athletes" on defense, putting face masks on helmets, and implementing the use of psychological tests, especially intelligence tests, in the selection of players.[20]

Paul Brown's Use of Psychological Testing

Recall that Brown was a very detail-oriented individual and had a system that he felt would almost ensure success in both life and in football if followed closely and deliberately. He did not tolerate mistakes within his system; therefore one of the most important characteristics his players could possess was intelligence (Kornspan 2006).

Given the importance placed on intelligence, one of the first tasks asked of players trying out for the team would be to complete a series of intelligence and psychological tests.[21] Brown's testing philosophy was accurately described by his son Mike Brown, now owner of the Cincinnati Bengals:

> Paul Brown provided a psychological test every year to his players. This test was more or less the Army test that was given to army personnel. The test took about 45 minutes to complete. It was aimed

at identifying the range of players' intelligence. Individuals who performed well were likely able to think quicker, be more poised in their thought under pressure, and would be able to consume/learn more. The less smart individuals would have a harder time consuming a lot of information and would be more susceptible to mental mistakes. His emphasis was on selecting players who could think quickly and effectively because he did not tolerate mental mistakes. After a warning [in response to a mental mistake], that was essentially it for a player. Thus, these tests alerted [Brown] and his coaching staff to those individuals who could handle the mental load.[22]

Types of Tests

According to Schlemmer, Brown required football players trying out for the Massillon High School football team to complete a full week of tests that assessed a variety of psychological traits that Brown felt were necessary for his players to possess: intelligence, aggression, character, personality and physical reaction.[23]

INTELLIGENCE

The test used to measure intelligence was the Terman Group Test of Mental Ability (Terman 1920), which was a widely used test of intelligence during the 1930s and 1940s (Minton 1988). Similar to today's intelligence tests, the purpose of this test was to determine an individual's ability to solve various types of problems.[24] This test had been used in education research literature to compare the intelligence of high school varsity athletes to nonathletes (Monroe 1929; Reals and Reess 1939). It would seem fitting that Terman's test was used to aid in the selection of athletes. In fact, Terman stated that he had used intelligence testing to aid in the selection of academic scholarships for students applying to Stanford University (Terman 1932).

AGGRESSION

Aggression was tested using the Aggressive-Submissive Reaction Study, which determined whether an individual was more likely to be aggressive or submissive.[25]

CHARACTER

The test used to assess a player's character was the Personal Index. The Personal Index measured the likelihood that players would have disciplinary problems (Loofbourow and Keys 1933). Brown wanted his athletes to be both "solid citizens and solid football players" (Brown and Clary 1979, 7); thus a test of character proved to be helpful to Brown in his selection of players for his squad.[26] It was common during this time for coaches to be interested in character, and some sought to use football's alleged role in developing character to justify their own jobs.

PERSONALITY

An athlete's personality was assessed using the Wisconsin Scale of Personality Traits (Stagner 1937b). This test measured an athlete's level of emotional control, confidence, and shyness.[27]

PHYSICAL REACTION

The last series of tests included the measurement of general motor ability — strength, speed, and peripheral vision, among others. Brown greatly emphasized the importance that his players possess strength, quickness, and speed because these attributes produced successful results on the field.[28]

Taking the Test

Although these tests were used by Brown during his days at Massillon High School, it is not known what tests he used when he was at Ohio State University and with the Cleveland Browns. Mike Brown suggested that the tests were similar to the Army tests that were commonly used.[29] Many of the recollections involving

Brown's use of testing with his Cleveland Browns players indicate that an intelligence test was given at the beginning of training camp (Rothman 1961). It included more than one hundred questions and was timed. Individuals rarely finished the whole test, and no one ever received a perfect score (Anonymous 1962). Sample questions from the test given on the first day of training camp included:

Q: "A man walks 2 ft. 6 in. per step and takes 100 steps per minute. How many feet does he walk in a half an hour?"

Q: "If a sequence of numbers is 4, 6, 3, 7, 9, 6, 10, what should be the next number?"

Q: "If a man pays $65 a month rent, and earns $3,120 a year, what percentage of his income does he pay for rent?"

Q: "If lemons sell at three for 10 cents, how much will a dozen and a half cost?"

Answers: 7,500 feet; 12; 25 percent; 60 cents. (Rothman 1961)

Former Players' Perspectives on the Tests

Not surprisingly many of Brown's former players have stories and reactions surrounding the use of these intelligence tests. Jack Oliver, a geophysicist at Cornell University, recalled his experience with Brown's intelligence test while trying out for the high school team at Massillon:

When I "went out" for the high school football team, Brown's unconventional style was immediately evident. On the first day, instead of strapping on pads and scrimmaging, or being measured for physical prowess, the candidates for that team were directed into a classroom and given a lengthy IQ test. Poor performers on that test were dropped from the squad. Brown demanded that his players learn, not just play, the game. He insisted that they work hard and do well as students as well as athletes, and he strongly encouraged, one might say insisted upon, entrance into college for his players following completion of their high school studies. In those days the squad numbered thirty-five players. All went "both ways" i.e. played offense and defense. That number meant that only about a dozen new players could be added each year. After some early practices complete with scrimmaging that permitted some evaluation of one's competitors, I was fairly certain that, if I made the team at all, I would be about number 33 or 34 or 35 on the list. At that age I didn't have the strength, or the coordination, or the crushing competitiveness of some of my fellow players, nor was I as old and physically mature as some of my classmates. I was clearly not in line to be a team leader and was at best marginal as a player during that first year. Then came the crucial day when the list of those who "made" the team was posted. I looked anxiously through the last few names on the bottom of the list and failed to find my name, I was about to leave in disappointment when a friend pounded me on the back and yelled "Congratulations, Oliver, you made it!" Of all things, my name was number one on the list! For a moment I thought Brown had become irrational as I was surely not the number one man on that team. Finally, it turned out that I had tied with two seniors for high score on the IQ test, and adjustments for my age made me first on that list. Brown had used that list to promote again his emphasis on academic performance by his players. He was never constrained by confidentiality. So I made the squad and managed to stay on it for three years, but I warmed the bench and didn't get to play much until I was a senior. (Oliver 1998, 159)

Former player Dick Schafrath also described Brown's use of intelligence as well as his own test-taking experience in his *Heart of a Mule*:

I passed Paul Brown's mental test. Paul had exceptionally high standards for his players. Each year, on opening day of camp at Hiram College, everyone had to take an IQ test. It was a tough four-hour military type test. Flunk it and you had a bus ticket home the next morning. No plane tickets in those days.

Paul would never reveal your grade. He did confide in those close to him that Frank Ryan, with an IQ of 156, scored the highest in Browns history, followed by Chuck Knoll and Paul Wiggin.

Paul used it [the IQ score] to check the learning capabilities of his players and their character. This helped to alert him on how to teach and prevent problems. He wanted to treat all players the same, and he felt the test was a useful tool for doing just that. He also placed great emphasis on character, behavior, class and intelligence-all necessary championship ingredients. His test today would be called a "psychological" or "personality" test.

Today the players' union does not permit testing of veteran players — only rookies and free agents. Before they sign a contract, they are asked to take the test. A player must be given the results of the test if he wants to know. Personally, I never knew or cared to know my results. I'd be surprised if I was more than average. (Schafrath 2006, 82)

Some humorous accounts on the utilization of intelligence testing by Brown are documented in Pluto's *Brown's Town 1964*.

Brown also tested you. In every training camp, Brown gave his players a football IQ test. The tests were infamous, a symbol of Brown's preparation and demands on the players. "The thing was, everyone cheated like crazy on those tests," said Bernie Parrish. "They used crib sheets with all the answers. Hell, I remember seeing Chuck Noll do it, and Paul would brag about how smart Chuck Noll was." In 1964, Jim Brown published a book in which he revealed the cheating. It was huge headlines; however Lou Groza said that he didn't remember anyone cheating. (Pluto 2003, 82)

Defensive back Ross Fitchner also recalled the tests vividly.

Because I played quarterback in college, I was tested with the quarterbacks. There were sixty questions on the test and you had about 25 minutes to finish it. They'd start out with basic stuff like a series of numbers: 1 . . . 2 . . . 3 . . . 5 . . . 6 . . . 8, and they'd ask you what two numbers were missing. That part was multiple-choice. Then there were football-related questions. Usually, I got 50–52 questions completed. The only [guy] I knew who was able to finish all the questions in the 25 minutes was Frank Ryan.

Fitchner remembered a rookie quarterback who took the test along with him. When they finished, the rookie asked how many questions Fitchner had answered.

"About fifty," Fitchner answered

"I only got six," said the rookie.

"The next day that rookie was gone," Fitchner said. "So, Paul did take those tests seriously" (Pluto 2003, 26).

Why Was Brown Committed to Psychological Testing?

It is evident that Brown used intelligence testing in the selection of his football players and that such a practice proved to be both beneficial and successful for him and his football teams (Kornspan 2006). Questions still remain regarding the reasons for Brown's commitment to intelligence testing. There are some well-known and well-documented events that help illustrate the connection between Brown and intelligence testing, but they by no means tell the whole story. In addition to these events, we will offer some hypotheses that might explain how Brown may have developed his interest in and began the utilization of intelligence tests.

The facts begin with Brown writing in his autobiography that "at Massillon I had a psychologist make up some tests and then combined the results with a boy's grade record. . . . Together they gave us an idea of the kind of boy we were coaching" (Brown and Clary 1979, 8). In 1940 J. Schlemmer wrote an in-depth newspaper article addressing Brown's use of intelligence testing in which he identified not only the types of tests that were used but also made mention of these "psychologists" that aided in the development, or at least utilization of these tests. In Schlemmer's article Robert Henderson and Ross Stagner were identified as being involved in the Massillon Tiger football testing program. Henderson received a master's degree in psychology from the University of Akron and was the advisee of Ross Stagner, a psychology faculty member at the University of Akron.[30] Upon graduation Henderson took a job as a faculty member at Massillon High School and also headed a similar testing program aimed at helping hospitals select nurses, and it was while at Massillon that Henderson headed the testing program for Brown.[31] It is unknown what Stagner's role was in the testing program outside of the utilization of one of his tests in this program (Wisconsin Test of Personality Traits), but Stagner (1937b) was especially interested in the study of personality, and his textbook on the subject was one of the first in the field. Thus many of the unanswered questions about Brown and testing surround his relationship with Henderson.

It is known that Brown and Henderson worked together in the development of Brown's football testing program.[32] It is likely that this collaboration resulted from their having played together on the same football team at Miami of Ohio, a connection noted also by archivist Bob Schmidt.[33] In addition, this connection may have been strengthened at Massillon High School because, according to Massillon Football archivist Junie Studer, Henderson taught chemistry at Massillon from 1935–40, a period that coincides with Brown's tenure there.[34] Thus it seems reasonable to suspect that Henderson and Brown had some knowledge of one another prior to the implementation of testing at Massillon.

The question remains how and why Brown began using intelligence and psychological testing with his players. To answer this question, it is important to understand the historical context of psychological and intelligence testing. After World War I colleges began collecting IQ data on incoming freshmen. In 1919 Miami University was one of the first schools to implement these testing procedures. Interestingly, the university was looking at traits that could be thought of as important to a football player, even though it was instead testing for these attributes in the entire student body. In fact, the physical education program used the tests in order to rank students based on both their physical and mental capabilities. The university wanted to make this program more scientific and so began testing all students. Thus the context at Miami University at this time was one that stressed the importance of testing in the selection of students and measuring their potential success. It is easy to suspect that such testing could be transferred to the selection of football players.

Brown received his BA in education in 1930 and Henderson his BA in psychology in 1932. Therefore it is likely that they had some knowledge of the use of testing in personnel selection. Miami University had implemented universal intelligence testing for all of its students by 1930; initially that testing was performed in the psychology department. Consequently, given that Henderson was a psychology major, he may have been involved in this testing in some way or would have been subject to the testing himself. Further, it is likely that Brown became knowledgeable about the use of testing in selection because of the large role it played at Miami. He would have likely either known that such practices were going on, or he would have been subjected to the testing himself upon entering the university.

After Miami Henderson went on to the University of Akron to receive his master's degree in psychology. While at Akron he was the advisee of Stagner, whose research was largely focused on personnel selection. So at Akron Henderson received a great deal of education on testing and selection that ultimately he could have used with the football team at Massillon. During this same period Henderson was also teaching chemistry at Massillon High School, where the relationship between Brown and Henderson likely continued. How the testing program actually began still remains a mystery. It seems reasonable that Brown, and especially Henderson, at least had knowledge of, if not an appreciation for, the use of testing in personnel selection from Miami University. Furthermore, Henderson's probable additional training in testing and selection made him a great asset to a testing program such as that created at Massillon for football.

Another hypothesis suggests that Brown found out about such testing programs through his wife Katy, who was a registered nurse (Brown and Clary 1979). It seems reasonable that Katy was introduced to intelligence testing when applying for nursing jobs around the Massillon area. Because Henderson coordinated testing programs for area hospitals to aid in the selection of nurses, Katy may have been exposed to such tests and perhaps communicated these practices to her husband, who then sought out Henderson.

Another possibility is that Brown learned of intelligence and psychological testing during his schooling in Ohio either at Ohio State University or Miami University. Perhaps Brown took a class in psychology or personnel selection that included discussion of intelligence and other psychological testing. Such knowledge may have sparked an interest in Brown and provided a realization that such tests could be utilized with the players and teams that he planned on coaching after graduation.

The Use of Testing beyond Massillon

It is well documented that Brown continued his psychological testing program in professional football with the Cleveland Browns and Cincinnati Bengals and that he has been credited with being one of the first to use it in the NFL. It is apparent that such testing programs soon caught on with other coaches because drafting the most talented and highly motivated players became essential in order to field successful football teams. Little information, however, has been located about Brown's use of intelligence testing at

Ohio State University. According to Reeder (1941), all students at Ohio State University took an intelligence test as part of the admissions process, and it is entirely possible that Brown used the results of these tests in analyzing potential players' abilities for success.

During this time others in the fields of psychology and physical education began to show interest in testing athletes on various psychological measures. One individual who emphasized personality traits was Franklin M. Henry, a psychologist who was part of the physical education faculty at the University of California–Berkeley. Henry was an instructor in the department of physical education while he was completing his doctorate at the University of California between 1936–38 (Park 1994). He began teaching a course related to the psychology of physical activity in 1942.

Henry (1941) became interested in analyzing the personality of athletes and published an abstract on that work titled "Personality differences in athletes, physical education, and aviation students." That he was still involved in that work in the late 1940s is evidenced by a newspaper article that stated that "a series of individual personality tests now being conducted by a University of California professor may show future athletic coaches how to develop champions by questions and answers" and continued by reporting that "these psychological quizzes, now useful in determining potential athletic ability, may also be successful in helping poorly adjusted students find a sport that will act as mental therapy."[35] Henry's research drew students who would develop into some of the leaders in contemporary sport psychology such as Andrew Ostrow, who directed the sport psychology program at West Virginia University and edited *Directory of Psychological Tests in the Sport and Exercise Sciences* (2002).

The Spread of Psychological and
Intelligence Testing in the NFL

In the 1960s the emergence of scouting organizations and alliances allowed teams to more effectively scout a great number of players. One such organization was Troika, a shared scouting organization consisting of the Dallas Cowboys, Los Angeles Rams, and San Francisco 49ers that used an IBM mainframe computer. Given the cost of such computers at that time, by sharing the computer the teams were able to afford the luxury of machine-calculated statistics by splitting the costs and results.[36]

As part of the scouting services teams would elicit the help of psychologists and psychological testing to aid in their scouting process. According to Thomas Tutko, a psychologist who worked with the Troika teams in the 1960s, Troika was beneficial because it would take into account what each team emphasized in a player. Based on that team's particular criteria, an individualized report on a particular athlete would be provided to that team.[37]

According to Gil Brandt, the Dallas Cowboys started by giving the Wonderlic Test, which the team would use essentially as a tiebreaker.[38] Initially, there would be expectations about how certain positions should score. Then, if a team had six to seven players who had very similar physical attributes, the club would use the Wonderlic to help decide among those players.

Brandt acknowledged that in 1962–63 the Cowboys began giving a battery of psychological tests administered and scored by Tutko and Bruce Ogilvie.[39] They would test players prior to the draft and those players at training camp who had not been tested. One goal was to find out how interested in the game of football players were and how they would need to be coached. Brandt noted that for some players the tests worked well, while for others they did not.[40] For instance, a test might indicate that a player wasn't interested in football, but then the athlete ended by staying in the league for thirteen years. On the other hand, a test might indicate that a player seemed psychologically fit for football, but then that player would quit after a week.

The goal of the psychological testing program was to make better draft selections. Tutko recalled that the Cowboys wanted players with athletic intelligence and a winning attitude. To accomplish these they provided a battery of tests such as the Wonderlic, the Jackson Personality Inventory, and the Athletic Motivation Inventory, which targeted such characteristics as desire for achievement, work habits, assertiveness, emotional control, and goal-setting ability.[41] Prior to drafting, the tests would be administered and the psychologists would come up with an individual diagnosis that they then relayed to the individuals in charge of making the picks for a particular team. Recall that these individualized reports were based on the criteria that the respective teams emphasized in their player selection, and thus the reports identified the extent to which the player matched the desired features.

It is unlikely that most football coaches today would share Paul Brown's belief in the critical importance of intelligence in producing successful football teams. Nor, given the frequent misconduct by professional football players, would most coaches agree with his emphasis on character. But Brown's reliance on measures of intelligence, personality, and character as a means of selecting his athletes contributed to a program of accomplishment at all levels of his coaching career. And it was perhaps this success that convinced other coaches to follow his lead in making psychological testing a part of the selection process, so much so that it has become institutionalized in the NFL Scouting Combine today.

Notes

1 "Study Starts; Students May Enroll; Applied Psychology among New Subjects Offered This Semester," *Hammond Times*, February 4, 1936.

2 "Warner and Allen Head Utah Aggie Coaching School Opening in June," *Helena Independent*, May 20, 1928.

3 "Big Athletes Alert, Speedy as Small Men, Coach Proves," *Charleston Gazette*, January 9, 1931.

4 *Reno Evening Gazette*, January 25, 1924.

5 B. Campbell, "Help! Aid! Also Assistance! Grizzlies Are Going to Pick a Quarterback thru Psychology," *Helena Daily Independent*, March 1, 1931.

6 "Al Sharpe Has Education Plan," *Syracuse Herald*, June 7, 1928.

7 D. Dillon, "Testing, Testing: Taking the Wonderlic," 2003, http://www.tsn.sportingnews.com.nfl/articles/20030417/469264-p.html (accessed November 20, 2006).

8 D. Arkush, "Make Way for the Combine," 2004, http://www.profootballweekly.com/PFW/NFLDraft/Scouting+Combine/2004/combineintro021804.htm (accessed November 21, 2006).

9 Dillon, "Testing."

10 Dillon, "Testing."

11 "Our History," Wonderlic, 2006, http://www.wonderlic.com/about/history.asp (accessed November 20, 2006).

12 J. Trotter, "Will Wonderlic Have Teams Wondering about Young?" 2006, http://www.signonsandiego.com/uniontrib/20060323/news_1s23wonder.html (accessed November 20, 2006).

13 G. Brandt, personal communication, June 2007.

14 "Paul Brown," Pro Football Hall of Fame, 2006, http://www.profootballhof.com/hof/member.jsp?player_id=34 (accessed November 20, 2006).

15 "Master Innovator: The Browns, Bengals and Entire NFL Owe Paul Brown a Debt of Gratitude," Pro Football Hall of Fame, 2006, http://www.profootballhof.com/history/release.jsp?release_id=732&print=yes (accessed November 20, 2006).

16 D. Steinberg, personal communication, June 2007.

17 G. Fekete, personal communication, June 2007.
18 "Master Innovator," http://www.profootballhof.com/history/release
    .jsp?release_id=732&print=yes.
19 "Paul Brown," Wikipedia, 2006, http://en.wikipedia.org/wiki/Paul
    _Brown (accessed November 20, 2006).
20 "Paul Brown," http://www.profootballhof.com/hof/member
    .jsp?player_id=34.
21 J. Schlemmer, "Massillon's Grid System Leaves Nothing Open to
    Chance; Here Is How Boys Are Selected," *Akron Beacon Journal*,
    March 7, 1940.
22 M. Brown, personal communication, October 2006.
23 Schlemmer, "Massillon's Grid System."
24 Schlemmer, "Massillon's Grid System."
25 Schlemmer, "Massillon's Grid System."
26 Schlemmer, "Massillon's Grid System."
27 Schlemmer, "Massillon's Grid System."
28 Schlemmer, "Massillon's Grid System."
29 Brown, personal communication.
30 Schlemmer, "Massillon's Grid System."
31 Schlemmer, "Massillon's Grid System."
32 Schlemmer, "Massillon's Grid System."
33 B. Schmidt, personal communication, June 2007.
34 J. Studer, personal communication, June 2007.
35 "U. C. Personality Tests May Help Find Athletes, Prescribe Mental
    Therapy," *Oakland Tribune*, May 1, 1949.
36 "Who Are BLESTO and The National?" n.d., http://www.draftdaddy
    .com/features/blesto.cfm#top (accessed September 18, 2007).
37 T. Tutko, personal communication, September 2007.
38 Brandt, personal communication.
39 Brandt, personal communication.
40 Brandt, personal communication.
41 Tutko, personal communication

References

Anonymous. 1962. Man for the season. *Sports Illustrated Magazine,* September 10.

Bean, C. H. 1927. Job-analyzing athletes. *Journal of Applied Psychology* 11:369–80.

Brown, P., and J. Clary. 1979. *PB: The Paul Brown story.* New York: Atheneum.

Griffith, C. R. 1926. *The psychology of coaching: A study of coaching methods from the point of psychology.* New York: Scribner.

———. 1928. *Psychology and athletics: A general survey for athletes and coaches.* New York: Scribner.

Henry, F. 1941. Personality differences in athletes and physical education and aviation students. *Psychological Bulletin* 38:745.

Kornspan, A. S. 2006. Applying psychology to football in the 1930s and 1940s. *Applied Research in Coaching and Athletics Annual* 21:83–99.

Loofbourow, G. C., and N. Keys. 1933. A group test of problem-behavior tendencies in junior high boys. *Journal of Educational Psychology* 24:641–53.

Minton, H. L. 1988. *Lewis M. Terman: Pioneer in psychological testing.* New York: New York University Press.

Monroe, W. S. 1929. The effect of participation in extra-curriculum activities on scholarship in the high school. *School Review* 37:747–52.

Natali, A. 2001. *Brown's Town: 20 famous Browns talk amongst themselves.* Wilmington OH: Orange Frazier.

Oliver, J. 1998. *Shakespeare got it wrong, it's not "to be," it's "to do": The autobiographical memoirs of a lucky geophysicist.* Ithaca: Internet-First University Press.

Ostrow, A. C., ed. 2002. *Directory of psychological tests in the sport and exercise sciences.* 2nd ed. Morgantown WV: Human Kinetics.

Park, R. J. 1994. A long and productive career: Franklin M. Henry—scientist, mentor, pioneer. *Research Quarterly for Exercise and Sport* 65:295–307.

Paterson, D. G., and I. E. Peterson. 1928. Athletics and scholarship. *University of Minnesota Department of Physical Education Research Bulletin* 1:1–16.

Pluto, T. 2003. *Browns Town 1964: Cleveland Browns and the 1964 championship*. Cleveland: Gray.

Reals, W. H., and R. G. Reess. 1939. High-school letter men: Their intelligence and scholarship. *School Review* 47:534–39.

Reeder, C. W. 1941. Academic performance. *Journal of Higher Education* 13:204–208.

Rothman, S. 1961. A study in Brown. *Blade Sunday Magazine*, December 3.

Schafrath, D. 2006. *Heart of the mule: The Dick Schafrath stories*. Cleveland: Gray.

Smith, W. 1930. Ruby and Lipe propose basketball rule changes. *Decatur Review*, April 5.

Stagner, R. 1937a. *Psychology of personality*. New York: McGraw-Hill.

———. 1937b. The Wisconsin scale of personality traits. *Journal of Abnormal and Social Psychology* 31:463–71.

Steinberg, D. 1992. *Expanding your horizons: Collegiate football's greatest team*. Pittsburgh: Dorrance.

Terman, L. M. 1920. Terman Test of Mental Ability for grades 7 to 12. *Elementary School Journal* 21:77–78.

———. 1932. Autobiography. In *A history of psychology in autobiography*, ed. C. Murchison, 297–331. Vol. 2. Worcester MA: Clark University Press.

9

Enhancing Performance in Sport

THE USE OF HYPNOSIS AND OTHER PSYCHOLOGICAL TECHNIQUES IN THE 1950S AND 1960S

Alan S. Kornspan

During the early twentieth century psychologists and physical educators became interested in how various psychological skills could be used to enhance athletic performance (Riley 1943). Even before the turn of the century E. W. Scripture in the early 1890s believed that psychology could be used to help an athlete compete at a higher level (Scripture 1894). More specifically, autosuggestion as a technique to improve athletic performance was discussed at the first International Congress of Sport Psychology in 1913 (Kornspan 2007).

Early Research on Relaxation and Athletes

Psychologists, physical educators, and medical professionals have long been interested in how the physical performance of athletes could be enhanced through various psychological techniques such as relaxation. Medical staff working with the U.S. Olympic athletes were well aware of the need to help athletes control their nervous tension before competition (Kornspan 2007; Lawson 1932). Physical educators also recognized the important psychological need of athletes to stay relaxed. Williams and Nixon (1932) wrote that "probably no one ever becomes a champion in any sport until he learns to relax" (106). They further stated that "relaxation in sports depends upon the cultivation of mental poise and emotional control. The player who is angry, fearful, or too anxious will lack this quality, and his performance will not be his best. By conscious effort we can all develop some measure of this poise and control. It will be more difficult for some than for others, but for anyone who hopes to become a skilled performer it is well worth trying for" (108).

One of the first studies on relaxation in athletes was by James Lawson of Ohio State University in 1933. Lawson was interested in comparing the relaxation of athletes to nonathletes. Using a pursuit-rotor task, he concluded that athletes were better in terms of their ability to relax.

R. W. Husband (1935), a former student of Walter Miles at Stanford University, asked varsity athletes a series of questions on their feelings before a competition. The athletes were asked about the physiological symptoms they experienced and about the onset of their excitement or nervousness before an athletic competition. Most of athletes in the study reported nervousness the day before the athletic event.

In 1935 sportswriter Grantland Rice interviewed physiologist Edmund Jacobson, the inventor of a technique known as progressive muscle relaxation, about relaxation and sports. The well-known golfer Alex Morrison was part of the interview as well. Rice wrote that "it might be stated in advance that Dr. Jacobson has made tests with football players and other athletes who are subjected to high tension and wasted energy motion."[1] Jacobson stated that "it is possible to be at high tension and then to relax completely, to relax every muscle in the body. Those able to do this will be much better athletes and will last much longer than those that don't, it is one of the most important factors connected with sport—with every branch of sport."[2] In the interview Morrison brought up the concept of visualization. Rice asked Jacobson whether picturing a free smooth flowing swing would help golfers. Jacobsen, in support of the importance of relaxation training for athletes replied, "Beyond any doubt. But if he could learn in advance just how to relax every muscle, which is not too difficult, it would be a great help. It would make golf much easier and much simpler, just as it would make any other sport much easier and much simpler."[3]

In the early 1940s psychological strategies that had initially been discussed in the early 1900s were applied to help athletes try to improve performance (Kornspan and MacCracken 2001). Dorothy Hazeltine Yates, a professor of psychology at San Jose State College, was asked by a boxer to teach him psychology in order to improve his boxing skill. She decided to help and began by conducting research with the college's boxing coach. Additionally, she taught a class to athletes and aviators and had individual consulting sessions with athletes. In her work with boxers in the early 1940s, Yates taught a relaxation method showing boxers how to progressively relax and to say positive affirmations to themselves.

Riley (1943) provided a coach's view of the work that Yates conducted with the San Jose State boxing team. Riley believed that a prime problem in boxing was for boxers to perform in competition as well as they did in practice. Riley reported that "last year one of our fighters, wondering why he couldn't enjoy his bouts the same as he did in his other sports visited Dr. Dorothy Hazeltine Yates, a psychologist on our faculty. She worked with him, and as a result the fighter fought the best fights of his career with greater relaxation than he ever had before" (95).

According to Riley, because of this initial success with one boxer, the coach was very interested and met with Yates. Coach and psychologist concluded that psychology could help boxers in reducing tension and thus also improve performance in competition (Riley 1943). Yates began to work with every athlete on the San Jose State College boxing team, applying relaxation and mental sets to aid in trying to improve athletic performance (Riley 1943).

Other psychologists contributed to the relaxation training as well. Clair Bee, football coach at Long Island University, and Richard Paynter, head of the psychology department at Long Island University, collaborated on the training of football players. In a 1940 newspaper article R. McGowen wrote that "Dr. Richard H. Paynter, head of the University's Department of Psychology, has been given carte blanche by Clair Bee, according to the LIU coach, to 'mental condition' the entire squad for the remaining five games of the schedule."[4] Coach Bee noted the previous work that Coleman Griffith and Walter Miles had conducted at the University of Illinois and Stanford University respectively. McGowen stated that "the doctor's contention, however, is that, all things being equal players who have developed the ability to relax will be better than opponents with identical physical abilities."[5]

In other work in the 1940s coach Bud Winter, a student in Yates's class on the psychology of athletics, was interested in how he could apply relaxation techniques to the athletes on the track team (Winter 1981). However, before Winter was able to provide the program developed by Yates to his athletes, he entered the Navy to serve during World War II. According to Winter (1981), when the Navy learned of his association with Yates, they asked him to chair a committee to study the use of relaxation for naval aviators during the Navy's preflight school. This 1943 study became one of the most advanced studies of the relaxation of individuals during athletic activities. Leading researchers and practitioners of relaxation were brought together by Winter to help with the research study. Winter pointed out that before the 1940s coaches realized that relaxation was important, but they did not provide systematic relaxation training (Winter 1981). He reported that "during World War II, we found the real scientific method for teaching relaxation. We also found that relaxation could be taught with good or even amazing results — to anyone" (2).

By the end of the 1940s the field of physical education had recognized the importance of relaxation in the improvement of athletic performance. Franklin Henry in conjunction with other psychologists and physical educators — including, Anna Espenschade, Pauline Hodgson, Peter Karpovich, Arthur H. Steinhaus, and Rheem F. Jarrett — wrote a chapter on psychology in a textbook of research methods for physical education (Henry et al. 1949). In their chapter they discussed the concept of muscular tension, highlighting the importance of studying relaxation and the importance of elements of muscular tension in relation to athletic performance. They stated that "the importance of this problem in physical education should not be overlooked. The frequent instructions to golfers, ball players and other athletes 'to relax' shows an awareness of the detrimental effect of too great tension. On the other hand, evidence of tension in athletes immediately preceding record-breaking performances is commonly observed. Both the inhibitive and the facilitative functions of tension under various circumstances need further investigation" (Henry et al. 1949, 281).

One psychological technique that gained attention in the 1940s as a method that could help athletes relax was hypnosis. Hypnosis had been used with athletes in the early 1900s to aid with performance issues, as noted in a 1913 article in the *New York Times*.[6] The *Times* described an athlete who would get so anxious that he could not even swing at the golf ball. A physician analyzed the golfer's physical condition and decided that nothing was wrong physically. So hypnotism was used to help the golfer overcome his problem. It was reported that hypnotism "is likely to become popular among golfers, most of whom suffered at one time or other from golf neurosis."[7] In addition, Hoberman (1992) has reported that hypnosis was an area of study in the German sports medicine literature by the early 1930s. A decade later use of hypnosis in working with athletes was clearly more widely accepted, for example, Richard Payne's work with a British soccer team.[8]

The importance of helping athletes relax for athletic competition continued to gain momentum during the 1950s. David Tracy's work with major league baseball's St. Louis Browns team gained much attention during the early 1950s. Tracy was hired to be a psychological consultant to the Browns during the 1950 season (Kornspan and MacCracken 2003; Tracy 1951). Tracy used various psychological techniques with the Browns including the teaching of relaxation, hypnosis, and autosuggestion. The main goal Tracy had in teaching these techniques to the baseball players was to help them play more relaxed (Kornspan and MacCracken 2003). It appears that Tracy's work with the baseball Browns drew much attention to the use of psychological techniques to sport performance.

The Application of Psychology to the St. Louis Browns

David F. Tracy is something of a mystery. The dust jacket of his book *The Psychologist at Bat* (1951) describing his work with the St. Louis Browns refers to him as a "noted New York psychologist." It indicates that he played quarterback for Tufts College and that his later studies in medical school "were interrupted by World War I." The Tufts University archives has no record of a David F. Tracy enrolled in the relevant years. There is no listing of him in directories of the American Psychiatric Association or American Psychological Association. Moreover, his name does not appear in the Social Security Death Index. Evidently Shirley Povich, the famed sportswriter, had his suspicions aroused because he was said to have questioned Tracy about his educational background, with the latter referring to himself as a doctor of metaphysics and claiming to have attended graduate school at the University of Southern California.[9] Yet no records can be found that would indicate that Tracy had any kind of a legitimate doctoral degree.

In July 1949 it was reported that Tracy offered to help the St. Louis Browns.[10] Tracy said that "if the Browns accept my invitation . . . I guarantee that it won't be long before every team has a staff hypnotist."[11] A few days later the St. Louis Browns left for New York. While in New York, Charles Dewitt, co-owner of the St. Louis Browns along with his brother Bill, was reported to have called Tracy and said, "This is no gag, doctor. . . . My brother Bill asked me to call you, take you to St. Louis for a conference. We believe you got a good idea."[12]

In late 1949 the national media reported that Tracy had been hired by the St. Louis Browns.[13] At this time Tracy claimed that he would help the athletes on the team learn how to use autosuggestion effectively. He said that this technique would help the ballplayers learn how to talk to themselves so that they would feel more confident.[14] Tracy was quoted as saying that "I've noticed a certain tenseness among the Browns. . . . I've watched them play at various times, and I predict they'll be a better club when I rid them of this tenseness."[15]

According to Tracy he had worked with individual athletes before, but this would be his first time working with a professional sports team: "I wanted to try something like this for years. . . . I've worked with busted-down business men, individual ball players, golfers and whatnot, but have always wanted a crack at a team."[16] Apparently, Tracy was intrinsically motivated to work with the team. Tracy stated that with the general population he worked seven-hour days and made $20 an hour. By contrast, in the two months he was originally contracted to work with the Browns, he reported he would lose a lot of money.[17]

In early January 1950, after the news had broken that Tracy would be working with the Browns, Tracy gave a speech at Carnegie Hall. He told the crowd that often coaches would not help young athletes when they were first starting out because the former felt that they might ruin the athletes' confidence. Also during this lecture Tracy argued that his work would change the sport world: "Maybe some of you folks think I'm crazy. I think we're going to revolutionize sports — not only baseball, but golf, basketball and all others where the individual is under constant tension."[18]

In January 1950 one of Tracy's main responsibilities was to raise awareness for what he would be doing with the Browns (Kornspan and MacCracken 2003). In addition to giving lectures at Carnegie Hall in New York, Tracy began lecturing on radio and television about the kind of work he would do with the baseball players. Tracy arrived in St. Louis on January 20 to begin his job with the Browns (Kornspan and MacCracken 2003). He then appeared on February 17 on *We, the People*, a television show that aired on NBC between 1948 and 1952.[19] It would not have been unusual for Tracy to be on this show. Other sports celebrities including Mickey Mantle, Babe Didrickson, Sam Snead, Yogi Berra, Floyd Patterson, and numerous football All-Americans made appearances on that show between 1950 and 1952.[20] The show's premise was the interviewing of individuals directly involved in interesting stories (Timberg 2002). On February 26, soon after appearing on *We, the People*, Tracy presented a lecture before 1,600 people on the work he would be doing with the St. Louis Browns.

On March 1 Tracy arrived in Burbank, California, to begin his work with the St. Louis Browns. The next day he began teaching classes twice a day to the players (Kornspan and MacCracken 2003). In the beginning it appeared that Tracy and Zack Taylor, the St. Louis Browns manager, got along well. Tracy's role was to help the athletes off the field, while Taylor had control of the athletes on the field.[21] In fact, published newspaper pictures show Taylor and Tracy sitting and talking together at the beginning of spring training.[22] At the beginning of spring training it appears that Tracy believed that Taylor did a good job of working with his athletes, whereas Taylor believed that Tracy's views and ideas about helping athletes were good.[23] Taylor appeared positive in an article in the *Sporting News* in which he stated, that "maybe I was responsible for the hiring of Dr. Tracy. At any rate — I sincerely believe he is going to help our club — and I made that statement to the DeWitts (President William O. DeWitt and Vice President Charely DeWitt) before they hired him."[24] On March 2 Taylor was quoted as saying, "I know that Dr. Tracy will do all that he can to give the boys the confidence that they need."[25]

Although it appeared that the relationship between Taylor and Tracy was a good one, published reports in the *Sporting News* suggested otherwise. Taylor stated that "I don't interfere with Dr. Tracy."[26] Also it was reported that Taylor believed that the things that Tracy was teaching were common sense and that the better athletes understood how to stay calm under pressure. Many years later, Taylor remarked that "matters got out of hand when my coaches came to me with complaints this hypnotist was giving players advice which contradicted what we were telling them . . . that's when I spoke up to Veeck and insisted that if Dr. Tracy stayed on, I would leave."[27]

In addition to Zack Taylor's initial belief that Tracy's ideas were sound, other managers and scouts during this time period also believed in the importance of having psychologists work with baseball players. For example, one manager during this time period who believed a psychologist could help baseball players was the Washington Senators manager Ossie Bluege. In 1947 Bluege suggested that every baseball team have a psychologist on staff, stating, "I mean it" and continuing with, "A psychologist is almost as necessary as a trainer or a coach. One of the greatest troubles with ball players is a mental slump. When they get in a rut, a hitting slump or have inferiorities the trouble mostly is upstairs. A psychologist is becoming almost a necessity in this game."[28]

One-time Brooklyn Dodgers manager Barney Shotton responded to Tracy's claim that Duke Snider could be helped by the methods that Tracy was teaching by saying that "Snider could come to be a great ball player overnight." Shotton continued, "He has what we call the tools. The only thing that has stopped him from arriving before this has been his own mind."[29] Interestingly enough, Duke Snider, a major league baseball Hall of Famer, believed that the mental game was an important part of success in baseball, and he was helped in that regard during the 1950s by a mentor, Pee Wee Reese. Snider recalled about Reese that "he helped me tremendously with the mental approach to the game. So much of baseball is mental alertness and anticipation to make the right play. And you had to maintain that level of sharpness over a season of 154 games. That's not easy even if you have the physical tools" (Snider and Gilbert 2002, 52).

During the first week of spring training Tracy taught classes to the Browns every day. Then after the first week he began to teach classes to the Browns' players every other day. Tracy focused on skills such as relaxation, autosuggestion, hypnosis, and techniques designed to build self-confidence (Kornspan and MacCracken 2003). It should be noted that these were the techniques being studied and applied by psychologists in universities. Perhaps Tracy was aware of the work that Franklin Henry and Anna Espenchade were doing at the University of California Berkeley or perhaps Tracy had heard about the work that Dorothy Yates had done with the San Jose State College boxers.

Henry and Espenchade were proponents of encouraging athletes to use mental practice based on their work conducted at the

University of California.[30] Fales (1952) in reporting on the work of Henry and Espenchade stated, "Tests show you can improve your golf swing, for example, by indulging in a few minutes of a mental practice, without touching a club" (7). Journalist E. D. Fales concluded that "it's the latest idea in sports improvement. It's no fad. Careful laboratory tests show it really works."[31] It is not clear to what tests Fales was referring, perhaps those tests used by Henry's student Twinning (1949). It should be noted that Franklin Henry has been described by Vealey (2006) as one of the few "key mentors for students who went on to become leaders in the emerging field of sport and exercise psychology" (138).

As discussed above, Henry, Espenchade, and others argued the importance of helping athletes relax (Henry et al. 1949). Tracy was now applying those important concepts by teaching the athletes the effects that pressure and nerves can have on performance. Tracy also focused on helping athletes change their thoughts from negative to more positive. He would use autosuggestion or thinking positively by having the pitchers step off the mound and take a deep breath and then have them say positive things to themselves (Kornspan and MacCracken 2003).

In Tracy's teaching the athletes various psychological skills such as autosuggestion, hypnosis, and relaxation, there were some humorous incidents. For example, at one point Tracy was helping an athlete overcome an injury to his arm. It was publicized that Tracy made an error in a hypnosis session with the team. Tracy asked a pitcher who had a sore arm to volunteer and come up to the front of the room. One of the players came to the front, and Tracy began helping him with his right arm. Tracy asked the athlete if his right arm felt better; the player replied, "My right arm feels great," but the "only trouble is I'm left-handed."[32]

Felker observed that Tracy's work was similar to what a coach does.[33] Tracy observed the athletes' behavior during the games and then would make notes on how the athlete performed from a mental perspective. Then after observing the athletes, he would help them correct various problems when working with them either in group or individual sessions.

After the first week of work with the team, Tracy was encouraged by their positive attitude toward what he was teaching them. The team did not require the athletes to attend the sessions, but most of them did. Tracy took this attendance as a sign of confidence in him and believed that the athletes felt that what he was teaching them was important for success.[34] His work with pitcher Bob Raney was reported as an example of Tracy's success. Manager Zack Taylor stated that Raney had difficulties controlling his pitches and had soreness in his arm. Taylor said that Raney and Tracy worked together for an hour and half before a game on March 23, 1950. In the contest Raney was very calm and performed very well. Raney was quoted as saying, "I'm so relaxed even now I could fall asleep standing up."[35] Just how much help Raney got from Tracy is debatable. Raney pitched in only one game in the 1950 season and lost it, giving up two runs on two hits and two walks in two innings of relief.

Other players on the St. Louis Browns also reported that their work together with Tracy was a positive experience. Owen Friend, a second baseman, believed that Tracy's work had helped him gain confidence.[36] Friend may have felt confident, but his batting average for the year was a meager .237 while his fielding percentage was not exactly stellar at .961. He was released at the end of the year. Pitcher Eddie Albrecht described how Tracy's work during spring training was helpful: "I was mightily depressed over arm trouble causing me to lose my chance." Albrecht continued, "The doc took the soreness out of my arm and convinced me I wouldn't be tense when I pitched the first time. I found myself remembering to take the deep breaths he suggested to relax on the mound, and I retired nine batters in a row on a total of 19 pitches."[37] However, during the season Albrecht didn't fare much better on the mound than his teammate Raney. For the 1950 season Albrecht pitched a little more than six innings, losing his only decision and achieving an earned run average of 5.40. He never pitched again in the Majors after that year.

Tracy was only contracted to work for the St. Louis Browns through spring training. Nevertheless, with spring training winding down, the Browns signed Tracy to a contract to continue working for the club during the baseball season.[38] Broeg reported that Tracy was originally signed for approximately $200 a week.[39]

The management of the Browns was happy with the work that Tracy had been doing.[40] They believed that Tracy had already helped some of their players and that he also earned the team more attention than it would have gotten otherwise. In fact a company in St. Louis had asked how much it would cost to have Tracy help improve the performance of their salesmen. The Browns' president replied that the cost would be 150 general admission tickets to a St. Louis Browns game.[41]

After being signed by the Browns for the regular season, Tracy hoped that he would be able to work with the pitchers immediately before competition.[42] Tracy's first project after spring training was to begin working with the Minor League teams. He was scheduled to meet with the highest level Minor League players at San Antonio, and then he was scheduled to work the Minor League athletes just starting out with the Browns organization at Pine Bluff, Arkansas.[43]

As the season began, Tracy traveled to the Minor League clubs for whom he provided lectures. He also took some credit as individual players on the Browns were successful. Tracy ended his time with the Browns on May 31 either when his contract was terminated by the Browns or when he resigned of his own free will — accounts differ.[44] Tracy believed that one of the problems that occurred after the regular season had begun was that he was not allowed to approach the players. Thus he could only work with the athletes if they scheduled an appointment with him. Tracy further felt that all he was doing after the season began was to just give lecture appearances.[45] He stated that the main reason he decided to leave the team was that he did not have the cooperation he wanted from manager Zack Taylor. Tracy indicated he would like the chance to work with another baseball team but only if he had good cooperation from the manager.

Tracy's period with the St. Louis Browns would not be the only time that he worked with a professional sports team. He briefly worked with the New York Rangers of the National Hockey League in November 1950. Tracy was asked to help the Rangers before and during the periods of play in the game with the Boston Bruins on November 15, 1950.[46] In order to begin working with the New York Rangers, Tracy had a meeting with Frank Boucher, the coach of the Rangers. It was reported that Boucher believed there was a lot that could be achieved by having a psychologist work with the team. Also, it was reported that the team's publicist most likely had told the Rangers about Tracy's use of positive suggestion through hypnosis (Kreiser and Friedman 1996).

Journalist J. Hand observed Tracy's work with the Rangers in the locker room. Hours before the game against the Bruins, Tracy came to the locker room, where the athletes on the team sat on the floor in a circle in front of Tracy. Their feet were on the floor flat, and there hands were folded in front of them while listening to Tracy.[47] Hand reported that Tracy said, "I want you to stop worrying." He continued, saying that "when you worry too much you block off the thinking process. When you are afraid you won't make a play, you tighten up. When you get behind a couple of goals you start to worry more. Forget about the score."[48]

After working with Tracy before the game, the Rangers looked very good on the ice, reportedly to the amazement of the crowd (Kreiser and Friedman 1996). However, the Rangers ended up losing the game 4–3. Kreiser and Friedman (1996) wrote that "that was all for Dr. Tracy, though he kept trying to convince the Rangers that he realized his mistake. You've got to let me at the 'goalie' he insisted. He's not relaxed" (Kreiser and Friedman 1996, 109).

Tracy after 1950

Tracy continued to receive attention from the media. As mentioned earlier, his book *Psychologist at Bat*, about his time with the Browns, was published in 1951. Over the years, Tracy's name continued to appear in the sports pages. Shirley Povich occasionally wrote articles discussing hypnosis, referring to Tracy's work with the Browns.[49]

Tracy occasionally generated publicity about himself. In one instance he wrote an editorial in the *Sporting News* suggesting that Duke Snider was giving bad advice to athletes just learning baseball because Snider was telling them to be overly focused on mechanical aspects of hitting.[50] Tracy was also interviewed for a magazine article in which he was critical of a well-known manager's coaching style. His critique received media attention at the beginning of the 1953 baseball season.

In 1961 Tracy was living in Miami, where he had started a school for hypnosis.[51] In the early 1960s, almost eleven years after working with the Browns, Tracy still believed he had helped the Browns' performance through the use of psychology.[52] The Browns in 1950 did improve their record over the 1949 season, winning five more games for a record of fifty-eight wins and ninety-six losses. Still, as in 1949 they finished next to last in the American League. Years after his season with the Browns, Tracy offered his services to the Miami Marlins, a Minor League team run by Bill Veeck. But Veeck declined, worried that having Tracy work with the team might be bad publicity.[53]

Tracy does not appear to have continued his work teaching

hypnosis and psychological techniques to other athletes in professional sports. Still, the publicity that his work received, despite lack of evidence that he was responsible for any athletic improvement, may have opened doors for other hypnotists and psychologists to work with athletes.

The Influence of Tracy's Work

What influence did Tracy's work have? It is possible that many psychologists, physical educators, and physicians heard about his work and decided to apply psychology and hypnosis to their specific team situations. For example, Tom Evans, a graduate student in psychology at Southern Illinois University, described his views about applying psychology to the field of sport, explaining that he believed that the St. Louis Browns' idea of having a psychologist work with the club's athletes was a good one.[54] Evans believed that Tracy may have had difficulty because successful work in psychology is based on the acceptance of the work by the individuals with whom one is working.

Evans also discussed his work with athletes at Southern Illinois University. As a graduate student working toward his doctoral degree in psychology, Evans used his psychological knowledge with five members of the university track team. He believed that he had a lot of success in working with the team.[55] The interventions Evans used included helping the athletes enter a hypnotic state and then providing them with positive suggestions. Evans saw these methods as helping the athletes gain confidence and as allowing them to relax more effectively.[56]

Another possible influence Tracy's work may have had was that some coaches considered the possibility of a psychologist helping to give their athletes an "edge." For example, the well-known early sport psychologist Bruce Ogilvie began to have coaches approach him to ask for help with their athletes:

I was an unusual faculty member because the coaches hadn't experienced men who were as devoted to fitness and sport as I had been all of my life. So my identification was as a member of the center staff and a jock. Coaches began asking me about problems that they were having with their athletes. They were open to me, and they would ask about issues and problems and crises. I was absolutely fascinated, and then, this was in the mid-1950s, they and other coaches started bringing athletes to sit with me to see if, through my training and background, I could provide any insight into performance decrements and performance problems. (cited in Simons and Anderson 1995, 454)

Ogilvie would go on to have a long and distinguished career in the field of sport psychology. His stature is such that some sources have labeled him the "Father" of applied sport psychology in North America.[57]

Another individual who saw the importance of sport psychology and was influenced by what the St. Louis Browns had done was George W. Crane. Crane had four degrees from Northwestern University, including an MD and a PhD in psychology.[58] Crane wrote a syndicated column called the "Worry Clinic," which at the peak of its popularity was in over 250 newspapers.[59] In this syndicated column Crane occasionally wrote about various psychological issues of athletes and coaches. In a 1955 installment Crane observed that "a few years ago I was greatly interested in reading that the St. Louis Browns were hiring a hypnotist to aid the team, for the idea is a fertile one. But a few weeks later I read that the arrangement had been discontinued. If I operated an athletic team, professional or amateur, I'd rely on a psychology coach as much as on rigorous batting practice or pitching drill."[60]

The 1950s and 1960s: The Use of Hypnosis in Sports

Many more stories and articles about the use of hypnosis in sport began to appear in media reports during the 1950s. For example, it was reported that the Vancouver Canucks of the minor Western Canada Hockey League had a hypnotist working with the team even before the New York Rangers brought in David F. Tracy.[61]

Another individual who became involved in providing hypnosis to athletes during the 1950s was Arthur Ellen. Ellen believed that Tracy's work had led to his being asked to provide services to professional baseball teams such as the California Angels and to working specifically with Hall of Fame pitcher, Nolan Ryan (Kornspan and MacCracken 2003).[62]

Ellen also worked with the University of Nevada football team in 1956. Paul Secord, the chair of the psychology department at the University of Nevada, commented on the use of psychology in sports: "It is conceivable that hypnotism could help by increasing the team's motivation and desire to win. However, hypnotism cannot enable a person to perform physical feats he could not perform in a normal state." Secord continued, saying that "Ellen would have to use a post-hypnotic suggestion. . . . He could not devise the plays or anything like that. He would have to put the team under his influence and then take them out of it before the game started."[63]

In addition to working with the University of Nevada football team, Ellen also received an offer to help the New York Giants baseball team in the early 1950s and worked with famed Dodger base stealer Maury Wills in the 1962–63 offseason. (Dodger pitcher Don Newcombe also used a hypnotist, Joseph Edelman, not to improve his pitching but to help overcome his fear of flying.[64])

Other hypnotists showed up in many sports during the 1950s. Other baseball teams that were reported as having hired hypnotists included the Kansas City Athletics.[65] In 1953 journalist O. Fraley reported on boxer George Adams' use of hypnosis in six straight victories in professional bouts.[66] In the sport of swimming it was reported that elite Australian athletes were using hypnosis in their training methods under famous Olympic swimming coach Forbes Carlisle.[67] In cross-country running it was reported that hypnosis was helpful in improving performance.[68] Soccer also had reports of the use of hypnosis in the 1950s.[69]

The use of hypnotism was not only being used in the United States, Canada, and Australia, but it was reported in the *New York Times* that Russia was also conducting studies on the use of hypnosis and autosuggestion to help athletes improve their performance.[70] After returning from a tour of Russia, Forbes Carlisle said that ski jumpers and other athletes were using hypnosis there. Carlisle reported being asked questions about his use of hypnotism with swimmers.[71] The study of sport psychology and physical education was prevalent in the Soviet Union during this time period as noted by psychology historian Josef Brozek (1968).

At the same time that there were many reports surfacing in the popular press on the use of hypnosis in sports, articles on the use of hypnosis were being published in scholarly books and journals. Maltz in his classic *Psycho-cybernetics* (1960) also mentioned the use of hypnosis by athletes, explaining how the technique could be used by athletes to enhance performance. Additionally, there began to be conferences held in the United States on the psychology of sports such as the one held at Yale University in 1953 (Ryan 1959).

Researchers such as Warren Johnson began studying hypnosis and emotional responses while a professor at the University of Maryland and even earlier as a doctoral student at the University of Denver. Johnson used hypnosis in his studies of the emotional reactions of university student-athletes. He would go on to train future leaders in the field of sport psychology at the

University of Maryland (Landers 1995). Johnson studied the use of hypnosis for six years.[72] He also published various articles on his research on hypnosis and presented research on hypnosis at the first International Congress of Sport Psychology in Rome in 1965 (Kornspan and MacCracken 2003).

Silva (2002) described the influence that Johnson had on the development of the field of sport psychology during the 1960s. At the same time that the first International Congress of Sport Psychology was taking place, at which Johnson presented his experimental studies on the use of hypnosis in sport, Johnson recommended that faculty teaching sport psychology in the United States come together to hold a meeting in North America (Silva 2002). According to Silva (2002), this group met in Chicago in 1966, and two very important results came out of this meeting. First came the decision to hold the International Society of Sport Psychology's second congress in Washington DC in 1968. Second came the development of the North American Society for the Psychology of Sport and Physical Activity, whose first gathering was held as part of the American Alliance for Health, Physical Education, and Recreation and Dance (AAHPERD) in Las Vegas, Nevada, in 1967 (Silva 2002).

As Johnson's work on the application of hypnosis to physical performance became better recognized, well-known psychologists took notice of the developments of the applications and research related to hypnosis and athletic performance. Ernest Hilgard (1968) referenced Johnson's studies that tested the effects of hypnosis on the enhancement of physical performance using athletes. Also, Hilgard described the case of a baseball player who used his skills in hypnosis to perform optimally (Hilgard 1968). Hilgard further wrote about sports and athletics in other books, among them *Hypnotic Susceptibility* (1965) and, with Atkinson, *Introduction to Psychology* (1967). In one of his texts (Hilgard and Hilgard 1994), he explained how he could use the sport experience during hypnosis to help individuals with a chronic illness relive a positive experience in their life when they were pain free. Such a reliving relieved them of pain at that moment.

As a pioneer in the study of hypnosis more broadly, it is notable that Hilgard addressed the application of hypnosis to sport performance in particular.[73] He may have known about the work that Coleman Griffith had conducted at the University of Illinois as he earned his bachelor's degree there in 1924. Later he became a faculty member at Stanford University, arriving one year after Walter Miles had left for Yale University. Hilgard was definitely aware of the work that Walter Miles conducted with athletes (Hilgard 1980).

In addition to books written by psychologists and physical educators, the use of hypnosis and other psychological techniques used by athletes was also discussed in the sports medicine literature. For example, Jokl (1964) in his textbook *The Scope of Exercise in Rehabilitation* discussed the use of hypnosis as did Dolan and Holladay (1961).

Popular books also were published in the 1960s on the use of hypnosis to enhance sport performance. For example, the books *How You Can Play Better Golf Using Self-Hypnosis* and *Super-Golf with Self-Hypnosis* were written by Jack G. Heise (Heise 1961b, 1962). Heise published *How You Can Bowl Better Using Self-Hypnosis* as well (Heise 1961a).

As can be seen, the use of hypnosis gained in popularity with coaches and athletes as well as by those interested in studying and researching the effects of hypnosis on the improvement of athletic performance. The American Medical Association took notice of the use of hypnosis in sport and published guidelines related to its use in athletics, with the chair of the committee on hypnosis suggesting that hypnosis not be used with athletes. Rosen wrote that "for obvious reasons self-hypnosis can be potentially dangerous. No one should hypnotize himself. Neither do we feel that ballplayers or other athletes should be hypnotized in an effort to win games. This too can be potentially dangerous."[74] He further stated that "in my opinion . . . there are no known conditions under which hypnosis is justified if the only object is to enhance one's athletic performance."[75]

As hypnosis became more popular, the American Medical Association published a report in the *Journal of the American Medical Association* suggesting that using hypnosis in sport was not good sportsmanship (Kornspan and MacCracken 2003). Warren Johnson responded to the report arguing that hypnosis was safe and fair to use in order to try to enhance sport performance. Psychologists were also aware of the committee report published by the American Medical Association and the American Council of Mental Health on the use of hypnosis in athletics (Moss, Logan, and Lynch 1962).

Interestingly, there were also different views from the medical profession as to whether hypnosis should be used in athletics.[76] Dr. Conrad Gale, a New York psychiatrist, believed that if hypnosis was administered properly, then an athlete could change his or her attitude consciously. He further believed that if a more positive attitude could help improve performance, then hypnosis for athletes could be effective. Dr. Gale felt that hypnosis would benefit athletes by helping them become more relaxed.[77]

The use of hypnosis and other psychological techniques to enhance performance continued during the 1960s. Many more reports of athletes and coaches using hypnosis continued to appear as well as reports of athletes using other psychological techniques. In the early 1960s there were reports of team physicians using hypnosis to help athletes with their mental game. For example, Dr. Huber Grim who was the Seattle University team physician helped a player before a basketball game.[78]

Arthur Ellen's work in the 1960s also continued to receive much attention, especially Ellen's work with Major League baseball players. Dodgers shortstop Maury Wills's work with hypnotist Ellen received attention during the 1960s. Wills had injured his leg and was having difficulty sliding when stealing bases.[79]

David Tracy's work also continued to be remembered. It was even mythologized in the popular movie *The Natural* starring Robert Redford, with the hypnotist brought on to help enhance the performance of the team being based on the work that Tracy did with the St. Louis Browns (Henry 1992).

This chapter has surveyed the use of relaxation techniques, especially hypnosis, to enhance the performance of athletes. The use of hypnosis in sport mirrored its use in medicine and psychiatry. Athletes sought such services in order to overcome injuries or anxieties or to improve athletic skills. Coaches and owners always looking for an edge to create more wins were willing to take a chance on these methods, even though their reputations for effectiveness and the reputations of the hypnotic practitioners were somewhat dubious.

David Tracy, a focus of this chapter, is a good example of the problems with the promise and expectations generated by such practitioners when compared to actual outcomes. Tracy's accomplishments were meager at best. His work with the Browns over the course of the 1950 season seemed to offer little to individual athletes with whom he worked or to the team in general. The New York Rangers worked with Tracy for a single game, a game the team lost, and consequently decided his services were no longer required.

Despite Tracy's accomplishments being minimal, there was considerable publicity surrounding his work, and much of it was positive. There seems no doubt that the publicity resulted in opportunities for other individuals — professionals with far more extensive and legitimate training than Tracy — to work in the field that would come to be known as sport psychology.

As the importance of professional sports escalated in the 1950s and 1960s, psychologists, hypnotists, and others who could offer to help the mental state of athletes were welcomed in greater numbers. These invitations opened the doors for the development of the profession of sport psychology and its development of a host of cognitive techniques that have demonstrated effectiveness for a number of elite athletes and Olympic, college, and professional teams. Yogi Berra was right: "ninety percent of this game is half mental," and that ninety percent (or is it fifty?) is the domain of the sport psychologist.

Notes

1 G. Rice, "Tension and Relaxing," *Syracuse Herald*, March 21, 1935.
2 Rice, "Tension and Relaxing."
3 Rice, "Tension and Relaxing."
4 R. McGowen, "Soft Music and Poetry Are Added to LIU's Football Curriculum," *New York Times*, October 16, 1940.
5 McGowen, "Soft Music and Poetry."
6 "Hypnotism Cures Golfer's Off Game," *New York Times*, January 26, 1913.
7 "Hypnotism Cures Golfer's Off Game."
8 "'You Will Win' Insists Hypnotist as He Puts Soccer Players to Sleep," *Nevada State Journal*, April 13, 1949.
9 S. Povich, "Putting Pump on Dr. Tracy," *Sporting News*, March 17, 1950.
10 "Browns' Troubles Solved," *Sporting News*, July 6, 1949.
11 "Browns' Troubles Solved"; "Hypnotist Wants to Aid Browns," *Portland Press Herald*, June 28, 1949.
12 H. Grayson, "Doctor Will Try to Hypnotize the Brownies into a Pennant," *Cochocton Tribune*, February 17, 1950.
13 R. Gillespie, "Metaphysics, Hypnosis, Psychology Injected into Browns' Plans for 50," *Sporting News*, December 28, 1949.
14 Gillespie, "Metaphysics, Hypnosis, Psychology."
15 Gillespie, "Metaphysics, Hypnosis, Psychology."
16 Grayson, "Doctor Will Try to Hypnotize the Brownies."

17 "Psychologist Is All Set for the Inferiority Complexes," *Sedalia Democrat*, February 1, 1950.

18 "Doctor Is Ready for His Patients; Hypnotism May Be Used on Some of the Browns," *Sedalia Democrat*, January 13, 1950.

19 "Today's Greater Washington Radio Programs," *Washington Post*, February 17, 1950; "We, the People," 2007, http://www.tv.com/we-the-people/show/21994/summary.html (accessed December 24, 2007).

20 See the episode list for 1951 and 1952 on TV.com for "We, the People," http://www.tv.com/we-the-people/show/21994/episode_listings.html?season=4&tag=nav_bar;4 (accessed December 24, 2007).

21 B. Myers, "Players, Doctor Dead Serious about Experiment," *Washington Post*, March 9, 1950.

22 See *Long Beach Press-Telegram*, March 2, 1950.

23 Myers, "Players, Doctor Dead Serious."

24 R. Gillespie, "Now It Can Be Told — Olde Zack Plugged for Brownie Hypnotist," *Sporting News*, March 1, 1950.

25 "Psychologist Begins Work on the St. Louis Browns," *El Paso Herald Post*, March 2, 1950.

26 B. Broeg, "I Don't Interfere with Dr. Tracy," *Sporting News*, April 5, 1950.

27 D. Meyer, "A Loquacious Chap Who Put Color Back in Baseball," *Elyria Chronicle Telegram*, July 1, 1961.

28 O. Fraley, "Managers Busy Making Money, Says Sen Pilot," *Port Arthur News*, March 4, 1947.

29 F. Eck, "Browns Fit Subjects for a Metaphysician," *New Port Rhode Island News*, February 18, 1950.

30 E. D. Fales, "What Makes a Good Athlete?" *Long Beach Press-Telegram*, July 20, 1952.

31 Fales, "What Makes a Good Athlete?"

32 "Psychologist 'Boots One' in Spring Work," *Walla Walla Union Bulletin*, March 15, 1950.

33 C. Felker, "Scribe Tells How It Feels to Be Hypnotized," *Sporting News*, April 5, 1950.

34 B. Broeg, "Dr. Tracy's There and the Brown's Loosen Up," *Sporting News*, March 15, 1950.

35 B. Broeg, "Psychologist to Be 'Tenth Man' in St. Louis Club's Lineup," *Sporting News*, April 5, 1950.

36 Broeg, "Psychologist to Be 'Tenth Man.'"

37 Broeg, "Psychologist to Be 'Tenth Man.'"

38 "Browns Sign Psychologist Tracy to Contract for the Rest of the Season," *Long Beach Press-Telegram*, March 26, 1950.

39 Broeg, "Dr. Tracy's There."

40 Broeg, "Dr. Tracy's There."

41 Broeg, "Psychologist to Be 'Tenth Man.'"

42 Broeg, "Psychologist to Be 'Tenth Man.'"

43 Broeg, "Psychologist to Be 'Tenth Man.'"

44 "Dr. Tracy Quits, Says He Didn't Get Cooperation," *Washington Post*, May 20, 1950.

45 "Dr. Tracy Quits."

46 "Rangers to Meet Bruin Six Tonight," *New York Times*, November 15, 1950.

47 J. Hand, "Now It's the New York Rangers Who Are Trying Out Hypnotism," *Ironwood Daily Globe*, November 16, 1950.

48 Hand, "Now It's the New York Rangers."

49 S. Povich, "This Morning with Shirley Povich," *Washington Post*, April 11, 1963.

50 "Voice of the Fan," *Sporting News*, January 28, 1953.

51 Myers, "Players, Doctor Dead Serious."

52 Myers, "Players, Doctor Dead Serious."

53 Myers, "Players, Doctor Dead Serious."

54 "Says Psychologist Can Help Athletes," *Edwardsville Intelligence*, June 12, 1950.

55 "Says Psychologist Can Help Athletes."

56 "Says Psychologist Can Help Athletes."

57 "Bruce C. Ogilvie, PhD," 2007, http://psych.sjsu.edu/faculty/emeritus/BOgilvie.html (accessed December 23, 2007).

58 R. Thomas, Jr., "George W. Crane Dies at 94; Advised with Horse Sense," *New York Times*, July 19, 1995, http://query.nytimes.com/gst/fullpage.html?res=990CR11D8153EF93AA25754C0A963958260 (accessed March 4, 2008).

59 Thomas, "George W. Crane."

60 G. W. Crane, "Worry Clinic," *Sheboygan Press*, September 26, 1955.

61 "No Miracle for Canucks?" *Ironwood Daily Globe*, November 7, 1950.

62 "Hypnosis Aids Nolan Ryan," *Burlington Times News*, July 18, 1977.

63 "Day and Night," *Reno Evening Gazette*, November 7, 1956.

64 "Talking Trouble," *Time*, December 23, 1957, http://www.time.com/time/magazine/article/0.9171.936775.00html?promoid=googlep (accessed March 4, 2008).

65 R. L. Sokolosky, "Looking and Listening; Movie Producers Take to Hypnotism," *Syracuse-Herald American*, October 4, 1959.

66 O. Fraley, "Hypnosis Does It Claims Boxer," *Redlands Daily Facts*, March 11, 1953.

67 "Australian Swimmers Get Hypnotism and Physiology during Their Training," *Port Arthur News*, February 24, 1955; "Sharks on Tail Make Aussies Sail," *Long Beach Independent*, March 9, 1956.

68 "Claims Hypnosis Won Meet for Griffith Squad," *Vidette Messenger*, October 20, 1955.

69 "Hypnotist Works on Winless Soccer Club," *Lethbridge Herald*, September 19, 1953; "Low Place Soccer Club Hires a Hypnotist," *Kansas City Times*, August 10, 1959.

70 "Russia Eyes Hypnotism in Sports, Aussie Says," *New York Times*, September 15, 1957.

71 "Russia Eyes Hypnotism."

72 "Experiments Ended," *Frederick Maryland News*, March 15, 1960.

73 M. Alexander, "Psychologist Ernest R. Hilgard, Hypnosis Pioneer, Dead at 97," *Stanford Report*, 2001, http://newsservice.stanford.edu/news/2001/october31/hilgardobit-1031.html (accessed December 24, 2007).

74 H. Rosen, "Hypnosis: The Cure That Can Be Dynamite!" *This Week Magazine*, July 16, 1960.

75 "Athletic Hypnosis Called Dangerous," *Washington Post*, July 10, 1960.

76 D. Hudson, "Warming Up," *Charleston Daily Mail*, March 18, 1960.

77 Hudson, "Warming Up."

78 "Hypnotized Hooper," *Modesto Bee*, January 1, 1960.

79 J. Ravich, "Wills' Speed Transformed the Game," July 19, 2004,

http://www.mlb.com/news/article.jsp?ymd=20040719&content
_id=803237&vkey=news_mlb&fext=.jsp&c_id=null (accessed
December 24, 2007).

References

Broeg, B. 1995. *Memories of a hall of fame sportswriter*. Champaign IL:
Sagamore.

Brozek, J. 1968. Spectrum of Soviet psychology: 1968 model. *American
Psychologist* 24:944–46.

Dolan, J. P., and L. J. Holladay. 1961. *Treatment and prevention of
athletic injuries*. Danville IL: Interstate Printers and Publishers.

Harris, J. C., and R. A. Swanson. 2005. History of physical activity.
In *Introduction to kinesiology: Studying physical activity*, ed. S. J.
Hoffman, 177–204. 2nd ed. Champaign IL: Human Kinetics.

Heise, J. G. 1961a. *How you can bowl better using self-hypnosis*. North
Hollywood CA: Wilshire Book Company.

———. 1961b. *How you can golf better using self-hypnosis*. North
Hollywood CA: Wilshire Book Company.

———. 1962. *Super-golf with self-hypnosis*. North Hollywood CA:
Wilshire Book Company.

Henry, F., A. Espenschade, P. Hodgson, P. Karpovich, A. Steinhaus, and
R. F. Jarrett. 1949. Psychological laboratory research. In *Research
methods applied to health, physical education, and recreation*, 275–
300. Washington DC: American Association for Health, Physical
Education, and Recreation.

Henry, H. 1992. Them Dodgers is my gallant knights: Fiction as history
in *The natural*. *Journal of Sport History* 19:110–29.

Hilgard, E. R. 1965. *Hypnotic susceptibility*. New York: Harcourt, Brace
and World.

———. 1968. *The experience of hypnosis*. New York: Harcourt, Brace and
World.

———. 1980. Walter Richard Miles: 1885–1978. *American Journal of
Psychology* 93:564–68.

Hilgard, E. R., and J. R. Hilgard. 1994. *Hypnosis in the relief of pain*.
2nd. ed. New York: Brunner/Mazel.

Hilgard, E. R., and R. C. Atkinson. 1967. *Introduction to psychology*. 4th ed. New York: Harcourt, Brace and World.

Hoberman, J. M. 1992. The early development of sports medicine in Germany. In *Sport and exercise science: Essays in the history of sports medicine*, ed. J. W. Berryman and R. J. Park, 233–82. Champaign IL: University of Illinois.

Husband, R. W. 1935. A study of the emotion of excitement. *Journal of Genetic Psychology* 46:465–70.

Johnson, W. R., ed. 1960. *Science and medicine of exercise and sports*. New York: Harper.

Jokl, E. 1964. *The scope of exercise in rehabilitation*. Springfield IL: Thomas.

Kornspan, A. S. 2006. Psychology applied to football in the 1930s and 1940s. *Annual of Applied Research in Coaching and Athletics* 21:83–99.

———. 2007. The early years of sport psychology: The work and influence of Pierre De Coubertin. *Journal of Sport Behavior* 30:77–93.

Kornspan, A. S., and M. J. MacCracken. 2001. Psychology applied to sports in the 1940s: The work of Dorothy Hazeltine Yates. *Sport Psychologist* 15:342–45.

———. 2003. The use of psychology in professional baseball: The pioneering work of David F. Tracy. *Nine: A Journal of Baseball History and Culture* 11:36–43.

Kreiser, J., and L. Friedman. 1996. *The New York Rangers: Broadway's longest running hit*. Champaign IL: Sports Publishing.

Landers, D. M. 1995. Sports psychology: The formative years, 1950–1980. *Sports Psychologist* 9:406–17.

Lawson, J. H. 1928. Report of medical officer. In *Report of the American Olympic Committee: Ninth Olympic Games, Amsterdam, 1928, second Olympic Winter Sports, St. Moritz, 1928*, 39–41. New York: American Olympic Committee.

———. 1932. Report of the American Olympic Medical Committee. In *Report of the American Olympic Committee: Games of the Xth Olympiad, Los Angeles, California, July 30–August 14, 1932, III Olympic Winter Games Lake Placid New York, February 4–13, 1932*, ed. F. W. Rubien. New York: American Olympic Committee.

———. 1933. A comparison of the differences of relaxation of athletes and non-athletes in pursuitmeter learning. Master's thesis, Ohio State University.

Maltz, M. 1960. *Psycho-cybernetics*. New York: Pocket Books.

Moss, C. S., J. C. Logan, and D. Lynch. 1962. Present status of psychological research and training in hypnosis: A developing professional problem *American Psychologist* 17:542–49.

Riley, B. G. 1943. Boxing and psychology. *Physical Educator* 3:95–96.

Ryan, F. J. 1959. Further observations on competitive ability in athletics. In *Psychosocial problems of college men*, ed. B. M. Wedge, 113–22. New Haven CT: Yale University Press.

Scripture, E. W. 1894. Tests of mental ability as exhibited in fencing. *Studies from the Yale Psychological Laboratory* 2:122–24.

Silva, J. M. 2002. The evolution of sport psychology. In *Psychological foundations of sport*, ed. J. M. Silva and D. E. Stevens, 1–26. Boston: Allyn and Bacon.

Simons, J. P., and M. B. Anderson. 1995. The development of consulting practice in applied sports psychology. *Sport Psychologist* 9:449–68.

Snider, D., and B. Gilbert. 2002. *The duke of Flatbush*. New York: Citadel Press.

Timberg, B. M. 2002. *Television talk: A history of the television talk show*. Austin TX: University of Texas Press.

Tracy, D. F. 1951. *Psychologist at bat*. New York: Sterling.

Twinning, H. W. 1949. Mental practice and physical practice in learning a motor skill. *Research Quarterly* 20:432–35.

Vealey, R. S. 2006. Smocks and jocks outside the box: The paradigmatic evolution of sport and exercise psychology. *Quest* 58:128–59.

Wheatley, G. M. 1961. Review of science and medicine of exercise and sports. *American Journal of Public Health* 51:786–87.

Williams, J. F., and E. W. Nixon. 1932. *The athlete in the making*. Philadelphia: Saunders.

Winter, B. 1981. *Relax and win: Championship performance*. San Diego: Barnes.

Conclusion

THE "PROPER" HISTORY OF
SPORT PSYCHOLOGY

Christopher D. Green and Ludy T. Benjamin Jr.

This book's focus is the prehistory of sport psychology because, properly speaking, the history of the discipline was not really established on a permanent, widespread basis until the 1960s, when as historians like to say, the disciplinary apparatus was finally put in place: academic departments, textbooks, scholarly journals, and professional associations, among other things. But as we have seen, decades earlier various individual psychologists had been conducting research into mental and behavioral aspects of sport in the absence of a substantial professional network. There had even been localized efforts to establish the discipline in Germany, the Soviet Union, and the United States in the 1920s. They, however, either faltered or remained local phenomena until approximately the last third of the twentieth century.

The key question for this final chapter then is how did we get from the point of Griffth's isolated work with the Cubs in the late 1930s to the point of a full-blown academic discipline in the 1960s? As the matter was succinctly put by Wiggins (1984) "a striking void exists between Griffith's productive years and the work of more contemporary researchers in sport psychology" (14). The story is, of course, rather complicated, involving global, social, and political trends as much as intellectual ones. Perhaps oddly, not many psychologists played key roles in the process of the professionalization of sport psychology. Instead, as has been detailed elsewhere, the leaders of the movement were in the main physical educators.

Physical education as it had been originally conceived for the American college in the 1900s was not a terribly scholarly enterprise. Rather than a source of research questions, physical education was seen as a way to round out the student's college experience. It was typically justified on moral grounds rather than on intellectual ones (see Coleman Griffith's words in Green, this volume). This justification began to change in the late 1940s. First, some physical educators were ambitious to be taken more seriously by their academic colleagues, and second, they were prodded, cajoled, and coerced by university administrations and governments who were not content to continue their support of traditional and intellectually flabby physical education departments.

Research-oriented motor learning laboratories were founded as early as the 1930s — at Pennsylvania State University by John Lawther and at the University of Wisconsin by Clarence Ragsdale — but research into the relation between psychology and sport was sporadic and took place under the often suspicious auspices of nonsport-oriented departments. The broad sociopolitical impacts of World War II, however, changed the situation dramatically. One important influence was the rapid expansion of the system of public postsecondary education, driven in no small part by the 1944 GI Bill, which among other benefits made provision for the postsecondary educations of veterans who otherwise would have been unlikely to attend college. Another was an exponential increase in the government's funding of scientific research. As the Cold War began to take shape in the late 1940s, Western governments, often through their militaries, began investing previously unheard-of amounts of money in preparedness for the confrontation then threatening to occur between the United States and the Soviet Union. The American trend toward government support for research leapt further, to near-desperate levels when the United States learned of the USSR's first nuclear weapons test in 1949 and then with the launch of Sputnik in 1957 (and probably more important, though less well known, the R-7 Semyorka ICBM in the same year). Although much of this money was poured into projects that had obvious and immediate military applications (such as missiles and computers), the idea of a much broader intellectual preparedness gained a great deal of currency in American government circles as well (Bakan 1994). Government funding rapidly overtook the role of traditional private funding agencies such as the Rockefeller and Carnegie Foundations in areas such as psychology, sociology, anthropology, and linguistics.

This newfound interest on the part of government in university research did not come without a cost to academics. Whereas certain areas of the university had traditionally been allowed, even expected, *not* to be actively engaged in primary research in the first half of the century — physical education among them — in the second half of the century there was a great deal more pressure brought to bear on departments to justify themselves in terms of their contribution to the national project of defending the country against its enemies, both real and imagined.

Traditional physical education departments did not measure up to these new expectations. In 1963 James Bryant Conant declared that if he "wished to portray the education of teachers in the worst terms, [he] should quote from the descriptions of some graduate course in physical education. To [his] mind, a university should cancel graduate programs in this area" (cited in Riba 2005, 101).

Conant was not one to be ignored. In addition to being a former president of Harvard University and a former U.S. ambassador to Germany, during the war he had led the National Defense Research Committee, from which vantage point he had overseen the Manhattan Project. The push was on to convert physical education, including its psychological aspect, from a relatively sleepy backwater of the academy into a full-fledged scholarly discipline.

But even if physical education were able to rapidly transform itself into the research-intensive academic discipline then being demanded, where best to publicly demonstrate its newfound intellectual muscle? There was, of course, varsity athletics, especially football, which was coming into its own as a significant part of the national athletic scene. In the context of the Cold War, however, a much more impressive display could be had by becoming a highly visible part of the American drive to dominate international athletic competition, especially the Olympics.

Just as in matters of scientific and technological prowess, the Soviet Union had come from nowhere (at least in the eyes of most Americans) to threaten U.S. leadership in the area of international sport. In 1948 the Soviet Union won no Olympic medals. However, in 1952 just four years later, the Soviets finished second in the medal count, just behind the United States, and in 1956 they passed the Americans to finish first, while in 1960 they extended that lead over the United States. Here was a perfect domain in which physical education research could demonstrate its mettle not only to a doubting academic establishment but also to the public at large.

Those interested primarily in studying psychological aspects of athletic performance were not far behind their more physically oriented colleagues in the race to prove themselves on the international stage. The impact of stress on athletic performance was one of the first coherent research programs in the nascent field of sport psychology. University of Maryland Health Education professor Warren R. Johnson started this line of work in 1949, and it gradually expanded into a general investigation of the relationships between personality factors and sport. Johnson's 1960 overview became one of the first popular textbooks on the topic, and it constituted an important step along the way of assembling the intellectual apparatus needed to found a new academic discipline. It was soon followed by textbooks by Bryant J. Cratty (1964, 1967) of the University of California–Los Angeles, Robert Singer (1967) of Florida State University, and Joseph Oxendine (1967) of Temple University. Another important book of the era was Ogilvie and Tutko's 1966 controversial *Problem Athletes and How to Handle Them*.

The topic of stress and sport was picked up in the 1950s by Franklin Henry of the University of California. One of Franklin's students, Maxwell Howell, brought this line of research to Canada when he took up positions first at the University of British Columbia (1954) and later at the University of Alberta (1961), where he established the first PhD program in physical education in Canada. Like the early textbooks, establishing independent graduate programs was crucial to gaining academic credibility. The sense of not being taken seriously by the rest of the academic world was quite pronounced among sport psychologists at this time. As the leading sport psychologist Robert Singer (1989) once put it, "the department that offered the graduate programs attempted to be academically rigorous and acceptable to other departments, to show that [sport psychology] was not merely a glorified 'jock' program, but rather a legitimate scientific area of study within sport sciences" (64).

In addition to textbooks and graduate programs, one of the most critical elements in the foundation of an academic discipline is the establishing of professional associations and journals. Many early sport psychologists regularly attended the convention of the National American Association of Health, Physical Education, and Recreation (NAAHPER). It was at the NAAHPER meetings of 1965 and 1966 that Warren Johnson began discussions with a number of individuals (including several of those mentioned above) about forming the North American Society for the Psychology of Sport and Physical Activity (NASPSPA). Using as a springboard the International Society of Sport Psychology, which had been founded in Rome in 1965, Johnson and others brought the NASPSPA into existence in 1967 (see Singer 1989, 63; Wiggins 1984, 19). As one of its first institutional acts NASPSPA established the *Sport Psychology Bulletin* to publish the research reports and other writings of its members. The *International Journal of Sport Psychology* would first appear soon after, in 1970.

It was also in 1970 that Walter Kroll and Guy Lewis of the University of Massachusetts formally revived the memory of Coleman Griffith in their article "America's First Sport Psychologist" (Kroll and Lewis [1970] 1978). Although Griffith had passed away only four years earlier, his activities related to the psychology of sport had ended three decades before. Kroll and Lewis's article provided more biographical information on Griffith than had previously been available, rounding him out into a kind of father figure. Their article, which is now cited nearly universally as authoritative, was a classic piece of celebratory history. It gloriously declared, for instance, that Griffith had "used every known means and all available opportunities to gather information" (17) but, more darkly, that "physical education associations . . . [had] failed to recognize the importance of his contributions" (18). Borrowing these tropes from the myth of the forgotten (or even maliciously suppressed) hero, Griffith's image was molded to the needs of the emerging discipline. The article established a foundation for sport psychology in the past; it "rediscovered" the kind of historical precedent that many nascent disciplines search for in order to establish their credibility. From this point forward, Griffith became a touchstone in the history of sport psychology, being cited in the historical sections of many sport psychology textbooks, journal articles, and, more recently, websites (see Wiggins 1984; Singer 1989; Gould and Pick 1995; Weinberg and Gould 2003).

The 1970s and 1980s saw a proliferation of specialized sport psychology associations such as the Association for the Advancement of Applied Sport Psychology (now just the Association for Applied Sport Psychology), the American Psychological Association's Division 47 of Exercise and Sport Psychology (see Swoap 1999), and the Sport Psychology Academy of the American Alliance for Health, Physical Education, Recreation and Dance. Along with these came what Singer (1989, 63) has described as an "avalanche of books" and several new journals, including the *Journal of Sport Psychology* (now the *Journal of Sport and Exercise Psychology*), the *Journal of Sport Science*, the *Sport Psychologist*, and the *Journal of Applied Sport Psychology*.

As discussed above, this expansion was driven in part by the demands of government and by the ambitions of sport psychologists themselves. One cannot discount, however, the impact of changes in the world of sport itself. The 1960s saw professional sports begin to become a truly continental enterprise. First, a small number of professional football (Rams, 1946), baseball (Dodgers and Giants, 1958), and basketball (Lakers, 1960, and Warriors, 1962) teams began to move to the west. Soon after, new franchises were established in all major team sports in California, Texas, Washington, and other western states (such as the 49ers, Texans, Cowboys, Raiders, Broncos, and Seahawks in football; the Angels, Colt .45s/Astros, Padres, and Pilots in baseball; the Supersonics, Suns, and Trailblazers in basketball; and the Kings and Seals in hockey). In the 1960s and 1970s the process of westward movement accelerated in baseball (for example, the A's, Senators/Twins, and Senators/Rangers) and expanded into other professional leagues (such as the Jazz, Royals/Kings, and Braves/Clippers in basketball). Further expansion was driven by the founding of replacements for some of the old eastern teams that had moved west (such as the Browns in football and the Mets and Royals in baseball) and by the growth of other eastern cities that desired either first time or additional Major League sports franchises (such as for New York, Buffalo, Cincinnati, New Orleans, Miami, Tampa, and Charlotte). Where rapid expansion was blocked by the established leagues, new professional leagues were formed (such as the AFL, WFL, USFL, ABA, and WHA). Some of these leagues failed, but others ultimately merged with their older competitors.

In addition, professional athletes started to unionize. Reserve clauses were struck down by the courts, opening the way for players to demand and receive increasingly enormous salaries. Owners responded by charging fans more for tickets, and television broadcast contracts began to balloon in cost. With so much money at stake the process of recruiting players became an ever more demanding, elaborate, and risky process. Players became, more than ever before, expensive investments to be carefully nurtured. Their training and broader care increasingly required special expertise that traditional scouts and coaches could not offer — expertise such as that possessed by sport psychologists.

In the amateur sporting arena as well, money gradually became the paramount concern. The Olympics has grown into a multibillion-dollar enterprise over the past few decades, and a progression of specialization similar to that in professional sports can be tracked there as well. For instance, in 1978 the United States Olympic Committee (USOC) created a Sports Medicine Council that included sport psychologists. It was even led by sport psychologist Robert Singer for a time. In 1982 the USOC founded a registry of sport psychologists. For a time there was some confusion over what qualification one must have in order to be listed on the registry. Within a decade, however, the AAASP began to offer a certification for sport psychologists, and the USOC then made the AAASP certification one of the key requirements for all those on their registry.

The inclusion of sport psychology into the amateur sport regimen was by no means limited to the Olympics. Indeed, because many sport psychologists already worked in college settings, college sports was a natural place for them to first apply and perfect their trade. As football and basketball in particular became important sources of revenue and reputation for many colleges, the demand for this sort of specialized expertise began to be felt in the schools, similar to what was seen earlier in the professional ranks. As money both became available to pay for such expertise and became a major incentive for college administrations to ensure that their teams did well on the field and the court, the demand for sport scientists grew as well. Sport psychologists have been among the most successful of this new breed of expert.

Today, we see more evidence of sport psychology's influence than ever before. Teams, both professional and amateur, continue to use the services of sport psychologists at an ever-increasing rate. The presence of sports psychologists is so pervasive that some leagues have felt the need to regulate their activity. The NCAA, for instance, which has strict rules about the number of coaches who are allowed on the field, has debated whether sport psychologists should be seen as another kind of coach (and therefore be limited) or as a new kind of consulting medical professional. In addition, we have seen individual athletes hiring sport psychologists as a standard part of their training team. The presence of sport psychologists has become so common — so expected — that we now see athletes who are being interviewed on television after a particularly important victory explicitly thanking their psychologist along with their coaches, trainers, and parents. Despite this recent explosive growth in the field, it is worth remembering, as we have aimed to demonstrate in this book, that it all started with isolated studies of men like Scripture, Triplett, Tissié, and Mosso over one hundred years ago. From such meager beginnings a new discipline and profession has been wrought.

References

Bakan, D. 1994. Reflections on fifty years of psychology. Paper presented at the annual meeting of Cheiron: The International Society for the History of the Behavioral and Social Sciences, Montreal.

Cratty, B. J. 1964. *Movement behavior and motor learning.* Philadelphia: Lea and Febinger.

———. 1967. *Psychology and physical activity.* Englewood Cliffs NJ: Prentice-Hall.

Gould, D., and S. Pick. 1995. Sport psychology: The Griffith era, 1920–1940. *Sport Psychologist* 9:391–405.

Johnson, W. R. 1949. A study of emotion revealed in two types of athletic sports contest. *Research Quarterly* 20:72–79.

———. 1960. *Science and medicine of exercise and sports.* New York: Harper and Row.

Kroll, W., and G. Lewis. [1970] 1978. America's first sport psychologist. In *Sport psychology: An analysis of athlete behavior,* ed. W. F. Straub, 16–19. Ithaca NY: Movement Publications. Originally published in *Quest* 12:1–4.

Ogilvie, B. C., and T. A. Tutko. 1966. *Problem athletes and how to handle them.* London: Pelham.

Oxendine, J. B. 1967. *Psychology and motor learning.* New York: Appleton-Century-Crofts.

Riba, T. 2005 *Applied sport psychology: Unearthing and contextualizing a dual genealogy.* PhD diss., University of Tennessee, Knoxville.

Singer, R. N. 1967. *Motor learning and human performance.* New York: Macmillan.

————. 1989. Applied sport psychology in the United States. *Journal of Applied Sport Psychology* 1:61–80.

Swoap, R. A. 1989. A history of Division 47 (Exercise and Sport Psychology). In *Unification through division: Histories of the divisions of the American Psychological Association*, ed. D. Dewsbury, 151–73. Vol. 4. Washington DC: American Psychological Association.

Weinberg, R. S., and D. Gould. 2003. *Foundations of sport and exercise psychology*. 3rd ed. Champaign IL: Human Kinetics.

Wiggins, D. K. 1984. The history of sport psychology in North America. In *Psychological foundations of sport*, ed. J. M. Silva and R. S. Weinberg 9–22. Champaign IL: Human Kinetics.

Contributors

DAVID BAKER, PHD, is the Margaret Clark Morgan Director of the Archives of the History of America Psychology and professor of psychology at the University of Akron. A contributing author to three books and more than forty scholarly articles and book chapters, he maintains an active program of research on the rise of professional psychology in twentieth-century America. He is a Fellow of the American Psychological Association and the Association for Psychological Science.

FRANK G. BAUGH, PHD, is a licensed psychologist in the state of Mississippi. He currently serves as the dean of Graduate Programs and dean of the School of Natural and Behavioral Sciences at William Carey University in Hattiesburg, Mississippi. In June 2008 Dr. Baugh was appointed the associate dean of Academics and Community Behavioral Medicine for the (proposed) William Carey University College of Osteopathic Medicine. Dr. Baugh has completed specialized training in sport and business psychology and has provided performance enhancement services to individuals and groups across a variety of sport, business, medical, and clinical environments. His professional and civic memberships include the American Psychological Association, the Mississippi Psychological Association, the Association for Applied Sport Psychology, and Rotary International. Dr. Baugh maintains special interest in sport and performance enhancement, organization development, health psychology, psychological preparedness, and emotional competence.

DR. GÜNTHER BÄUMLER is professor emeritus at the Technische Universität, München, Germany, where he was head of sport psychology from 1973 to 2003. He studied psychology in Marburg/Lahn and Würzburg and was an assistant at university clinics of psychiatry-neurology as well as psychology (Würzburg) and ergonomics (Munich). His special interests are experimental psychology, psychology of individual differences, and history of sport psychology. He is the author of psychological tests, founder and editor of the journal *Sportonomics*, and former chief editor of the journal *Psychologische Beiträge* (Psychological Contributions) from 1972 to 2002. He is also a cofounder of the German Society of the History of Sport Science.

ANGELA H. BECKER is an associate professor of psychology in the Social and Behavioral Sciences department at Indiana University–Kokomo.

LUDY T. BENJAMIN JR. is professor of psychology and Presidential Professor of Teaching Excellence at Texas A&M University. His published works include 23 books and more than 150 journal articles and book chapters, the majority of those on the history of psychology. He was elected a Fellow of the American Psychological Association (APA) in 1981 and has served as president of two of APA's divisions, including the Society for the History of Psychology and the Society for the Teaching of Psychology. In 2007 he received the Distinguished Lifetime Achievement Award from APA's Society for the History of Psychology.

STEPHEN F. DAVIS is emeritus professor at Emporia State University. He served as the 2002–3 Knapp Distinguished Professor of Arts and Sciences at the University of San Diego. Currently he is visiting distinguished professor of psychology at Texas Wesleyan University and distinguished guest professor at Morningside College. Since 1966 he has published over 290 articles, 27 textbooks, and presented over 900 professional papers; the vast majority of these publications and presentations include student coauthors. He has served as president of the Society for the Teaching of Psychology of the American Psychological Association (APA) Division 2, the Southern Society for Philosophy and Psychology, Southwestern Psychological Association, and Psi Chi. Additionally, he was selected as the first recipient of the Psi Chi Florence L. Denmark Faculty Advisor Award. He is a Fellow of APA divisions 1 (General), 2 (Society for the Teaching of Psychology), 3 (Experimental), and 6 (Behavioral Neuroscience and Comparative Psychology), as well as a recipient of the American Psychological Foundation's Distinguished Teaching in Psychology Award.

DONALD A. DEWSBURY is professor emeritus of psychology at the University of Florida. He received an AB degree from Bucknell University and a PhD from the University of Michigan; he did postdoctoral work at the University of California–Berkeley. His early career emphasized comparative psychology, but he later shifted to the history of psychology. He has been elected president of three American Psychological Association divisions and the Animal Behavior Society. He is the author or editor of 16 volumes, including *Comparative Animal Behavior* (McGraw-Hill, 1978), *Comparative Psychology in the Twentieth Century* (Von Nostrand Reinhold, 1983), and *Monkey Farm* (Bucknell University Press, 2006) and has published more than 350 articles and chapters.

ALFRED H. FUCHS is professor emeritus of psychology. He grew up as a fan of the (then) New York Giants and became enthusiastic about the Boston Red Sox after his move to Maine in order to join the faculty of Bowdoin College. His teaching and research interests in the history of psychology coincided with his interest in baseball and led to the discovery of Ruth's participation in laboratory tests that took their place in the history of psychology, of baseball, and of the prehistory of the psychology of sport.

C. JAMES GOODWIN is a professor of psychology at Western Carolina University in Cullowhee, North Carolina. He earned a bachelor's degree from Holy Cross College and a master's and doctorate in experimental psychology from Florida State University, specializing in memory and cognition. He is a Fellow of the American Psychological Association divisions 2 (teaching) and 26 (history) and past president of the Society for the History of Psychology. His major research interest is in the early history of experimental psychology in the United States.

STEPHEN T. GRAEF is a doctoral student in counseling psychology at the University of Akron and is currently an intern at the Ball State University Counseling Center. He is doing a specialization in sport psychology while at Ball State and hopes to continue working with athletes and teams after graduation. He has research interests pertaining to men and masculinity, the athlete population, and career issues. He was also a member of the 2002 Ohio State Buckeyes National Championship football team.

CHRISTOPHER D. GREEN is a professor in the history and theory of psychology program at York University (Toronto). He is 2009 president of the Society for the History of Psychology American Psychological Association Division 26 and past editor of the *Journal of the History of the Behavioral Sciences*. His publications include *Early Psychological Thought: Ancient Accounts of the Mind and Soul* (with P. R. Groff; Praeger, 2003), "Was Babbage's Analytical Engine Intended to Be a Mechanical Model of the Mind?" (2005), and "Johns Hopkins' First Professorship in Philosophy: A Critical Pivot Point in the History of American Psychology" (2007).

MATTHEW T. HUSS, PHD, MLS, is currently a professor at Creighton University in Omaha, Nebraska. He also is a graduate of the University of Nebraska law and psychology and clinical psychology training programs. He is the author of over fifty different scholarly publications and a forthcoming textbook on forensic clinical psychology, *Forensic Psychology: Research, Clinical Practice, and Applications* (Blackwell, 2008). His primary research interests focus on the prediction of violence, domestic violence, psychopathy, and sex offenders. In addition, he has significant interests in training and education in law and psychology.

ALAN S. KORNSPAN received his doctorate in sport behavior from West Virginia University. He is an associate professor in the Department of Sport Science and Wellness Education at the University of Akron, where he teaches courses related to the mental and behavioral aspects of sport, coaching, and measurement and evaluation. His research interests include the historical aspects of sport and exercise psychology, the psychosocial development of student-athletes, and the scientific aspects of coaching. His new book *Fundamentals of Sport and Exercise Psychology* was published by Human Kinetics Publishers in 2009.

Index

United States Olympic Committee (USOC), 290–91

Van der Mars, H., 138
Vealey, R. S., 263
Veeck, Bill, 220, 261, 267
Vernon, Philip Ewart, 26, 32, 41, 51nn21–22
Virgilio, S. J., 135
Voigtländer, Else, 40, 57n62

Wagner, Ludwig, 28, 53n32
Wang, M. Q., 136, 137
Warner, Glenn S. "Pop," 14, 169, 173–75, 178, 181, 186–87, 190–91, 193
Washburn, Margaret, 92
Watson, John B., 6, 12, 116–17; *Behavior*, 121; experiment discussion of, 131–33; experiment results of, 127–31; research methods of, 123–27; research of, with Karl Lashley, 121–33, 138–39
Watterson, J. S., 170
We, the People, 260
Weber, Ernst, 98
What Research Tells the Coach about Football (Paige), 195
Whitley, M. T., 120
Wiggam, Albert, 174
Wiggin, Paul, 241

Wiggins, D. K., 284
Wilkinson, Charles "Bud," 196
Williams, J. F., 254
willpower, goal-oriented, 26–27
Wills, Maury, 270, 275
Winter, Bud, 256–57
Wisconsin Scale of Personality Traits, 238
Wonderlic, E. F., 233
Wonderlic Personnel Test (WPT), 233–34, 248
Woodworth, R. S., 132, 153
Wrigley, Phillip K., 15, 210–20, 223n21, 226n52
Wrigley, William, Jr., 210
Wundt, Wilhelm, 21, 78, 83, 92, 98, 151; *Grundzüge der Physiologischen Psychologie*, 21; *Lectures on Human and Animal Psychology*, 92

Yates, Dorothy Hazeltine, 255–56
Yerkes, Robert M., 107
yoga, 27
Young, O. G., 134, 135

Zen Buddhism, 137
Zervas, Y., 137
Zuppke, Robert Carl, 172–73, 205, 209; *The Psychology of Football*, 173